Sharks of the
Mediterranean

Sharks of the Mediterranean

An Illustrated Study of All Species

Alessandro De Maddalena
with Harald Bänsch
and Walter Heim

McFarland & Company, Inc., Publishers
Jefferson, North Carolina

ALSO BY ALESSANDRO DE MADDALENA
AND WALTER HEIM

Mediterranean Great White Sharks: A Comprehensive Study Including All Recorded Sightings (2012)

Great White Sharks in United States Museums (2009)

LIBRARY OF CONGRESS CATALOGUING-IN-PUBLICATION DATA [new form]

Names: De Maddalena, Alessandro, 1970– , author. | Bänsch, Harald, 1966– , author. | Heim, Walter (Walter D.), author.
Title: Sharks of the Mediterranean : an illustrated study of all species / Alessandro De Maddalena with Harald Bänsch and Walter Heim.
Description: Jefferson, North Carolina : McFarland & Company, Inc., Publishers, 2016. | Includes bibliographical references and index.
Identifiers: LCCN 2015041892 | ISBN 9781476663579 (softcover : acid free paper)
Subjects: LCSH: Sharks—Mediterranean Sea.
Classification: LCC QL638.9 .D4293 2016 | DDC 597.3—dc23
LC record available at http://lccn.loc.gov/2015041892

BRITISH LIBRARY CATALOGUING DATA ARE AVAILABLE

**ISBN (print) 978-1-4766-6357-9
ISBN (ebook) 978-1-4766-2294-1**

© 2016 Alessandro De Maddalena, Harald Bänsch and Walter Heim. All rights reserved

All drawings © 2015 Alessandro De Maddalena

No part of this book may be reproduced or transmitted in any form or by any means, electronic or mechanical, including photocopying or recording, or by any information storage and retrieval system, without permission in writing from the publisher.

Front cover: a blacktip shark (*Carcharhinus limbatus*) (photograph by Nicolas Barraqué)

Printed in the United States of America

*McFarland & Company, Inc., Publishers
Box 611, Jefferson, North Carolina 28640*
www.mcfarlandpub.com

To Alessandra and Antonio

Table of Contents

Acknowledgments   ix

Preface   1

Biology and Ecology of Sharks   3

Status of Sharks in the Mediterranean Sea   39

Research on Sharks in the Mediterranean Area   51

Classification of Sharks Living in the Mediterranean Sea   66

Species Identification   70

Between pages 76 and 77 are 16 color plates containing 49 images

Species Profiles   77

Glossary   191

Bibliography   193

Index   205

Acknowledgments

Many people have contributed to this book. We thank the following people for freely sharing their observations and for their assistance in assembling material for this book: Jim Abernethy (Jim Abernethy's Scuba Adventures, Palm Beach, Florida), Richard Allan (Requins en Péril, Saint-Mards-de-Fresne, France), Greg Amptman (San Diego, California), Cynthia Awruch (Tasmania Aquaculture and Fisheries Institute, University of Tasmania, Taroona, Tasmania, Australia), Nicolas Barraqué (Hyères, France), Dominique Barray (Hyères, France), Joan Barrull (Laboratorio Vertebrats, Secciò Ictiologia, Museu de Zoologia, Barcelona, Spain), Miguel Berrios (NOAA Fisheries, Pacific Islands Region Observer Program, United States), Pascal Bertin (France), Ferdinando Boero (Dipartimento di Biologia, Università degli Studi di Lecce, Lecce, Italy), Nicola Bressi (Museo Civico di Storia Naturale, Trieste, Italy), Michèle Bruni (Musée Océanographique de Monaco, Monaco), Clay Bryce (Western Australian Museum, Perth, Western Australia), Pedro Miguel Niny Cambraia Duarte (Lisbon, Portugal), Christian Capapé (Laboratoire d'Ichtyologie, Université Montpellier II, Sciences et Techniques du Languedoc, Montpellier, France), Capitaneria di Porto di Piombino (Piombino, Italy), José I. Castro (Mote Marine Laboratory, Sarasota, Florida), Giorgio Cataldini (Centro Studi Cetacei, Gallipoli, Italy), Gioacchino Cataldo (Favignana, Italy), Antonio Celona (Istituto di Ricerca Aquastudio, Messina, Italy), Seinen Chow (National Research Institute of Far Seas Fisheries, Shizuoka, Japan), Franco Cigala Fulgosi (Dipartimento di Scienze della Terra, Universita' degli Studi di Parma, Parma, Italy), Antonio Celona (Istituto di Ricerca Aquastudio, Messina, Italy), Geremy Cliff (Natal Sharks Board, Umhlanga Rocks, South Africa), Ralph Collier (Shark Research Committee, Van Nuys, California), Tobey H. Curtis (Florida Program for Shark Research, Florida Museum of Natural History, Gainesville), Stefano D'Apote (Italy), Pascal P. Deynat (Laboratoire d'Ichtyologie Générale et Appliquée, Museum National d'Histoire Naturelle de Paris, Paris, France), Gilles Di Raimondo (France), Manuela Domingues (Alianza Tiburones de Canarias, Spain), Giuliano Doria (Museo civico di Storia Naturale "G. Doria," Genoa, Italy), David A. Ebert (Pacific Shark Research Center, Moss Landing Marine Laboratories, Moss Landing, California), Eddy Eneman (Noordzeeaquarium Oostende, Ostende, Belgium), Roberto Farkas (Rome, Italy), Ila France Porcher (Papeete, Tahiti, French Polynesia), Alexander Gelman (Fishery Products Laboratory, Kimron Veterinary Institute, Bet Dagan, Israel), E. Gilat (Israel), Thomas Gloerfelt-Tarp (Bangalow, New South Wales), Viktor Goushterov (Turkey), Stéphane Granzotto (France), Katie Grudecki (Brooklyn Park, Minnesota), Christine Gstoettner (Gablitz, Austria), Javier Guallart (L'Elasmogrup, Valencia, Spain), Farid Hemida (Faculté des Sciences Biologiques, Université des Sciences et Techniques Houari Boumediene,

Algeria), Carlos L. Hernández Gonzaléz (Instituto Español de Oceanografía, Santa Cruz de Tenerife, Spain), Alan Hill (Hopwood Hall College, Manchester, United Kingdom), Ruggero Ilgrande (Mercato Ittico, Milan, Italy), Claus Qvist Jessen (Holmegaard, Denmark), Philippe Joachim (France), Hakan Kabasakal (Ichthyological Research Society, Istanbul, Turkey), Stephen M. Kajiura (Ecology and Evolutionary Biology, University of California, Irvine), Marcelo Kovacic (Natural History Museum Rijeka, Rijeka, Croatia), Michel Krafft (Musée cantonal de Zoologie, Lausanne, Switzerland), Friedhelm Krupp (Senckenberg Research Institute and Natural History Museum, Frankfurt am Main, Germany), David W. Kulka (Northwest Atlantic Fisheries Centre, St. Johns, Newfoundland, Canada), Patrick Lelong (Institut Paul Ricard, Six-Fours-Les-Plages, France), Robert Lindner (Haus der Natur, Salzburg, Austria), Lovrenc Lipej (Marine Biological Station, National Institute of Biology, Piran, Slovenia), Patrick Louisy (France), Luis O. Lucifora (Instituto Nacional de Investigación y Desarrollo Pesquero, Mar del Plata, Argentina), Walid Maamouri (Tunisia), Renato Malandra (Mercato Ittico, Milano, Italy), Vincent Maliet (Corsica-MSRG, Appietto, Corse, France), Barb Marshall (Northwest Atlantic Fisheries Organization Secretariat, Dartmouth, Nova Scotia, Canada), Richard Aidan Martin (ReefQuest Centre for Shark Research, Vancouver, Canada), Isabel Mate (Laboratorio Vertebrats, Secció Ictiologia, Museu de Zoologia, Barcelona, Spain), Persefoni Megalofonou (University of Athens, Department of Biology, Section of Zoology Marine Biology, Athens, Greece), Glauco Micheli (Italy), Lorenzo Millan, Stéphane Moity-Banchard (France), Alec Moore, Juan Antonio Moreno (Universidad Complutense de Madrid, Madrid, Spain), Gabriel Morey (IMEDEA–Mediterranean Institute for Advanced Studies, Esporles, Spain), Martino Motti (Underwater and Travel Photography, Genoa, Italy), Sarah Muttoni (Montpellier, France), Marco maria Navoni (Biblioteca Ambrosiana, Milano, Italy), Eric Olijnyk (Recanati, Italy), Claudio Perotti (Brescia, Italy), Luigi Piscitelli (Mercato Ittico, Milano, Italy), Antonella Preti (Southwest Fisheries Science Center, NMFS, San Diego, California), John E. Randall (Bernice P. Bishop Museum, Honolulu, Hawaii), Frank Reckel (Zoologisches Institut der Ludwig-Maximilians Universität, München, Germany), Sonia Rottichieri (Bergamo, Italy), Keith Sainsbury (CSIRO, Hobart, Tasmania, Australia), Radek Šanda (Department of Zoology, National Museum, Prague, Czech Republic), Igor Shestopal (Polar Research Institute of Marine Fisheries and Oceanography, Murmansk, Russia), Jeff Shindle (San Antonio, Texas), Alen Soldo (Institute of Oceanography and Fisheries, Split, Croatia), Erling Svensen (Egeroya, Norway), Skip Theberge (NOAA Central Library, Silver Spring, Maryland), Egidio Trainito (Loiri Porto San Paolo, Italy), Stefania Vannuccini (FAO, FIDI, Roma, Italy), Giorgio Volpe (Apnea Magazine, Italy), Sabine Wintner (Natal Sharks Board, Umhlanga Rocks, South Africa), Alberto Zanoli (Italy), Nicolas Ziani (Mediterranean Shark Research Group, Montpellier, France) and Marco Zuffa (Museo Archeologico "Luigi Donini," Ozzano dell'Emilia, Italy).

For their help, support and friendship, Alessandro De Maddalena's sincere gratitude goes to Alessandra Baldi, Antonio De Maddalena, Pinuccia De Maddalena, Emilio De Maddalena, Eleonora De Maddalena, Elisabetta De Maddalena, Isabella De Maddalena, Sauro Baldi, Chiara Serino, Federico Serino, Gianfranco Della Rovere, Gaspare Schillaci, Andrea Del Coco, Claudio Perotti, Francesco Guerrazzi, Matteo Messa, Walter Heim, Sean R. Van Sommeran, Marie Levine, Ralph Collier, Chris and Monique Fallows, Andrew and Rodney Fox, Joan Barrull, Isabel Mate, Hakan Kabasakal, Lovrenc Lipej, Antonella Preti, Gianni Laudati, Simona Fiume, and Andy Dellios.

Preface

There is no other marine creature, except maybe the great whales, that attracts man's interest and stimulates his imagination as the shark. Indeed, sharks are wonderful animals that can be described as living artworks, with their perfect hydrodynamic shape, shining skin and silent graceful movements. Additionally, some sharks are the largest fish swimming in the oceans and among the largest animals that ever lived on Earth. Consequently, it is normal that we are fascinated by these fishes.

For a long time, research on these fascinating predators in European waters was scarce compared to the many wide and long term studies conducted in the United States on the same animals. However, the situation is rapidly changing and the number of interesting and detailed studies on sharks inhabiting the Mediterranean has grown. We are now filling in the gaps in our knowledge of morphology, biology, ecology and etology of the Mediterranean sharks.

This research is due to the efforts of the few dedicated ichthyologists, because the interest shown by European governments for marine biological research is very scarce (unfortunately, the same lack of interest is shown by the same countries for other natural resources). Most studies (and funds) on fish are concentrated on the few species considered to have high economic importance. The conservation of the natural world, the world we also inhabit, and their living components are considered as "optional." If we kill the marine predators we kill the marine world. According to recent estimates, we have already destroyed 90 percent of the sharks in the past few decades.

The aim of this book is to present a concise, accurate and up to date compendium of our knowledge on the sharks that inhabit the Mediterranean Sea. The content is widely based on the work made by many shark specialists who worked on the sharks described in the Mediterranean. The authors themselves are long-time researchers on sharks.

We wrote this book primarily for the general public. Of course, the text is scientific and detailed, but all technical terms are explained. We avoided preparing a technical work directed toward ichthyologists. We suggest that readers interested in digging deeper into the study of the Mediterranean sharks find a copy of the excellent books "Tiburones del Mediterráneo" by Joan Barrull and Isabel Mate and "Requins de Méditerranée et d'Atlantique" by Jean Cadenat and Jacques Blache. Also, take a look at the references in the bibliography.

The text is supported with many pictures, and the illustrations are the result of a lifetime portraying sharks. To produce the numerous drawings, Alessandro De Mad-

An oceanic whitetip shark (*Carcharhinus longimanus*) (photo by Dominique Barray).

dalena examined an immense amount of shark specimens at fish markets and museums of natural history in Europe, as well as many hundreds of photographs. The book also features beautiful photos of live specimens taken by Harald Bänsch and other photographers from around the world. There are also several pictures of rare Mediterranean specimens from several sources.

We hope that the readers will find this book interesting and useful. Through these pages and illustrations, we hope to be able to pass a little bit of the love and passion we have for these wonderful and mysterious creatures.

Biology and Ecology of Sharks

Classification

Starting at the top, sharks belong to the Phylum Chordata, the Subphylum Vertebrata, the Class Chondrichthyes, the Subclass Elasmobranchii and the Superorder Selachimorpha. Sharks, together with rays and chimaeras, are called Chondrichthyes or cartilaginous fishes. These fishes have skeletons composed of cartilage, a light and flexible tissue that is present in the human skeleton but in a much smaller amount. In fact, the only bony tissues present in the shark body are found in their teeth and scales. The other class of fish, the Osteichthyes, is called bony fishes having skeletons made of bone.

Sharks are classified into eight orders: Hexanchiformes (frilled and cow sharks), Squaliformes (dogfish sharks), Pristiophoriformes (saw sharks), Squatiniformes (angel-

Sharks, as well as rays and chimaeras (who are in a different subclass), are called Chondrichthyes because they have skeletons composed of cartilage. Above, a bull ray (*Pteromylaeus bovinus*) off Belvidè-Campumuru, Corse, France (photo by Pascal Bertin / Corsica-MSRG).

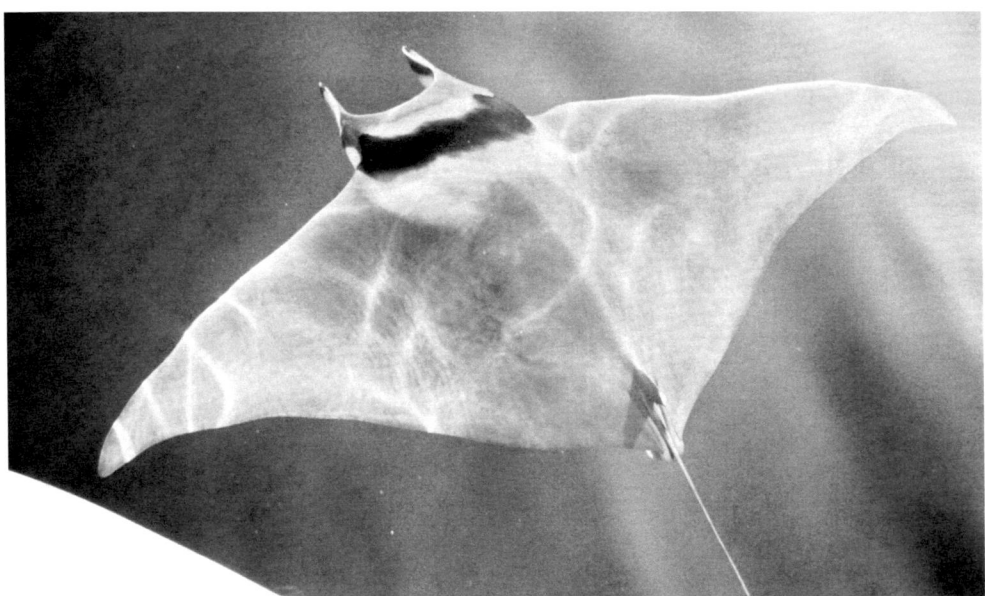

Chondrichthyes (sharks, rays and chimaeras) all have skeletons composed of cartilage. Above, a devil fish (*Mobula mobular*) off Lampedusa, Italy (photo by Antonio Celona).

sharks), Heterodontiformes (bullhead sharks), Orectolobiformes (carpet sharks), Lamniformes (mackerel sharks), and Carcharhiniformes (ground sharks). These orders are divided in 34 families that include 479 species of sharks. With the discovery of unknown species and an increase in knowledge of shark morphology, this classification is in continuous change.

Evolution

The origin of sharks is very ancient as they are thought to have arisen some 425 million years ago. This occurred between the Silurian and the Early Devonian periods. Sharks are thought to have evolved from the placoderms, a group of extinct armored bony fishes. A large amount of fossil remains of sharks have been found throughout the world. Although shark vertebrae can occasionally be preserved as fossils because of partial calcification, complete skeletons are preserved only in very rare cases because the cartilaginous skeletons rapidly disinte-

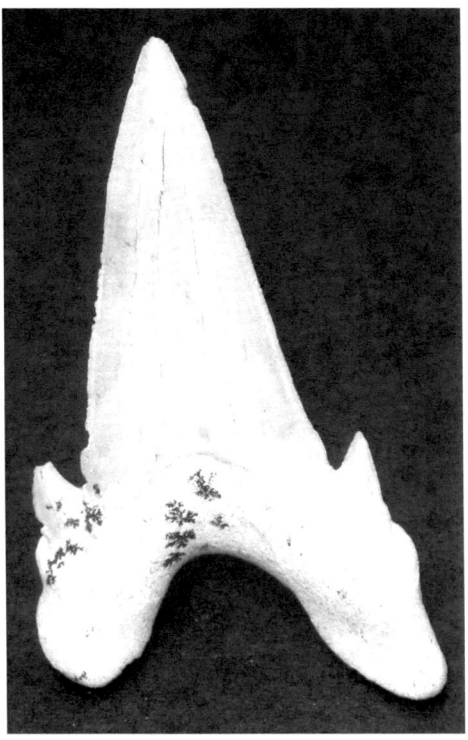

Fossil teeth like this, belonging to an extinct Lamnid shark (*Otodus obliquus*), are very common in the Morocco region (photo by Eric Olijnyk).

grate after death. However, shark teeth fossilize easily because they are highly calcified. Fossil teeth are extremely numerous and are the only remains of an extinct species. Sharks have not changed very much throughout the fossil record. This fact suggests that these creatures have characteristics that make them very well adapted to their environment. Consequently, sharks are considered as a highly evolved group.

Size

The smallest shark found in the Mediterranean is the velvet belly (*Etmopterus spinax*). At birth, it is 10–11 cm long and reaches a maximum size of 83 cm. Contrary to the popular opinion that all sharks are large animals, most sharks are small, reaching a length of less than 1.5 meters. However others are actually huge. In the Mediterranean Sea there are at least 10 very large species that have been confirmed to exceed 4 meters in length. They are the basking shark (*Cetorhinus maximus*), great white shark (*Carcharodon carcharias*), tiger shark (*Galeocerdo cuvier*), great hammerhead (*Sphyrna mokarran*), common thresher shark (*Alopias vulpinus*), bluntnose sixgill shark (*Hexanchus griseus*), bigeye thresher (*Alopias superciliosus*), shortfin mako (*Isurus oxyrinchus*), longfin mako (*Isurus paucus*) and smalltooth sand tiger (*Odontaspis ferox*). The basking shark (*Cetorhinus maximus*) is the second largest living fish, attaining lengths of at least 9.8 m and probably up to 12 m. Only the whale shark (*Rhincodon typus*), that grows to 20 m in length is larger, but it is not a Mediterranean species.

An enormous female great white shark (*Carcharodon carcharias*), about 597–613 cm, caught off Enfola, Isola d'Elba, Italy, on 12 August 1938 (photo courtesy Alberto Zanoli).

Some of the typical Mediterranean sharks represented in scale to show their maximum size compared with a man (top right): (1) bluntnose sixgill shark (*Hexanchus griseus*); (2) velvet belly (*Etmopterus spinax*); (3) common angelshark (*Squatina squatina*); (4) smalltooth sand tiger (*Odontaspis ferox*); (5) nursehound (*Scyliorhinus stellaris*); (6) common thresher (*Alopias vulpinus*); (7) small-spotted catshark (*Scyliorhinus canicula*); (8) basking shark (*Cetorhinus maximus*); (9) small blackmouth catshark (*Galeus melastomus*); (10) piked dogfish (*Squalus acanthias*); (11) common smooth-hound (*Mustelus mustelus*); (12) great white shark (*Carcharodon carcharias*); (13) porbeagle (*Lamna nasus*); (14) shortfin mako (*Isurus oxyrinchus*); (15) blue shark (*Prionace glauca*); (16) smooth hammerhead (*Sphyrna zygaena*); (17) tope shark (*Galeorhinus galeus*).

Excluding the basking shark that feeds on plankton, the largest predator species (meaning an animal that catches, kills and eats large prey) is the great white shark (*Carcharodon carcharias*). It has been confirmed to attain at least 6.6 m (this size is reported from specimens caught off France, Italy and Malta), but it is estimated to exceed 8 m in length. Female sharks attain larger maximum sizes than males.

Morphology, Swimming and Buoyancy

Body shape varies considerably among species of sharks. Most of these fish have a streamlined body, long flattened snout, ventral parabolic mouth, asymmetric caudal fin with the upper lobe much longer than the lower lobe. However, body shape does vary and is related to habitat and way of life. For example, benthic catsharks (*Scyliorhinus sp.*) have long and slender bodies, pelagic fast-swimming makos (*Isurus sp.*) have spindle shaped bodies, and benthic angelsharks (*Squatina sp.*) have flattened (depressed) bodies. "Benthic" refers to all animals living on the sea bottom, and "pelagic" refers to those living in the open sea or not relating to the sea bottom.

The fins of a shark are essential for swimming. Most shark species have eight fins, which include a pair of pectoral, a pair of pelvic, first dorsal, second dorsal, anal and

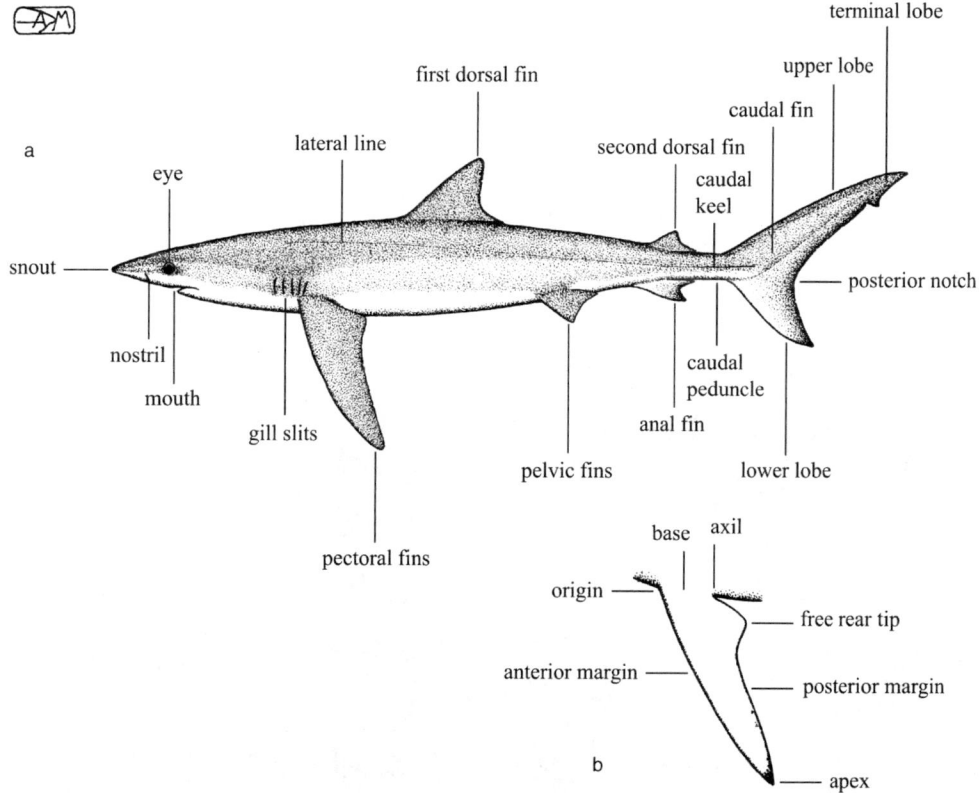

The external anatomy of a blue shark (*Prionace glauca*).

A blacktip shark (*Carcharhinus limbatus*). This species perfectly corresponds to the "typical shark," having a streamlined body, long flattened snout, ventral parabolic mouth, and asymmetric caudal fin with the upper lobe much longer than the lower lobe (photo by Nicolas Barraqué).

caudal fin. The caudal fin is used for propulsion. Besides the upper and lower lobes of the caudal fin, there is usually a terminal lobe at the end of the upper lobe. Forward motion is achieved by moving the caudal fin from side to side. The longer upper caudal fin lobe drives the shark down during swimming, but this is balanced by upward lift generated from the flattened head and the almost horizontal wide pectoral fins. One function of the wide head of the hammerhead sharks (*Sphyrna sp.*) is to provide more lift. In some benthic species, such as the small-spotted catshark (*Scyliorhinus canicula*), the lower lobe is almost absent, while in some fast-swimming species, such as the porbeagle (*Lamna nasus*) the upper and lower lobes are nearly of equal size (lunate) and the snout is conical. The large pectoral fins of the blue shark (*Prionace glauca*) make it very maneuverable. The other fins have stability functions.

In order to improve their hydrodynamic design, some sharks have lateral keels on the sides of the caudal peduncle, at the base of the caudal fin, which are flattened and laterally expanded. Usually there is one pair of caudal keels, but the porbeagle

To reduce its specific weight, the sandtiger shark (*Carcharias taurus*) gulps air into its stomach (photo by Nicolas Barraqué).

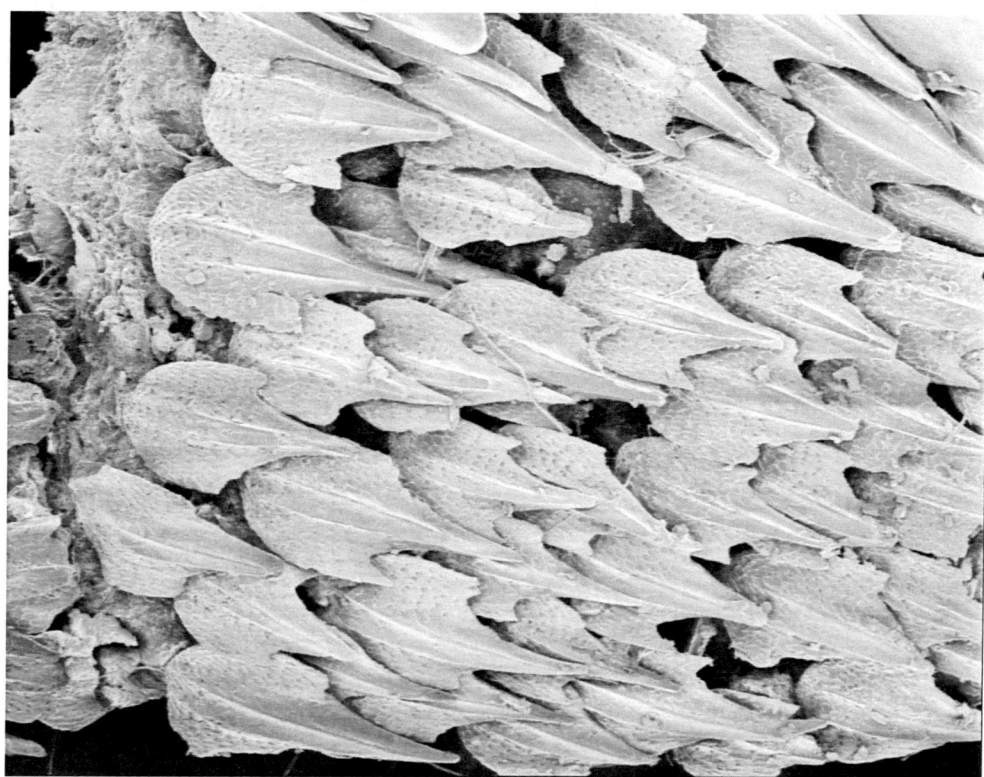

The dermal denticles (also called placoid scales) of a blackmouth catshark (*Galeus melastomus*) (photo by Pascal Deynat / Odontobase).

(*Lamna nasus*) and the longfin mako (*Isurus paucus*) have two pairs of caudal keels (the second pair is much smaller and located on the sides of the caudal fin, immediately below the caudal peduncle). The fastest species may be the blue shark (*Prionace glauca*) and the shortfin mako (*Isurus oxyrinchus*), with maximum speeds of 69 km and 56 km per hour, respectively. However, sharks usually swim slowly and even the fastest species have a relatively low average speed.

Some sharks have a spine before the dorsal fins. For example, the piked dogfish (*Squalus acanthias*), can use the dorsal fin spines as a defensive weapon against predators. Growth rings from a section of the second dorsal fin spine have been useful to study the age of some species, such as the velvet belly (*Etmopterus spinax*).

Most bony fishes have a gas bladder. This is a gas-filled sac located in the upper part of the body cavity to offset the weight of heavier tissues such as bone allowing the fish to be neutrally buoyant. Sharks lack a gas bladder, but because of the light cartilaginous skeleton and a huge oily liver of very low specific gravity, they are only slightly heavier than sea water. Certain species have developed additional ways of increasing buoyancy. For example, the sandtiger shark (*Carcharias taurus*) gulps air into its stomach. The difference in the density of various sharks is also related to their habitat. In fact, pelagic species are less dense than benthic species. Because sharks are negatively buoyant, they have to constantly swim to stay neutral. However, the benthic sharks lie

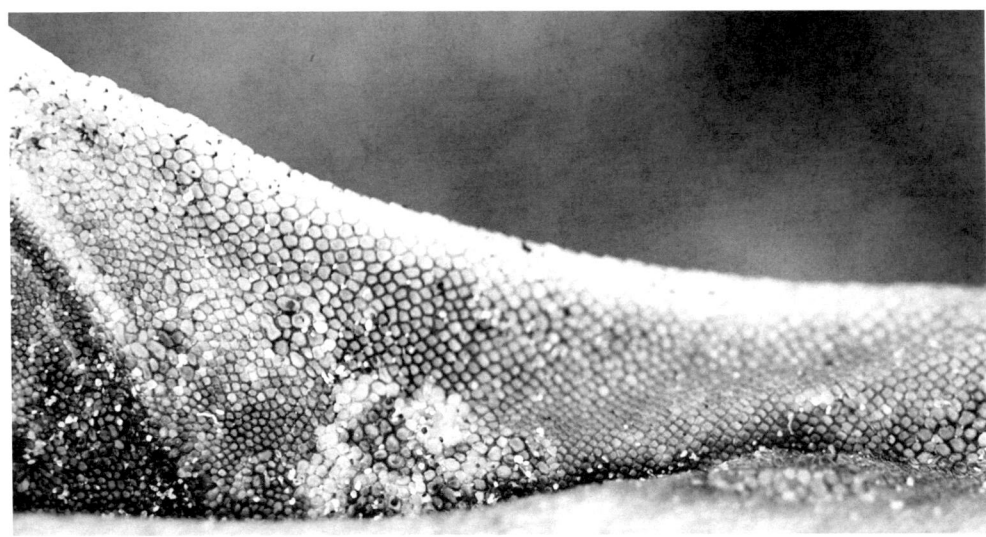

The dermal denticles of a gulper shark (*Centrophorus granulosus*) stranded near Bastia, Corse, France (photo by Vincent Maliet / Corsica-MSRG).

on the sea bottom for long periods. A typical example is the angelshark (*Squatina sp.*) that lies buried in the sand for a long time waiting to ambush prey. For those benthic sharks, neutral buoyancy is not important.

Shark skin is rough and abrasive, because it is covered by very small to moderately large structures called "dermal denticles" or "placoid scales." These dermal denticles are actually modified teeth rather than true scales. A denticle is composed of a pulp, dentine and enamel-like vitrodentine over a bony basal plate or root that is set into the skin. Dermal denticles are oriented to give the shark skin its sandpaper texture in one direction, yet smooth in the opposite direction. Grooves in the dermal denticles are aligned with the flow and reduce skin drag during swimming when the flow is turbulent. In fact, this drag reduction has been applied in engineering applications as "riblet" grooves on surfaces, which reduce turbulent fluid drag. The shape of dermal denticles varies from species to species and from body part to body part. Their shape is also of importance in the identification of a species, especially when it is not possible to examine the whole specimen, such as fish markets where sharks are often delivered cut in pieces.

Mouth and Teeth

Mouth size, tooth shape and jaw morphology are well adapted to the prey that is available to each shark species. The mouth of almost all sharks is located on the undersurface of their head (an exception is the angelsharks that have a terminal mouth) and varies in size, from small to very large, and in shape, from parabolic to almost straight. Usually there are upper and lower labial furrows at the corners of the mouth that can be very short to very long (in the smooth-hounds their length is useful to help in the species identification). Jaws vary considerably in size. Some sharks have spectacularly

Alessandro De Maddalena showing the jaws of a great white shark (*Carcharodon carcharias*) caught in the Mediterranean Sea and preserved in the Museo civico di Storia Naturale "Giacomo Doria" in Genoa, Italy (photo by Stéphane Granzotto, courtesy Museo civico di Storia Naturale "Giacomo Doria," Genoa).

wide jaws, for example the huge basking shark (*Cetorhinus maximus*), great white shark (*Carcharodon carcharias*) and tiger shark (*Galeocerdo cuvier*). Other sharks, like the commom thresher (*Alopias vulpinus*), have relatively small mouths with small teeth for such a large shark because they prey on small fish.

Shark jaws seem to be a modification of the first gill arch. In the most primitive sharks, the cladodonts, the mouth was terminal rather than ventral, the jaws were long and the upper jaw was fixed tightly to the chondrocranium (braincase). This kind of jaw suspension is called amphistylic and allows little independent movement. In advanced sharks, the jaws are shortened and the upper jaw does not have the tight connection to the chondrocranium being loosely suspended from it. This made the upper jaw highly mobile and enabled the shark to protrude it. This kind of jaw suspension is called hyostylic. Most modern sharks have a hyostylic jaw suspension.

The ventral position of the mouth is not an impediment to feeding. The snout lifts up and the upper jaw protrudes forward carrying the mouth to an almost terminal position. The best example is the bite action of the great white shark (*Carcharodon carcharias*). Its bite action is comprised of a sequence of jaw and snout movements: (a) snout lift, (b) lower jaw depression, (c) upper jaw protrusion, (d) lower jaw elevation, (e) snout drop. The great white shark removes large chunks of prey by biting and shaking the head laterally (large specimens can easily remove 20 kg of flesh in a single bite).

Jaw set of an approximately 300 cm pigeye shark (*Carcharhinus amboinensis*) caught off Crotone, Italy, Ionian Sea, in the summer of 2003.

The teeth of sharks are modified and enlarged dermal denticles, consequently they are composed of a pulp, dentine and enamel-like vitrodentine over a bony base. Each tooth has a root and a crown and the pointy projection of the crown is called the cusp. Many species have teeth with a large main cusp flanked by one or more auxiliary cusplets. A few species, such as the bluntnose sixgill shark (*Hexanchus griseus*), are provided with a row of cusps on a single tooth that resemble a saw. The tooth is not fixed into a socket but is implanted in the connective tissue (tooth bed) of the jaw with the root. The teeth of sharks are often broken and easily detached, but these fish have a perfect system of regular tooth replacement. Teeth are formed in a groove along the inner jaw surfaces, and behind the front row of teeth are several parallel rows of replacement teeth. There are 5 to 15 rows of teeth in each jaw. The teeth are continuously replaced throughout life. Whaler sharks (*Carcharhinus sp.*) replace each tooth every eight to fifteen days during the first year of life, but in adults replacement slows and each tooth is probably replaced every month. Sharks with small teeth usually have more than one functional row

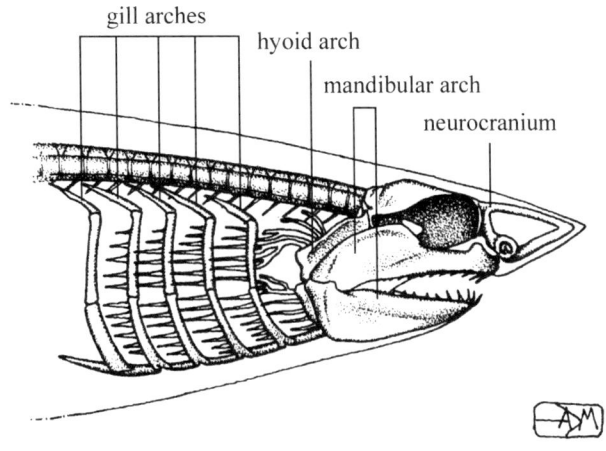

Skull of a shortfin mako.

in the jaws, while species with large teeth usually have one or two functional rows.

The number of teeth in the outer row of the upper and lower jaws is used to help identify species. In order to present the number of teeth in a shark's mouth, a dental formula is used. For example, the great white shark's dental formula is usually 13–13/11–11. This dental formula is read as 13 teeth in the right side of the upper jaw–13 teeth in the left side of the upper jaw / 11 teeth in the right side of the lower jaw–11 teeth in the left side of the lower jaw. Moreover the dental formula often shows variability. For example, great white shark's formula has variability of 12 to 14–12 to 14/10 to 13–10 to 13. Sometimes a third term is added to the formula. Blue sharks (*Prionace glauca*) have a dental formula of 15-1-15/14–1-14. The added tooth between the right and left sides of each jaw resides in the symphysis.

The teeth exhibit a wide variety of shape, since the shape varies between species according to what they eat. Teeth are an invaluable means

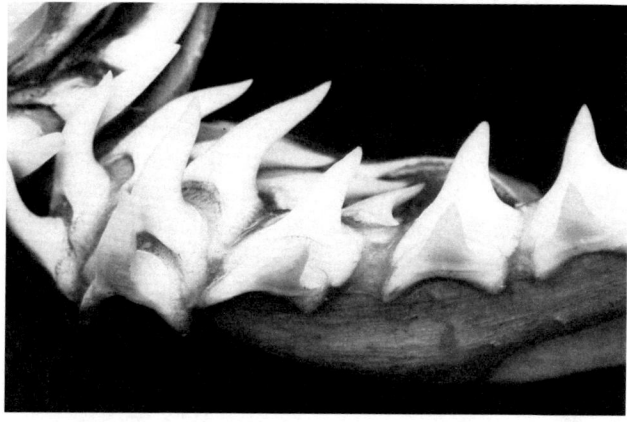

Functional rows of teeth in the lower jaw of a shortfin mako (*Isurus oxyrinchus*) (photo by Eric Olijnyk).

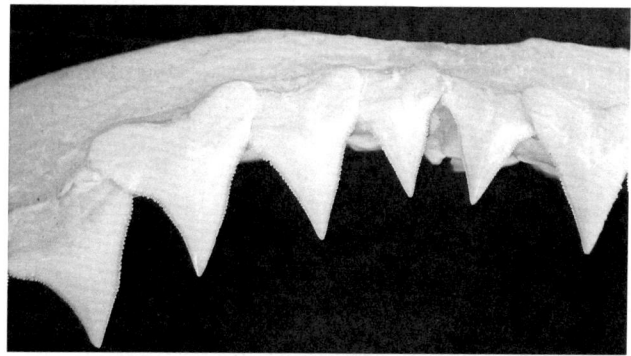

Upper teeth of a sandbar shark (*Carcharhinus plumbeus*) caught in Italian waters. These triangular teeth with serrated margins are adapted for sawing pieces from prey (photo by Alessandro De Maddalena).

Lower teeth of a common smooth-hound (*Mustelus mustelus*) caught in Italian waters. Its teeth are arranged in a pavement formation and are adapted for crushing hard prey such as mollusks and crustaceans (photo by Alessandro De Maddalena).

of identification. There are three main tooth shapes common to sharks with similar feeding ecologies and several variations.

(a) Teeth adapted for shearing or sawing pieces from large animals such as large fishes and marine mammals. These teeth are large, triangular, sharp and with or without serrate edges. For example, the great white shark (*Carcharodon carcharias*) and tiger shark (*Galeocerdo cuvier*) have this kind of teeth;

(b) Teeth adapted for seizing smaller fast prey such as small schooling fishes. These teeth are narrow and curved and tend to be moderately to very long. For example, the shortfin mako (*Isurus oxyrinchus*) and sandtiger shark (*Carcharias taurus*) have teeth with this shape.

(c) Teeth adapted for crushing hard prey such as molluscs and crustaceans. These teeth are smooth or arranged in a pavement formation. For example, the smooth-hounds (*Mustelus spp.*) have this kind of teeth.

Shark teeth have been modified in a number of ways. In most species, the teeth of the upper jaw are very different in shape from those of the lower jaw. Teeth in the lower jaw are often smaller and narrower and anterior teeth are larger than the teeth that follow them. Teeth vary considerably in size. Some species have spectacularly large teeth, like the great white shark and the mako shark (*Isurus sp.*). The largest great white shark teeth measured 6.4 cm total height.

Tooth shape is also related to the age of the sharks. The tooth shape can change as they grow larger and change their diet. In order for the shortfin mako (*Isurus oxyrinchus*) to eat fast pelagic fishes, it is born with narrow teeth. As it grows, these teeth become thick and strong to accommodate larger prey such as swordfish (*Xiphias gladius*) and small cetaceans. Young specimens are sometimes mistaken for other shark species because of their tooth shape. For example teeth of young porbeagles (*Lamna nasus*) are sometimes mistaken for those of shortfin makos (*Isurus oxyrinchus*) because they lack cusplets, and the teeth of young white sharks (*Carcharodon carcharias*) can be mistaken for those of porbeagles because they have small cusplets and partially lack serrated edges.

Respiration

The respiratory organ of sharks is the gills. While the gills of bony fish are covered by a flap called an opercu-

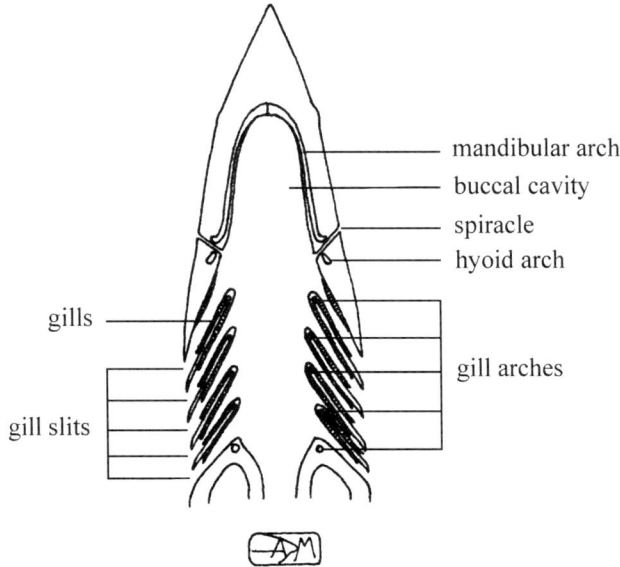

Section of the head of a shortfin mako (*Isurus oxyrinchus*), showing its respiratory system, with the spiracle and the five gill slits with their gill arches and lamellae.

The wide five gill slits of this shortfin mako (*Isurus oxyrinchus*) are well evident (photo by Walter Heim).

lum, shark gill slits are uncovered. Consequently, they are external and clearly visible. Sharks have five to seven pairs of gill slits. In the Mediterranean, there is only one species that has seven pairs of gill slits, the sharpnose sevengill shark (*Heptranchias perlo*) and two species that have six, the bluntnose sixgill shark (*Hexanchus griseus*) and the bigeyed sixgill shark (*Hexanchus nakamurai*). All others have five. Water flows into the mouth of the shark and downstream to the buccal cavity and to the pharynx where gills are located. Oxygen is extracted from the water and carbon dioxide released thanks to highly vascular membranes called gill lamellae. Many sharks have two small openings located behind or below the eyes, one per side, called spiracles. Spiracles are rudimentary gill openings and are used as entrance for water instead of the mouth. These openings are especially useful to those species that live on the sea bottom. Consequently, the spiracles are large in benthic species, such as the in the angelsharks (*Squatina sp.*) and very small in pelagic species, such as the thresher sharks (*Alopias sp.*). They are absent in some sharks, such as in the whaler sharks (*Carcharhinus sp.*). Fast pelagic sharks, such as the makos (*Isurus sp.*) that are very active, require large amounts of oxygen and must constantly swim to stay alive. As the shark Swims With An Open Mouth, The Water Is Channeled To The Gills Through Ram Ventilation.

Circulation

Sharks have a simple circulatory system. The heart is divided into two parts, the auricle and the ventricle. The blood goes from the ventricle to the ventral aorta, onto the branchial arteries then to the capillaries located in the gills (where gaseous

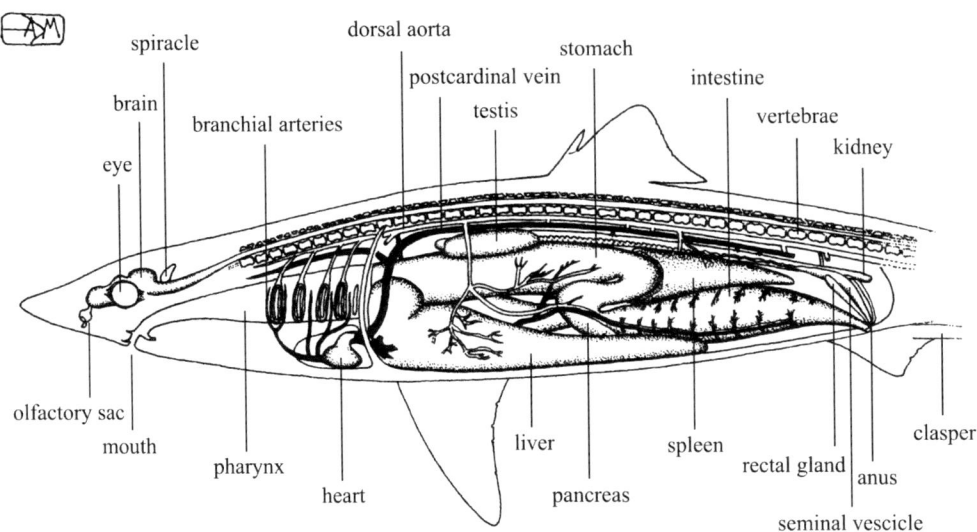

Internal anatomy of a piked dogfish (*Squalus acanthias*).

exchanges occur and the blood becomes oxygenated). Then, the blood continues to the dorsal aorta enroute to the rest of the body through the smaller arteries. After the oxygen and nutrients have been delivered to the organs via the capillaries, the blood enters the venous system and returns to the heart through the cardinal veins.

While most sharks have body temperatures equal to that of the surrounding seawater, some species of the Order Lamniformes exhibit regional endothermy meaning they maintain a higher body temperature than the seawater because they have a heat-retaining system. In the Mediterranean, the species that show endothermy are the shortfin mako (*Isurus oxyrinchus*), great white shark (*Carcharodon carcharias*), porbeagle (*Lamna nasus*) and thresher sharks (*Alopias sp.*). Red muscles are the most powerful

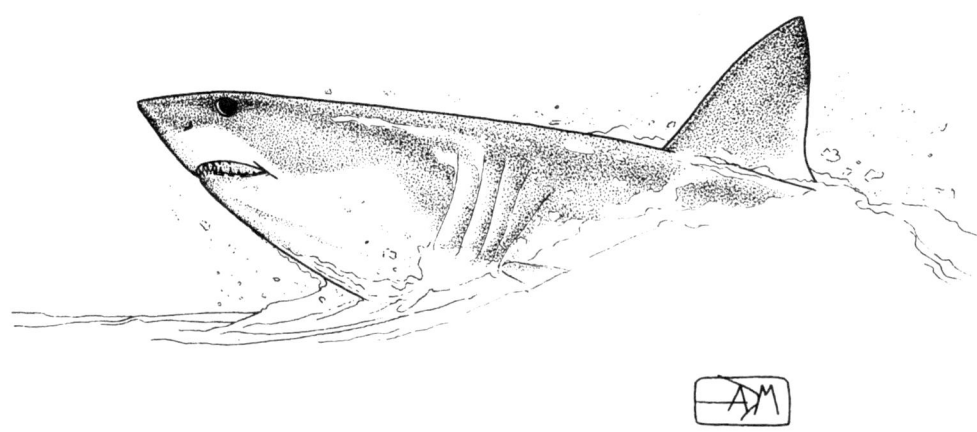

The porbeagle (*Lamna nasus*) is a particularly powerful swimmer because it is among those few sharks that are able to maintain a higher body temperature than the seawater thanks to their physiological heat-retaining systems.

during normal swimming. Endothermic sharks have larger amounts of red muscle tissue located deep in the musculature close to the vertebral column, while other species have this red muscle located closer to the skin. The red muscle tissue is connected to the circulatory system by a complicated network of arteries and veins called "rete mirabile" and heat generated in the red muscles by swimming warms the blood. As the outgoing warm blood passes through the venules in the rete mirabile, the heat is transferred to incoming cold blood in the parallel arteries. So the heat is retained in the shark's body, rather than dissipating to the environment. Metabolism is a function of temperature, so warm blooded sharks have more energy at their disposal allowing them to swim fast and leap from the sea's surface. The metabolism of these very active species requires a large amount of oxygen, so their gills have a large surface area.

Digestive System

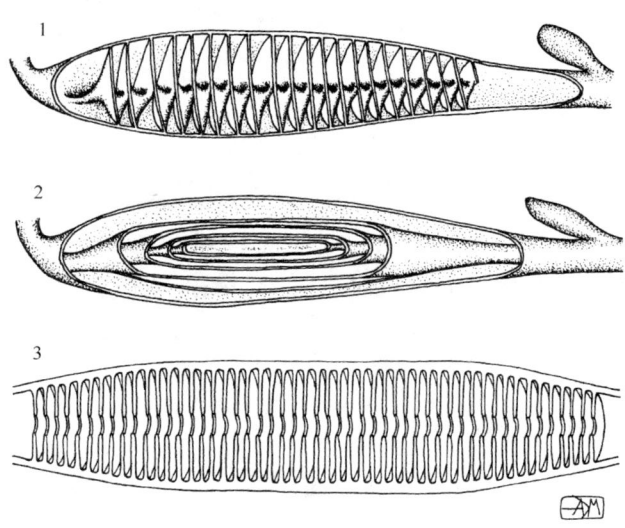

Section of two shark intestines, at the ileum level, showing the three kinds of intestinal valves: (1) **spiral valve**; (2) **scroll valve**; (3) **ring valve**.

Similarly to other vertebrates, digestion takes place in the mouth, stomach and intestine. The food that enters the stomach is acted on by the digestive juices. The shark stomach is very large, enabling these formidable predators to ingest whole animals, large chunks of prey and a large amount of smaller prey (some great white sharks captured in the Mediterranean had in their stomachs dolphins and large tunas whole or bitten in half). Consequently, sharks are able to ingest large amounts of food at a time and they do not need to feed often. After digestion, sharks are able to evert their stomachs, possibly to eliminate indigestible objects.

The products of digestion are absorbed in the relatively short intestine. The most important portion of the intestine is the ileum, which contains the intestinal valve. The intestinal valve is an internal structure that serves to increase the absorptive surface of the intestine without increasing the volume. This compact intestine provides sharks with the necessary space for a very large liver and stomach. There are three basic types of intestinal valves in sharks: the spiral valve, which resembles an auger in shape; the ring valve, which resembles a series of tightly packed lamellae (plates) with a hole in their center; and the scroll valve, which resembles a loose roll of paper in shape.

Studies have shown that digestion is slow in sharks compared to that for bony fishes. In fact, initial digestion of the food is relatively fast, taking around 24 hours, but usually it takes 1.5 to 5 days for the food to be completely processed. However, the rate at which

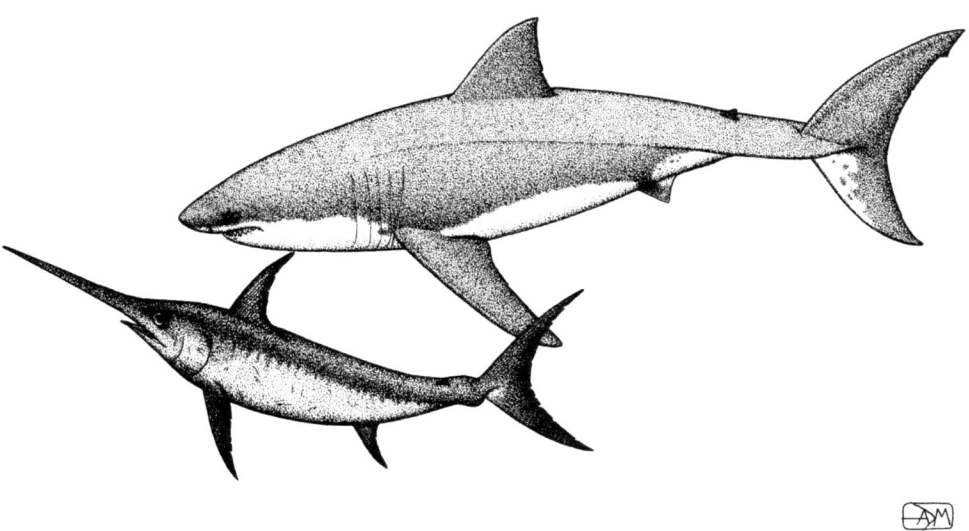

A shark's stomach is very large, allowing large individuals, such as the great white shark (*Carcharodon carcharias*), to ingest enormous prey, such as swordfishes or tunas, whole or in large pieces.

food is digested is closely related to the activity level of each species and its physiology.

Reproduction

Sharks live fairly long lives. Most species live about 12 to 27 years, but there are some species, such as the piked dogfish (*Squalus acanthias*), that have a maximum life span of at least 40 years and possibly up to 100 years. Sharks have a slow rate of growth and consequently have long sexual maturation times. Depending on species, a shark can reach sexual maturity in 2 to 20 years.

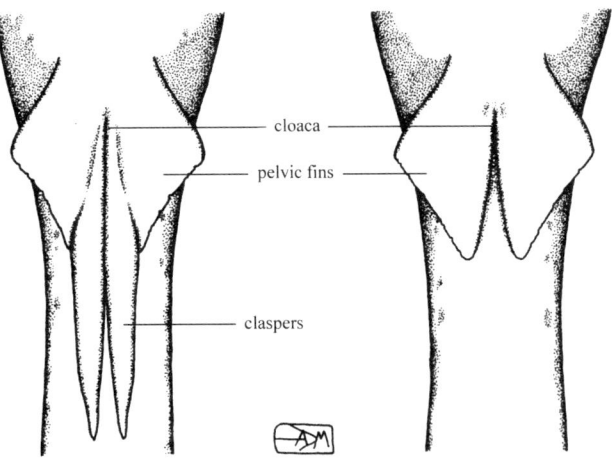

Pelvic region of a male (left) and a female (right) great white shark (*Carcharodon carcharias*).

Fertilization for sharks is accomplished internally. The males have two organs called claspers located at the base of the pelvic fins. They serve to impregnate females. In young male specimens, the claspers are short and soft, while in adult specimens they become calcified and long (consequently the sex of a shark is easy to identify by the presence or the absence of clasper). During mating, the male inserts one clasper into the female cloaca. In order to stimulate the female to copulate, the male bites the female both during courtship and copulation. Consequently, scars called "love bites" or mating scars can be seen on the body (flanks, gill region, belly, back, caudal peduncle and fins) of female specimens.

Three different reproductive methods have been observed in sharks:

(a) oviparity where the female lays horny egg cases containing embryos nourished by the yolk sac.

(b) aplacental viviparity where the female produces live young nourished in the uterus by a yolk-sac.

(c) placental viviparity where the female produces live young nourished in the uterus by a placenta formed by a modified yolk-sac attached to the uterine wall.

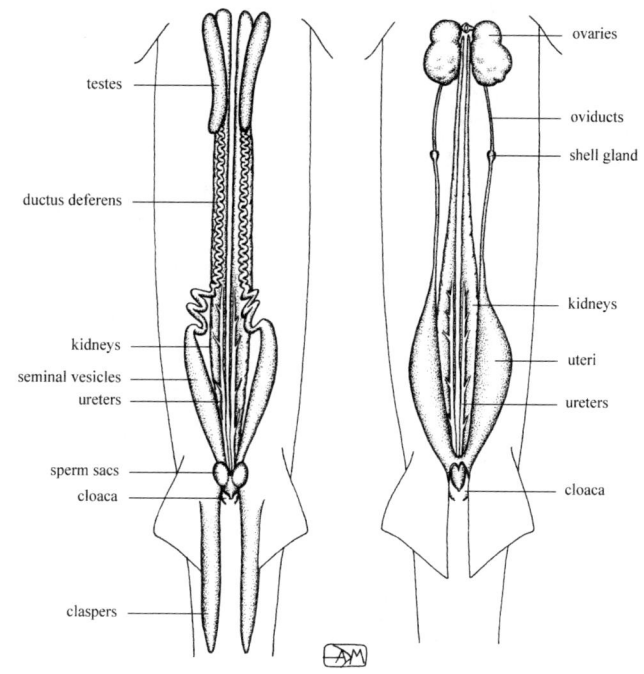

Urogenital system of sharks: male (left) and female (right) (redrawn from illustrations in Castro, 1983).

Small-spotted catsharks (*Scyliorhinus canicula*) mating; on exhibit at the National Sea Life Centre, Birmingham, England, 2000 (photo by Alan Hill).

Aplacental viviparity is the most common reproductive method and there are two additional ways to nourish the embryos. In oophagy, embryos in the uterus feed on unfertilized eggs produced by their mother. This nourishing method has been observed in many Mediterranean species, including the bigeye thresher (*Alopias superciliosus*), common thresher shark (*Alopias vulpinus*), basking shark (*Cetorhinus maximus*), great white shark (*Carcharodon carcharias*), shortfin mako (*Isurus oxyrinchus*), porbeagle (*Lamna nasus*), and sandtiger shark (*Carcharias taurus*). In embryophagy, also called intrauterine cannibalism, embryos in the uterus feed on their siblings. This has been observed in the sandtiger shark.

In oviparous sharks, the female lays horny egg cases containing embryos nourished by the yolk sac (photo by Harald Bänsch).

Gestation periods for sharks are among the longest of any living vertebrates. The average gestation is 9 to 12 months, but can be up to 24 months for the piked dogfish (*Squalus acanthias*), and it has been hypothesized that it could reach three years for the basking shark (*Cetorhinus maximus*) and the gulper shark (*Centrophorus granulosus*). Litter sizes of Mediterranean sharks vary from a single pup to a maximum of 135 for the blue shark (*Prionace glauca*), but most species produce relatively small numbers of young, usually from 2 to 20 pups. When pups are born, they are fully formed and able to catch food without any assistance from their mother. Many shark species segregate by sex and size. Nursery areas for some species are often coastal waters, lagoons or estuaries, where only newborns and juveniles live. These nursery areas reduce the risk of cannibalism, and usually have an abundance of suitable prey for the pups. Many sharks reproduce only every other year.

Senses

Sharks have a highly developed nervous system and sense organs used to find prey. These senses are separated into four types: chemoreception, mechanoreception, photoreception and electroreception.

An example of chemoreception is olfaction. Feeding areas are often located via olfaction. The nostrils are located on the underside of the snout and lead to the olfactory bulb. Sharks have a keen sense of smell. The slick produced by a large cetacean carcass attracts large sharks, such as blue sharks (*Prionace glauca*) and white sharks (*Carchar-*

odon carcharias) from a long distance. Some species weave across the odor trail as they navigate toward the prey, while others swim straight up the trail. Stimulated by blood and food in the water, the shark becomes increasingly aggressive as they approach the prey.

As for mechanoreception, the lateral line system and the ears enable sharks to detect movements in the water. The lateral line is a row of sensory receptors located along the flanks and head of the shark. These sensors are pressure-sensitive, enabling the shark to detect vibrations in the water.

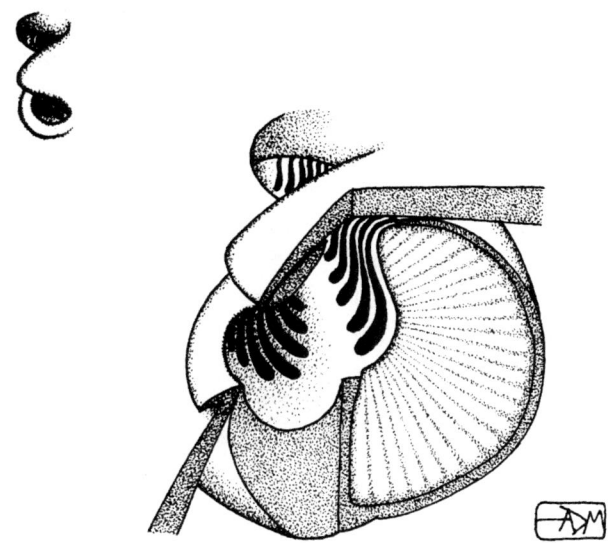

The nostril (left) and the olfactory organ (right) of a shark (redrawn from an illustration in Gilbert, 1962).

They are able to detect both direction and the intensity of the movement in the water from great distances. A wounded creature, for example a speared fish, sends out vibrations that are received by the predator indicating that the animal is in trouble and therefore easy prey. These predators also use this sense to detect water currents. Sharks have

Like many other sharks, the blue shark (*Prionace glauca*) has wide nostrils, because the olfaction is particularly important allowing this animal to find its prey. In the photo, the openings of the electrical sensors called ampullae of Lorenzini can be clearly seen (photo by Walter Heim).

two inner ears, connected to the exterior by narrow canals called endolymphatic ducts. The ears of the shark are integrated with the lateral line system, and are very sensitive to low-frequency vibrations, like those produced by struggling prey.

As for photoreception, prey detection depends heavily on vision. The vision of a shark is excellent. Different parts of their retina are adapted for bright and dim light. Consequently, sharks are able to use their eyes even in low light conditions. The retina contains cone and rod photoreceptors (cones function in bright light while rods function in dim light.) The tapetum lucidum is a structure that lies under the retina that reflects incoming light back through the retina to

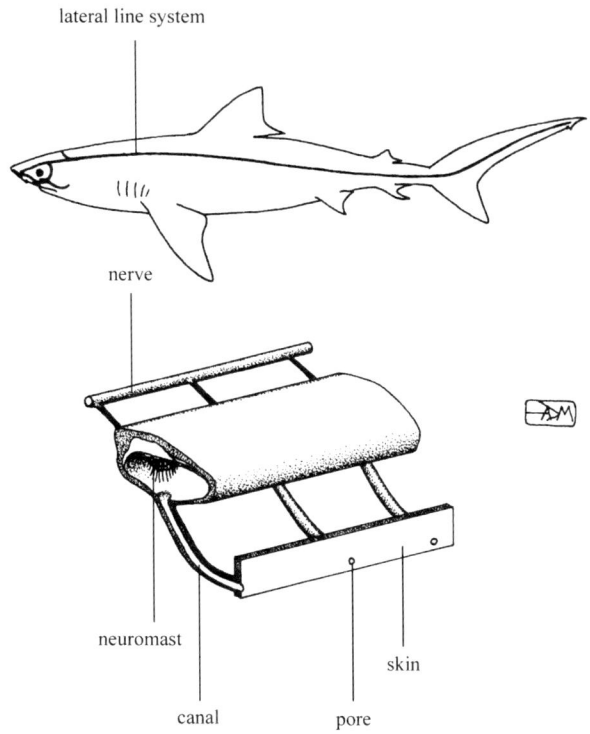

Location (above) and internal structure (below) of a shark's lateral line.

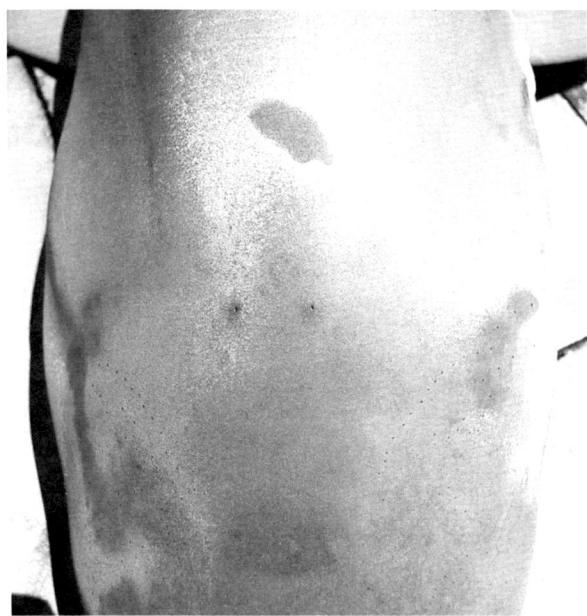

Dorsal view of a whaler shark's head showing the external openings of endolymphatic ducts (photo by Harald Bänsch).

restimulate photoreceptors, thus increasing the sensitivity of the eye. At least some sharks have color vision.

Sharks have immovable eyelids, but many species have a third eyelid, called the nictitating membrane, formed by an additional fold of the lower eyelid. This structure is movable and when the shark is feeding, the membrane closes over it for protection. However many species lack the nictitating membrane. The great white shark (*Carcharodon carcharias*) is among these, and in order to reduce the risk of injury, it rolls its eye backward during the attack.

As for electroreception,

when sharks are in close proximity to their prey, they can detect the minute electrical currents generated by the nervous systems of their prey by using electrical sensors called ampullae of Lorenzini. The ampullae are numerous small organs containing a sensory hair cell and are filled with an electrically conductive jelly. The external openings to the electroreceptors are small pores located over the head and are particularly abundant on the underside of the snout. For the great hammerhead (*Sphyrna mokarran*), these sophisticated sensors are very useful for finding prey buried under sand. Sharks also use this sense to navigate using the Earth's magnetic field. The ampullae of Lorenzini cause sharks to be attracted to metals, as a response to the galvanic currents produced by electrochemical interactions between seawater and metals.

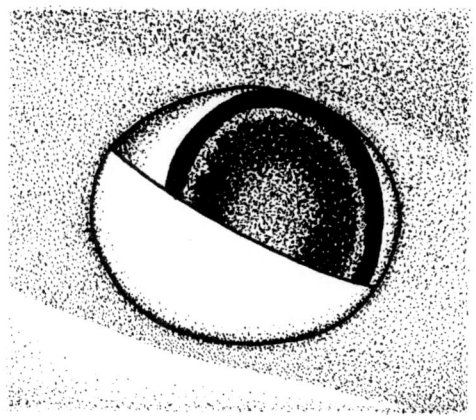

A shark eye showing the nictitating membrane.

Touch receptors are located over the entire body of the shark and this sense is used to obtain information by bumping the prey. Taste receptors enable the shark to discrim-

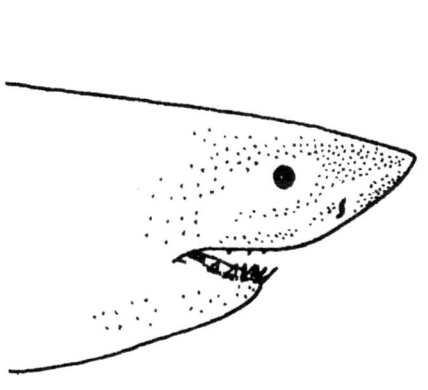
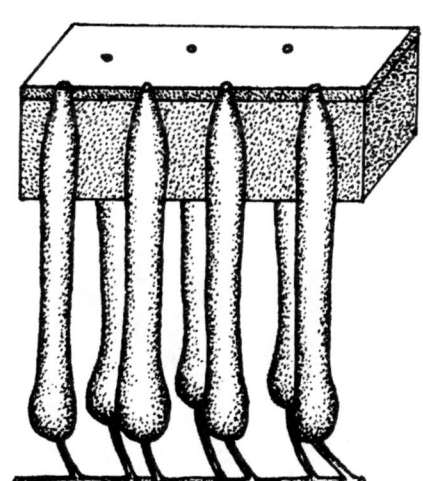

Location of the ampullae of Lorenzini on the head of a great white shark (left) and their internal structure (right).

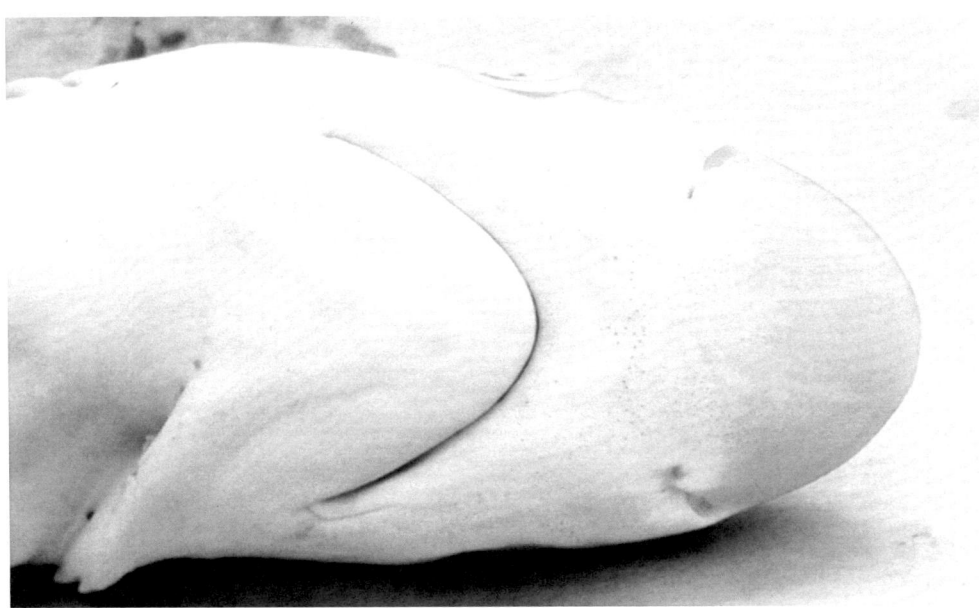

Ampullae of Lorenzini on the underside of a whaler shark's head (photo by Harald Bänsch).

inate the food before it is ingested. Some sharks, like the great white shark, decide the palatability of the food while it is lodged in its mouth. Gustatory receptors are located in the shark's mouth and pharynx.

Color

The body of the shark is dark on the dorsal surfaces (usually grey, brown, greenish or blue) and white on the ventral surfaces. This color pattern is called countershading and serves to render these fish less visible to their prey and to their predators, when viewed from below or from above. The fins on some species show different coloration

The young tiger sharks (*Galeocerdo cuvier*) have black spots, then dark vertical stripes and patches, but this color pattern gradually fades in adults and is almost absent in the largest specimens (photo by Harald Bänsch).

at their apex and posterior margin. This is very evident in species such as the oceanic whitetip shark (*Carcharhinus longimanus*) and blacktip reef shark (*Carcharhinus melanopterus*). Some species show dark or light spots on body, such as the starry smoothhound (*Mustelus asterias*) and the sandtiger shark (*Carcharias taurus*). In the case of the angelsharks (*Squatina sp.*), the spotted pattern serves as camouflage on the sandy sea floor. A more complex mottled color pattern can be found in the catsharks (*Scyliorhinus sp.*). In very rare cases, albinism has been recorded in a few shark species found in the Mediterranean, including the basking shark (*Cetorhinus maximus*), great white shark (*Carcharodon carcharias*), tope shark (*Galeorhinus galeus*), scalloped hammerhead (*Sphyrna lewini*) and great hammerhead (*Sphyrna mokarran*).

Distribution and Habitat

Sharks are found throughout the Mediterranean Sea on any type of sea floor. In the Mediterranean, large sharks usually stay offshore, but some prefer the area close to shoals or the straits where they can find prey easily. Sometimes, the large pelagic sharks venture into very shallow waters. Records of great white sharks (*Carcharodon carcharias*) or blue sharks (*Prionace glauca*) swimming a few meters from shore exist in the Mediterranean, but these are very rare cases. This happens occasionally, especially if the shoreline is located very close to a nearshore drop off into deep water. Most sharks dwell on the continental and insular shelves and upper slopes. However, some of these predators can visit the deeper parts of the sea. The deepest accurate record of a shark in the Mediterranean was a Portuguese dogfish (*Centroscymnus coelolepis*) at 2718 m depth.

The Northeastern Tyrrhenian Sea coast (Italy) is particularly frequented by large sharks such as the great white shark (*Carcharodon carcharias*) (photo by Alessandro De Maddalena).

Feeding

Sharks typically consume a small amount of food with the average meal being 3 to 5 percent of the body weight. They feed intensively for a short time and then feed very little for a longer period of time. Most sharks feed at one or two day intervals and are also able to stop feeding for several weeks. During this time, they live on oil reserves

The blacktip shark (*Carcharhinus limbatus*) is a very active species and consumes more food than that required by less active species (photo by Dominique Barray).

in their large liver. Obviously, food consumption is related to the activity level of a given species, so the food consumption per day is different for each species. Sedentary sharks, such as the catsharks (*Scyliorhinus sp.*), require a small amount of food, while more active species such as the sandbar shark (*Carcharhinus plumbeus*) and blue shark (*Prionace glauca*), consume more and some very active warm blooded species such as the shortfin mako (*Isurus oxyrinchus*) consume even more.

Most sharks are nocturnal and feed in the darkness. However, daytime feeding by nocturnal species is often reported (even these sharks eat when given an opportunity). Other species, such as the great white shark (*Carcharodon carcharias*) hunt both day and night. Certain species are vertical migrators on a diel cycle, so they stay in deep zones during the day and ascend to the surface at night to feed. In the Mediterranean, the bluntnose sixgill shark (*Hexanchus griseus*) and the velvet belly (*Etmopterus spinax*) are diel migrators.

Sharks usually inflict deep wounds to their prey. Sometimes, their prey can be found stranded dead or alive, or observed floating at the sea surface with wounds that are evidence of a shark attack. Tooth enamel fragments are sometimes found in the carcasses. In the Mediterranean, shark bite scars are frequently found on tunas, swordfishes and dolphins. These animals are often thought to have been hit by a boat, because sometimes the lacerations are similar to those inflicted by boat propellers. Shark bite scars and fresh wounds are used to identify the species of sharks responsible for predation and scavenging, however proper identification is complicated.

The great white shark (*Carcharodon carcharias*) hunts day and night (photo by Nicolas Barraqué).

Diet

Sharks are carnivorous and feed on a wide variety of prey. Most sharks feed mainly on live prey, some attacking healthy prey and others feeding on diseased, wounded or dead animals. All sharks usually prey on animals of comparable or smaller size. Sharks eat bony fishes, cartilaginous fishes, molluscs, crustaceans, echinoderms, worms, pinnipeds, cetaceans, marine turtles, sea snakes, sea birds and other animals. The list includes even planktonic organisms such as euphasiids, copepods and jellyfishes.

Many sharks are opportunistic feeders, preying on a variety of species depending on their availability in a given area. When a particular prey is scarce, they feed on other species. A common species or one that is easily captured may dominate the diet of the opportunistic sharks. According to studies conducted on Mediterranean sharks, most opportunistic sharks are benthic species. There are also numerous sharks that show dietary preferences and some species have a highly specialized diet. The common thresher (*Alopias vulpinus*) feeds mainly on anchovies, hakes and mackerels, while the great hammerhead (*Sphyrna mokarran*) favors stingrays. Great white sharks (*Carcharodon carcharias*) and blue sharks (*Prionace glauca*), seem to feed selectively on the energy-rich blubber layer when scavenging a whale carcass.

Sharks prey primarily on fish. Bony fishes are the preferred food for most sharks and they supply a very important part of their diet. Examination of shark stomachs has shown that for most species, about 70 to 80 percent of the diet consists of bony fishes. Prey size ranges from small pilchards to the large bluefin tuna (*Thunnus thynnus*) and

A porbeagle (*Lamna nasus*) catching Atlantic mackerels (*Scomber scombrus*). Bony fishes are the most important food for sharks.

swordfish (*Xiphias gladius*). However, the small species are the most common prey. Elasmobranchs are the most important prey item for many shark species that seem to prefer cartilaginous fishes over bony fishes. Most sharks have no enemies except other sharks and man. Moreover, sharks are also the main predators of rays. Some species also feed on elasmobranch eggs, such as the angular roughshark (*Oxynotus centrina*) that eats the small-spotted catshark (*Scyliorhinus canicula*) eggs.

Most sharks also eat a certain percentage of invertebrates, especially cephalopods

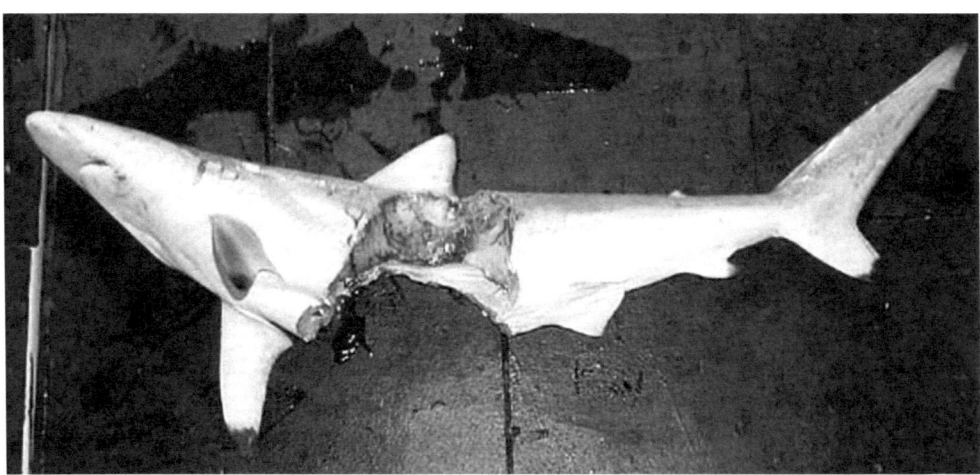

A spinner shark (*Carcharhinus brevipinna*) after a massive attack by a larger shark (photo by Harald Bänsch).

The bottlenose dolphin (*Tursiops truncatus*). Some Mediterranean sharks, especially the great white shark (*Carcharodon carcharias*), catch live cetaceans, but feed primarily on dead specimens (photo by Alessandro De Maddalena).

and crustaceans. The small-spotted catshark (*Scyliorhinus canicula*) feeds primarily on invertebrates, including hermit crabs, cockles and whelks. Crustaceans are the most important prey items of the common smooth-hound (*Mustelus mustelus*), that favors mantis shrimps (*Squilla mantis*). Cephalopods form also the main item in the diet of the blue shark (*Prionace glauca*) and young bluntnose sixgill sharks (*Hexanchus griseus*).

Some sharks feed on marine mammals, but while some of these species feed on both live and dead specimens, such as the great white shark (*Carcharodon carcharias*) and tiger shark (*Galeocerdo cuvier*), most sharks eat only dead animals. Large cetacean carcasses are an important food for species such as the oceanic whitetip shark *(Carcharhinus longimanus)* and blue shark (*Prionace glauca*). A few sharks also eat marine turtles and sea birds. In the Mediterranean there is even a plankton eater, the basking shark (*Cetorhinus maximus*) that filters the plankton from the water like a whale.

Diet is also related to age and size of the shark and there is considerable variation in the diet of many sharks as they grow. Larger prey becomes increasingly important in the diet of sharks as they grow larger. Change in the diet is accompanied by a change in tooth shape. Many young sharks feed mainly on bony fishes and molluscs, but the amount of that prey declines when the sharks grow and start to eat larger prey such as cartilaginous fishes and marine mammals.

There is considerable variation in the diet of several sharks from one location or season to the next. Regional differences in diet are attributable to the higher presence of particular prey. In fact, many sharks focus their hunting activity on the most abundant species. In many locations of the world, such as California, South Africa and South Australia, elasmobranchs and pinnipeds are the major components in the diet of great white sharks. In the Mediterranean Sea, where there are almost no pinnipeds or other

Some sharks occasionally catch sea birds. Shortfin makos (*Isurus oxyrinchus*) and great white sharks (*Carcharodon carcharias*) have been observed pursuing gulls at the sea surface, and remains of these birds have been found in their stomachs (photo by Alessandro De Maddalena).

sharks, great white sharks feed heavily on cetaceans, bony fishes and marine turtles. In the Catalan Sea, Spain, kitefin sharks (*Dalatias licha*) prey primarily on small sharks during the spring and winter, crustaceans during the summer and cephalopods during the fall.

Mutualisms

Mutualism is a relationship between two individuals of different species, where both benefit from the relationship. The relationships between pilot fishes (family Carangidae) and sharks and between remoras (family Echeneidae) and sharks are cases of mutualism, because both species benefit from the relationship. Remoras have a dorsal suction disk (formed from its modified dorsal fin) that is used to attach themselves to sharks, mantas, marine turtles and other large aquatic animals. This suction attachment is only used when the large animal changes direction or slows down. In the Mediterranean, the common remora (*Remora remora*) accompanies sharks. The pilot fish (*Naucrates ductor*) is found in the Mediterranean and is frequently observed close to large cartilaginous fishes, bony fishes and marine turtles. Remoras and pilot fishes benefit from these relationships by eating food scraps, excrements and parasites (sharks are hosts to several external parasites), as well by riding the shark bow wave. The sharks benefit from these relationships by being cleaned of parasites.

A remora attached to an oceanic whitetip shark (*Carcharhinus longimanus*). The relationship between remoras and sharks is a case of mutualism (photo by Dominique Barray).

Shark Attacks on Humans

People are occasionally killed or injured by sharks. These rare cases provoke extreme emotional reactions from most people and the media irrationally amplifies each incident. As a consequence, tourism suffers where the attack occurred and sharks are killed by people longing to capture the shark responsible for the attack. Clearly, shark attacks occur in the Mediterranean Sea, but they are very rare and the number of deaths from other forms of water-related activities, far surpass those caused by shark attacks. In fact, only 110 attacks have been recorded in these waters. Considering the large number of people who frequent the beaches and the fact that potentially dangerous sharks can be found throughout the Mediterranean, clearly shows that human beings are not part of the diet of any shark.

As a result of some data collection programs, information on historical and recent shark attacks has been collected. One of these programs is the International Shark Attack File (ISAF), based at the Florida Museum of Natural History in Gainesville. According to the ISAF, worldwide there are 70 to 100 shark attacks annually and only 5 to 15 are fatal. But the recorded shark incidents represent only a part of the actual total as several shark attacks go unrecorded. The goal of the ISAF is to create a compilation of all known shark attacks worldwide. However, the ISAF is based in United States, and the files are almost complete for attacks that occur in North American waters, but are incomplete for the rest of the world. More detailed data of shark attacks in the Mediterranean have been recently collected by scientists working in this geographical area. The Italian Great White Shark Data Bank, a program of data collection on the great white shark in the Mediterranean Sea including a compilation of great white shark incidents in these waters, is based in Milan, Italy (the great white shark is the species responsible for most unprovoked attacks occurring in this area).

Shark attacks can occur in shallow, deep, warm or cold waters. As stated previously, large sharks, including the dangerous species, occasionally come close inshore, usually in zones where the bottom drops off very rapidly, such as islands, straits, channels and shoals. The majority of attacks recorded in the Mediterranean occurred along the Italian coasts for various reasons.

Pilot fish (*Naucrates ductor*) accompanying an oceanic whitetip shark (*Carcharhinus longimanus*). Even the relationship between pilot fish and sharks is a case of mutualism (photo by Christine Gstoettner).

The Italian peninsula extends deep into the Mediterranean with many miles of coastline. The waters off Italy are popular waters for swimming and other water based sports. In the past, potentially dangerous sharks like the great white shark, were more common along the Italian and Croatian coasts than in other areas. The North African Countries

It seems that the Baie des Anges, on the Côte d'Azur (France), derived its name from "ange de mer," the French name for the angelshark (genus *Squatina*), evidently once common in these waters. Considering the enormous number of people who frequent famous beaches such as these, and the fact that much more dangerous sharks than angelsharks live in these waters, it seems strange that attacks on humans are extremely rare (photo by Alessandro De Maddalena).

The great white shark (*Carcharodon carcharias*) is without any doubt the most dangerous shark species inhabiting the Mediterranean Sea. In rare cases, this large predator can be aggressive toward humans without provocation (photo by Nicolas Barraqué).

may have many shark attacks that are not reported. In some countries, reports of attacks are intentionally suppressed to prevent a reduction in tourism.

A few shark species can be dangerous without provocation. Only three species have been implicated in many attacks worldwide, which include the great white shark (*Carcharodon carcharias*), tiger shark (*Galeocerdo cuvier*) and bull shark (*Carcharhinus leucas*). Of these sharks, only the great white shark is a stable presence in the Mediterranean. The tiger shark is extremely rare in these waters and the bull shark is not present in the Mediterranean. Great white sharks are responsible for the majority of attacks. Sometimes these animals are extremely aggressive to humans without provocation. However, there are many cases of great white sharks approaching divers and bathers without attacking.

Other species in the Mediterranean are known to sometimes be aggressive towards humans, which include the blue shark (*Prionace glauca*), shortfin mako (*Isurus oxyrinchus*), great hammerhead shark (*Sphyrna mokarran*), oceanic whitetip shark (*Carcharhinus longimanus*), dusky shark (*Carcharhinus obscurus*), bronze whaler shark (*Carcharhinus brachyurus*), blacktip reef shark (*Carcharhinus melanopterus*), blacktip shark (*Carcharhinus limbatus*). Except for the blue shark and shortfin mako, the others species cited are so rare in the Mediterranean that they can not be considered a real danger. Most of the common Mediterranean shark species are harmless to humans. Even so, they need to be treated with caution and respect. Usually sharks fear and avoid man if there are no fishing activities or blood in the water.

An estimated 7 m great white shark (*Carcharodon carcharias*) sighted in the Gulf of Baratti, Italy, on 27 December 1998. In the same waters, on 2 February 1989, a scuba diver, Luciano Costanzo, was killed by a great white shark estimated to be over 6 m long (photo courtesy Capitaneria di Porto di Piombino).

In most cases, an attack ends after the initial contact and the shark does not kill or eat the victim. The fatality rate is low and when the victim dies, it is usually the result of shock or blood loss. Shark attacks can be divided into two categories; provoked and unprovoked attacks. Almost all sharks are capable of inflicting wounds when harassed or injured. Most provoked attacks involve scuba divers or fishermen catching sharks. Unprovoked attacks can be attributed to various causes, mainly feeding, defense or social behaviors. In many unprovoked attacks, the shark bites the victim (usually with little or no loss of flesh) and then swims away. Maybe after biting, the shark realizes that the human is an unusual prey item and immediately releases it. Some attacks could be related to social behaviors unrelated to feeding. This pertains to many species, especially whaler sharks (*Carcharhinus sp.*). In other cases, the shark executes repeat attacks with multiple bites (with large loss of flesh), resulting in wounds that are very serious or fatal. This type of attack is likely the result of feeding or antagonistic behaviors. Sometimes the shark circles and bumps the victim before executing the attack. However, the great white shark often attacks suddenly without warning, and is responsible for most of the serious incidents.

Shark nets are the most effective method of protecting beaches from dangerous sharks. Shark nets have protected beaches in Croatia during the past century. However, beach nets are no longer used, due to the scarcity of dangerous sharks. For the same reason, other means of protection, such as electrical repellants or sharkproof suits, are virtually unknown in the Mediterranean Countries.

The blue shark (*Prionace glauca*) is known to rarely be aggressive towards humans and usually avoids them if there are no fishing activities or blood in the water (photo by Alessandro De Maddalena).

The oceanic whitetip shark (*Carcharhinus longimanus*) is so rare in the Mediterranean that it cannot be considered a real danger (photo by Christine Gstoettner).

Behavior

Until recently, the behavior of these predators was essentially unknown. Slowly, scientists are filling in the gaps of knowledge concerning this fundamental aspect of sharks.

Most sharks hunt alone, but they can occur in pairs or in small or large groups, depending on species. Some sharks, such as the smooth hammerhead (*Sphyrna zygaena*), feed in groups. Many behaviors have a communication function. These predators often attempt to communicate with other animals (man included) using particular signals warning of an attack. These behaviors may function as a means of defending the shark,

Scalloped hammerhead sharks (*Sphyrna lewini*). Most sharks are frequently encountered individually or in pairs, but some species can form enormous groups (photo by Nicolas Barraqué).

its food or its territory. Consequently, the correct interpretation of the behavior, particularly threat displays, can prevent many incidents. Often, the shark circles the prey or even bumps it before attacking. Sometimes as does the great white shark (*Carcharodon carcharias*) and the shortfin mako (*Isurus oxyrinchus*) show a threat display with partial opening of the jaws called gaping. The shortfin mako also swims rapidly in figure eight pattern as a threat display.

Complex social behavior has been observed in large groups of scalloped hammerheads (*Sphyrna lewini*). Studies have revealed a dominance hierarchy, where the larger females compete for the prime social position at the center of the group via various behaviors. These behaviors include jaw gaping, hitting other individuals with their head, accelerated swimming and headshaking. Sometimes, when two great white sharks attempt to feed on the same carcass, one will slap the surface with its caudal fin, splashing water towards the other individual. This behavior has been interpreted as an agonistic display, with one shark trying to force the competitor to flee avoiding a fight. Many sharks eat other shark species as well as members of their own species. Social hierarchies serve as anti-predatory tactic with the subordinate sharks yielding to more dominant sharks. These hierarchies are size-dependent. Smaller individuals move away from larger individuals. Social hierarchies between different species and among members of the same species have been reported when sharks are feeding. Great white sharks are dominate over blue sharks (*Prionace glauca*) when both species are feeding (it has been observed that blue sharks do not scavenge on a whale carcass when white sharks are feeding on the carcass) and oceanic whitetip sharks (*Carcharhinus longimanus*) are dominate over silky sharks (*Carcharhinus falciformis*) of similar size.

The oceanic whitetip shark (*Carcharhinus longimanus*) has conspicuous white spots at the apex of the fin that might be lures for attracting prey. These sharks are always accompanied by many pilot fish (*Naucrates ductor*), and their presence could help to increase the visual effect and attract the prey into the strike zone (photo by Philippe Joachim).

The study of shark behavior shows that these fishes have a wide variety of predatory strategies. Many active sharks, such as the shortfin mako, simply pursue and overtake their prey to capture it. Others attack by surprise and violently, as does the great white shark, White sharks execute horizontal or vertical oriented attacks by swimming fast from deep waters without warning. Other sharks, such as the angelsharks (*Squatina sp.*) lie motionless on the sea bottom in wait of passing prey. When the prey is in range, they strike suddenly and very rapidly. Other species execute strategies to feed on schooling prey. For example, thresher sharks (*Alopias sp.*) slash the water with the incredibly long upper lobe of their caudal fins in order to herd and disorient the prey fish. Blue sharks swim through closely schooled squid with their mouths wide open ingesting squid that inadvertently swim into their mouths. However no shark relies exclusively on a single tactic to capture its prey.

Ecological Importance of Sharks

Sharks are apex predators, at the top of most of the marine food chains. Consequently, they play an important ecological role in marine communities. As predators, they are fundamental instruments of natural selection. They contribute to the stability of the marine ecosystems and maintain biodiversity. Shark predation is an important natural control on the population size of many species. Knowing the diet and biology of sharks is fundamental in understanding how these predators are integrated into the marine ecosystems.

If we exclude other sharks, just a few creatures prey on sharks. The orca (*Orcinus orca*) is one of the few animals that occasionally attack and eat various species of sharks (photo by Alessandro De Maddalena).

To be located at the top of the food chain means that sharks have no enemies. In reality, the eggs and young are susceptible to predation by some fishes and molluscs. Only a few creatures prey on adult sharks, such as other sharks, a few bony fishes like large groupers, and in rare cases, a few marine mammals like the orca (*Orcinus orca*) and sperm whale (*Physeter macrocephalus*). In fact, sharks are totally susceptible to the massive attack by humans, who are decimating many species.

Status of Sharks in the Mediterranean Sea

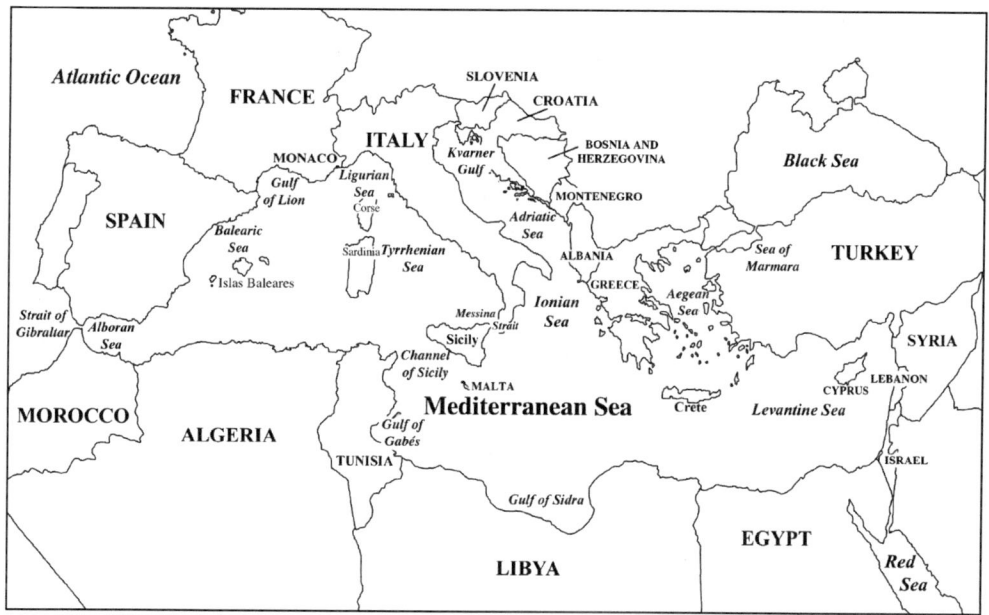

The Mediterranean Sea

Abundance

Almost all shark species have noticeably diminished abundance in the Mediterranean Sea. Most sharks in these waters are now incredibly scarce. The only exception is probably the basking shark (*Cetorhinus maximus*), that for some reason has noticeably increased its abundance in the Mediterranean.

In addition to the species normally recorded in the Mediterranean, some tropical species have entered this sea from the Atlantic Ocean and the Red Sea in recent years. This could be due to global warming and the heating of the Mediterranean Sea (a phenomenon called "tropicalization"). This could explain recent reports of the presence of individuals of species such as the tiger shark (*Galeocerdo cuvier*), the oceanic whitetip

The great white shark (*Carcharodon carcharias*) is among the shark species that have greatly decreased in number in the Mediterranean Sea because of fishing for them and their prey. This photo shows a 594 cm specimen caught off Isola La Formica, Egadi Islands, Italy, in May 1974 (photo courtesy Nitto Mineo).

shark (*Carcharhinus longimanus*), the pigeye shark (*Carcharhinus amboinensis*). There are unconfirmed reports of the whale shark (*Rhincodon typus*), that do not belong in this sea.

There is evidence that many species of sharks have strongly declined during the twentieth century likely due to overfishing of them or their prey. Included in this category are the sandtiger shark (*Carcharias taurus*), smalltooth sand tiger (*Odontaspis ferox*), great white shark (*Carcharodon carcharias*), shortfin mako (*Isurus oxyrinchus*), porbeagle (*Lamna nasus*), tope shark (*Galeorhinus galeus*), common smooth-hound (*Mustelus mustelus*), starry smooth-hound (*Mustelus asterias*), sandbar shark (*Carcharhinus plumbeus*), blue shark (*Prionace glauca*), smooth hammerhead (*Sphyrna zygaena*), piked dogfish (*Squalus acanthias*) and common angelshark (*Squatina squatina*).

Species at risk of total disappearance from the Mediterranean area include some of the species cited above and some that have always been rare even before the overexploitation of the marine fauna. Those species that need immediate total protection are the bramble shark (*Echinorhinus brucus*), angular roughshark (*Oxynotus centrina*), little sleeper shark (*Somniosus rostratus*), bigeyed sixgill shark (*Hexanchus nakamurai*), sawback angelshark (*Squatina aculeata*), smoothback angelshark (*Squatina oculata*), common angelshark, sandtiger shark, smalltooth sand tiger, great white shark, porbeagle, sandbar shark and smooth hammerhead.

In addition to the species normally recorded in the Mediterranean, some tropical species have entered this sea from the Atlantic Ocean and the Red Sea in recent years. This could be due to global warming and the warming of the Mediterranean Sea. This could explain exceptional reports of the presence of individuals of the tiger shark (*Galeocerdo cuvier*), the pigeye shark (*Carcharhinus amboinensis*), and the oceanic whitetip shark (*Carcharhinus longimanus*) (photo by Christine Gstoettner).

The most common species in the Mediterranean are the piked dogfish (*Squalus acanthias*), small blackmouth catshark (*Galeus melastomus*), small-spotted catshark (*Scyliorhinus canicula*), nursehound (*Scyliorhinus stellaris*), common smooth-hound (*Mustelus mustelus*), starry smooth-hound (*Mustelus asterias*), velvet belly (*Etmopterus spinax*), blue shark (*Prionace glauca*), bluntnose sixgill shark (*Hexanchus griseus*) and basking shark (*Cetorhinus maximus*).

Shark Fishery

Man is the only predator impacting shark survival. Many shark species are of economic importance. Today, sharks are decreasing in all oceans because of human activities, and the Mediterranean is a sad testimony to this.

In the past, Mediterranean fishermen captured few sharks and few people consumed their meat. However, the market for shark meat has dramatically increased in the last few decades. As the fishery for bony fish has been depleted, fishermen have compensated by targeting shark. For example, the people of Turkey, in part for their religious belief and in part for lack of tradition, only consumed small quantities of shark meat in the past. But the recent reduction of commercially important bony fishes compelled fishermen to intensely fish for sharks.

A great hammerhead (*Sphyrna mokarran*) has been hooked (photo by Harald Bänsch).

Many sharks are fished commercially and are being overfished throughout the world. Species such as the porbeagle (*Lamna nasus*), shortfin mako (*Isurus oxyrinchus*), piked dogfish (*Squalus acanthias*), smooth-hounds (*Mustelus sp.*), requiem sharks (family Carcharhinidae) are heavily exploited. The piked dogfish (*Squalus acanthias*) is the leading shark taken commercially worldwide. An estimated 50 percent of the world shark catch is believed to be taken incidentally while fishing for other species, such as tunas and swordfish. This unplanned capture of marine animals is called "bycatch." Pelagic longlines are single-stranded fishing lines 18 to 72 km long with an average 1500 hooks attached. This terrible gear is widely used in many parts of the world (including the Mediterranean) to catch tuna and swordfish. In some areas, the number of sharks caught by longliners reaches 90 percent of total captures. Species such as the blue shark (*Prionace glauca*) and shortfin mako are the most impacted by this fishing method, but many others, such as the common thresher shark (*Alopias vulpinus*) and the smooth hammerhead (*Sphyrna zygaena*), are also taken occasionally.

Sharks are more vulnerable to commercial fishing than bony fishes as they have long sexual maturation times, low fecundity, long gestation periods and they produce small numbers of young. Moreover many shark species segregate by size and sex. The exploitation of sharks in a nursery area, where only newborns live, can be particularly devastating. These fishes are unable to withstand overexploitation since this has long term effects as rebuilding shark populations takes many years.

Nobody knows how many sharks are caught in the world, but the number is staggering. Annual landings of cartilaginous fishes reported to the Food and Agriculture Organization of the United Nations (FAO) amount to around 820,000 tons, but the

A 5.2 meter great white shark (*Carcharodon carcharias*) caught in the tuna trap off Sidi Daoud, Tunisia, in April 2001 (photo by Walid Maamouri).

actual total is surely much higher since much of catch is not recorded. This estimate does not include several thousands of sharks that are boated by fishermen annually and thrown-back because in many countries, numerous shark species are considered not suitable for market.

Several shark species are caught by recreational anglers. Many years of unregulated and unmonitored sportfishing in the blue shark nursery area located in the Adriatic Sea, Central Mediterranean, has been devastating. Other species that are strongly affected by sportfishing are the thresher sharks (*Alopias sp.*).

The catches and landings of sharks in the Mediterranean in the past decades have been much higher than today. Both researchers and fishermen agree on this point. Unfortunately, exhaustive data collection on shark captures has not been done in the past for the Mediterranean Sea. The scarce and incomplete data collected considered only a few species, such as porbeagle (*Lamna nasus*), catsharks (*Scyliorhinus spp.*), smooth-hounds (*Mustelus spp.*) piked dogfish (*Squalus acanthias*), dogfish sharks (family Squalidae), angelsharks (family Squatinidae) and large sharks (Squaliformes). Data for these few categories are insufficient to provide information for all shark species that inhabit the Mediterranean Sea. Having no information from the past to compare with that from the present for capture by species, scientists are unable to assess the status of any shark species in the Mediterranean. This is a big problem and the governments and the institutes that collect fisheries data are responsible for the terrible situation of shark decline in the Mediterranean.

The Italian Ichthyological Society has recently presented data on the past and present abundance of the smooth hammerhead in the Sicilian waters. In the area off Palermo, that once was an area where hammerhead sharks were captured in high numbers, shark captures diminished at least 96 to 98 percent in the last 30 years. Hammerheads were once abundant in these waters, and 300 to 400 specimens were caught incidentally each year during summer months in drift nets used to capture swordfishes, while another 50 hammerheads were caught each year on pelagic longlines. The fishermen themselves are aware that the main reason for this disaster has been the use of drift nets called "spadare." The "spadare" has been banned in Italy since 1998 following resolutions by the General Assembly of the ONU (UNGA) and the International Commission for the Conservation of Atlantic Tunas (ICCAT) that prohibited the use of this kind of drift net. But the ban arrived too late. It is likely that many other shark species have faced a tragic destiny similar to the one of the smooth hammerhead.

Human Consumption of Shark Meat

Humans catch sharks for meat, cartilage, skin, oil and other products. Shark meat is consumed in almost all European and Mediterranean Countries. In some of these nations, shark meat is a significant part of the human diet. Together with China, Spain and Italy are the leading importers of sharks in the world, according to recent statistics from the FAO. Moreover, Spain and France are among the leading shark fishing nations worldwide. In the Mediterranean, sharks are sold fresh, chilled, frozen, smoked and dried-salted.

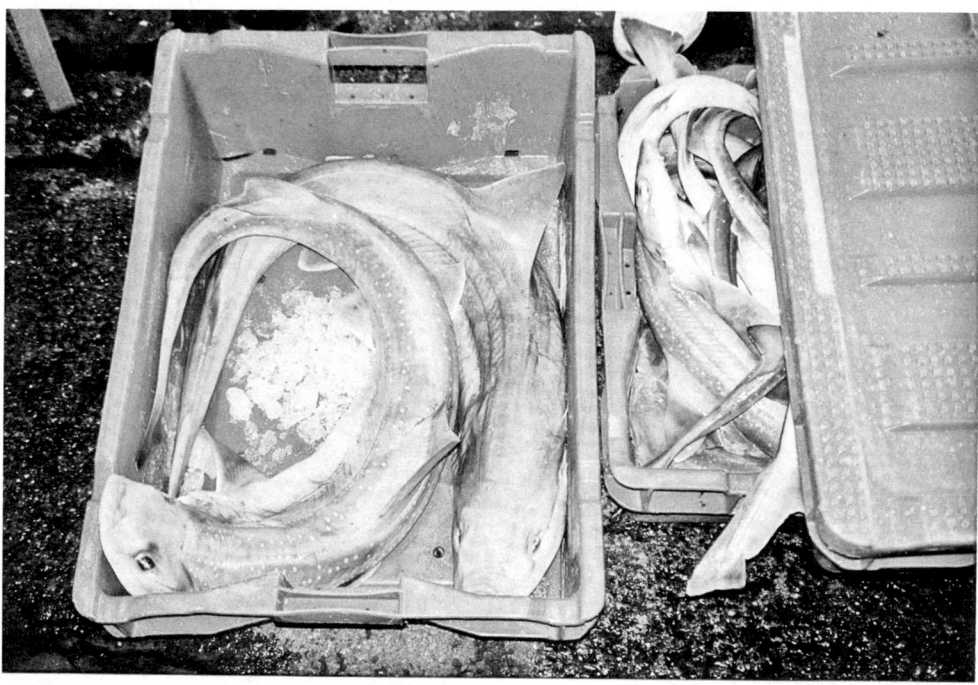

Common smooth-hounds (*Mustelus mustelus*) and starry smooth-hounds (*Mustelus asterias*) in a fish market (photo by Harald Bänsch).

A 158 cm male porbeagle (*Lamna nasus*) at the Milan fish market (Italy). The meat of this species is highly desired in European countries (photo by Alessandro De Maddalena).

An about 300 cm common thresher shark (*Alopias vulpinus*) in a market in Corfu (Greece), caught in the Aegean Sea in early October 1999 (photo by Alec Moore).

The higher quality meat is that of the shortfin mako (*Isurus oxyrinchus*), while other desired species include the porbeagle (*Lamna nasus*), the piked dogfish (*Squalus acanthias*) and the smooth-hounds (*Mustelus sp.*). In Mediterranean Countries, the meat of most sharks is sold under incorrect names, usually as smooth-hound. Exceptions to this practice are dogfish (*Squalus acanthias*) and catshark (*Scyliorhinus sp.*), which are usually sold under their correct common names. In some countries, this has changed recently due to new laws regarding the fish trade that now require proper identification of the species. However, since it has not happened yet, many people will continue to eat shark meat without knowing what they're really eating. Consequently, there is little awareness of the threats to sharks among European consumers.

Conservation

Humans also have an indirect, but just as harmful effect on Mediterranean sharks due to depletion of resources, environmental pollution, global warming and habitat destruction. Toxic chemicals can be absorbed or ingested by animals and passed up the food chain through feeding. Consequently, top predators like sharks are at higher risk

An approximately 300 cm great hammerhead (*Sphyrna mokarran*), caught in the tuna trap off Camogli, Italy, Ligurian Sea, on 21 September 1969 (photo by Soc. An. Coop. "La tonnarella").

An estimated 500 cm female great white shark swims in a tuna cage on June 12, 2002, off Tripoli, Libya (photo by Lorenzo Millan).

since several toxins accumulate in each organism along the food chain, becoming most concentrated at the top. For example, mercury, a toxic metallic element, has been shown to accumulate especially in long-lived predator muscle tissue. Accumulation of mercury increases with the age of the shark, as a result of the inefficient elimination from its tissues. Therefore sharks, tunas and swordfishes can represent an unwanted dietary source of mercury for humans. For this reason, regular monitoring of shark meat is done by health professionals.

A few species are now protected in some countries, but the short list of protected species is far from complete. Moreover, fishing vessels often operate in flagrant violation of fishing regulations. Even the few protected species are still captured, like the basking sharks (*Cetorhinus maximus*) in Italian waters. Researchers are aware of this situation, but the European governments show a total lack of interest in shark conservation. Shark conservation and shark fishery regulation is considered a problem of secondary importance. In the Mediterranean, shark research is neglected in favor of study of more commercially important fishes, such as tuna and swordfish.

The rapid decline in sharks warrants an urgent investigation into the status of many species. Effective conservation and management of shark fisheries should be based on research of biology, ecology, distribution, abundance and exploitation of sharks. Understanding the biology and ecology of sharks can provide significant insights into protecting them from extinction. No country in the Mediterranean records accurate capture data by species. A continuous long-term study could provide fundamental information on occurrence, relative abundance and fisheries status of all Mediterranean shark species. There is the need for biological information on the life history of many shark species, including feeding ecology and predator-prey relationships, to better assess stock status and harvest impact. It is also necessary to better manage fisheries in which sharks constitute a significant bycatch. Existing fisheries laws need to be enforced. Lack of research and management in many countries is leading to extinction of several shark species. The removal of sharks will lead to increases in some prey populations and consequently in declines in other prey species. The stability of the Mediterranean marine ecosystems is in danger.

Shark Conservation Associations Active in the Area

SharkProject

Address: Frankfurter Str. 111 b, 63067 Offenbach, Deutschland
Website: www.sharkproject.org
Email: info@sharkproject.org

Sharks Mission France

Address: 193, rue des Acacias, 01190 Sermoyer, France
Website: www.sharks-mission.fr
Email: Sharksmissionfrance@gmail.com

Requins En Péril

Address: Le sentenier, 27230 Saint Mards de Fresne, France
Website: www.requinsenperil.com
E-mail: requinsenperil@gmail.com

Research on Sharks in the Mediterranean Area

About Research

Sharks are difficult to study and there are many gaps in knowledge concerning these creatures. Considering the wide distribution and large size of many sharks, the amount of data on many Mediterranean species was surprising scarce until a few years ago. The number of scientists working on Mediterranean sharks has always been relatively small. There are many difficulties encountered when studying these animals. Field research is expensive and funds are often very restricted or nonexistent. Sharks are very difficult to study in the wild, and many species are uncommon. Most sharks are elusive and avoid people and most species are difficult to keep in captivity. However, most studies cannot be done in the artificial conditions of captivity.

Many young biologists wish to study sharks, but change their mind when they see the difference between the excitement of cage diving with great white sharks in South African waters and the day to day work of taking measurements on dead 40-cm catsharks in a fish market at night. Documentaries on television present the most dramatic view of the shark specialist's work, but most of what is know about sharks and most of the present research on sharks worldwide has been done on dead specimens. Most shark research is not a dramatic underwater encounter with a 5-m great white shark. But, if the passion for sharks is real, the study of dead sharks will be quite satisfying.

As we have said previously, effective conservation and management of shark fisheries is based on research that advances the knowledge of Mediterranean sharks. The sharks of these waters have been the subject of periodic and discontinuous studies. Important scientific works have been published by some researchers for the Mediterranean, such as those by Enrico Tortonese, Christian Capapé, Juan Antonio Moreno, Franco Cigala Fulgosi, Jean Cadenat, Jacques Blache, Joan Barrull and Isabel Mate, just to name a few. These works are the products of individual researchers, while extensive research programs led by large institutions or collaboration of several researchers are rare.

The lack of large scale data collection programs on sharks has been identified recently by many organizations, primarily the Food and Agriculture Organization of the United Nations (FAO) and ecological institutions such as WildAid, based in the United States. These organizations promote initiatives in the Mediterranean countries

Most research on sharks, especially in the Mediterranean, has to be done on dead specimens. The photo shows a 293 cm female bluntnose sixgill shark (*Hexanchus griseus*), caught by a commercial fishing vessel off Pace, Sicily, Italy, on 29 October 2000. This shark was studied as part of a research program on the biology of this species in Northeastern Sicilian waters (photo by Antonio Celona).

to promote research on sharks in these waters. Unfortunately, the barriers to effective shark research still persist. The first barrier is a scientific community that is too closed, with little collaboration among researchers. The second is the lack of funds for research in the field of zoology. On a positive note, there is a recent increase of studies and scientific publications on Mediterranean sharks. The most important examples are articles in the scientific journals *Annales* (published by the Science and Research Centre of the Republic of Slovenia, Koper, Slovenia) and *Acta Adriatica* (published by the Institute of Oceanography and Fisheries, Split, Croatia), which are publishing a long series of important studies focused on the sharks inhabiting the Mediterranean, including various aspects of the biology, morphology and distribution of these fishes.

Methods For Studying The Sharks

There are different ways to study the sharks in the Mediterranean area.

One way is to study sharks captured by commercial fishermen. Sharks are often present in markets, especially in those of great size. Unfortunately, most sharks are

In the recent years, the scientific journal *Annales*, published by the Science and Research Centre of the Republic of Slovenia, has been particularly important for the advancement of knowledge of the Mediterranean sharks (photo courtesy *Annales*).

Spanish shark specialist Joan Barrull shows a specimen of angular roughshark (*Oxynotus centrina*) (photo by Joan Barrull and Isabel Mate).

already gutted and often without head, skin and fins. In that case, they are obviously not useful for any study. Whole sharks are found more frequently in some fish markets in cities along the coast and in the largest fish markets of the bigger towns. The specimens examined can be useful for a wide spectrum of studies, including external morphology, systematics, anatomy, diet and reproduction. Some of these studies are not possible on large specimens because medium and large sized sharks are generally eviscerated by fishermen immediately upon capture and the viscera are discarded at sea. When reliable capture data is available from fishermen or is collected by on-board researchers, knowledge of the species geographical and bathymetric distribution is obtained and even information about segregation by sex and size and existence of nursery areas may be evident. An additional source of useful information about the diet of sharks comes from the examination of shark predation and scavenging on carcasses of other animals. In some cases, shark specimens are caught during cruises aboard research vessels. Even specimens caught by sportfishermen are sometimes the object study.

Another precious source of specimens and data for the ichthyologists that study the sharks of the Mediterranean are the numerous museums present in the area. European countries often keep large and important shark collections in their museums of Natural Science, Zoology and Comparative Anatomy. Most of these materials are historical pieces, acquired by the museums mainly during the nineteenth century and in the first half of the twentieth century. Most specimens preserved in these collections have not been studied yet. Unfortunately, those collections are often inadequately pre-

A taxidermied basking shark (*Cetorhinus maximus*) preserved in the Museo civico di Storia Naturale "Giacomo Doria" in Genoa, Italy. Museum collections are precious sources of material for the researchers that study sharks (photo by Alessandro De Maddalena, courtesy Museo civico di Storia Naturale "Giacomo Doria," Genoa).

served and the museum catalogues are sometimes lost or lack important data. Specimens are preserved in different ways. Whole specimens are taxidermied or preserved in liquid (alcohol or formalin), as well as their skeletons (usually only the jaws are preserved). Towns such as Florence and Genoa in Italy, Monte-Carlo, and Prague, Czech Republic, have museums that host collections containing many hundreds of specimens from the Mediterranean and other parts of the world.

Another way to study sharks is in captivity. Observation of captive specimens permits the study of swimming, reproduction and sensorial abilities. The study of the shark behavior under these conditions has been rightly criticized because the behavior of a shark forced to live in a tank can be considerably different from that of a free specimen. Aquaria are now common throughout the Mediterranean area, including some historical aquaria, such as the aquarium of the Oceanographic Museum of Monaco, Principauté de Monaco) or that of the Zoological Station of Naples, Italy. Other aquaria are very modern, such as the Aquarium of Genoa, Italy and L'Oceanografic of Valencia, Spain. Most aquaria keep some sharks, but they are often tropical sharks. Sharks are difficult to keep in captivity as they require large tanks and high water purity. Under these unnatural conditions, they consume a very small amount of food and can stop feeding for many weeks or months and sometimes die. For these reasons and others related to their physiological needs, many shark species, especially large sharks and

This 522 cm female great white shark (*Carcharodon carcharias*) caught in Kvarner, Croatia, on 29 May 1906 and preserved in the Museo civico di Storia Naturale di Trieste, Italy, is one of the largest taxidermied specimens preserved worldwide and is the largest skin-mounted specimen in Europe (photo by Alessandro De Maddalena, courtesy Museo civico di Storia Naturale "Giacomo Doria," Genoa).

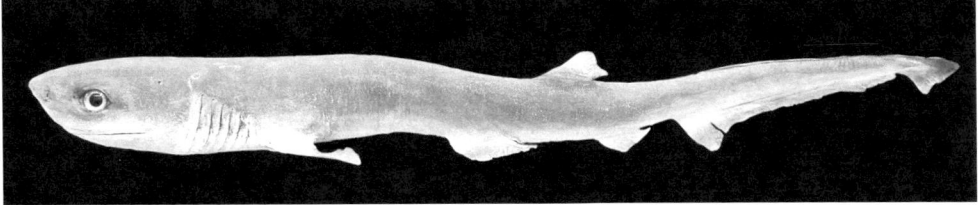

An 82 cm bigeyed sixgill shark (*Hexanchus nakamurai*) caught in an unknown location in the Mediterranean Sea and preserved in the Národní muzeum in Prague, Czech Republic (photo by Radek Šanda, courtesy Národní muzeum, Prague).

those that are pelagic, rarely survive in aquaria. Unfortunately, most European aquaria only exhibit the animals and are not places where serious research is conducted. This needs to change. Keeping sharks in captivity is morally unacceptable, but it can be partially justified if the sharks are object of studies that could be important to advancement of knowledge and promote conservation for the species.

The last way to studying sharks is in their natural environment. That can provide useful data about shark behavior, distribution, movements and seasonality, especially through long term studies and tagging programs. However, it is still a great problem to conduct this kind of study in the Mediterranean, due to lack of funding (fundamental for expensive field research) and the scarcity of most sharks in these waters. An alternative way to gather data from the field is to network with coast guards, professional and sport fishermen, diving clubs and associations as well with other marine biologists working in the field on other species. The data collected in this way forms a database that can be analyzed by shark specialists.

Shark Research Programs Active in the Area

The Mediterranean Shark Research Group (MSRG) was created in summer of 2000 by four shark researchers: Alessandro De Maddalena (Italian Great White Shark Data Bank, Italy), Lovrenc Lipej (Marine Biological Station of Piran, Slovenia), Joan Barrull and Isabel Mate (Barcelona Museum of Zoology, Spain). The MSRG promotes a web of information exchange between ichthyologists who study sharks of the Mediterranean Sea, with the intent of complete collaboration. The MSRG has grown over the years to include 55 researchers from 13 countries (Spain, France, Italy, Germany, Slovenia, Croatia, Malta, Turkey, Tunisia, Algeria, Ireland, the United States and Brazil). The activity of the Mediterranean Shark Research Group is a positive change, but the group is facing serious problems in conducting its research projects. The governments still show little interest in these research activities. The MSRG researchers participate on a voluntary basis, but this will not ensure the conservation of Mediterranean shark populations. Governments of major European shark fishing countries should put far more resources

Alessandro De Maddalena about to present a lecture at the Maison des Océans in Paris, France. De Maddalena is one of the founding members of the Mediterranean Shark Research Group (photo by Richard Allan).

into research on shark biology and fisheries. Mediterranean nations should take the responsibility to facilitate research on all shark species and Europe must finally assume an important role in shark conservation.

To contact the Mediterranean Shark Research Group, write Monte Nebbio—l'Orsala 20167 Appietto, Corse, France, or email corsica-msrg@sfr.fr.

Several other research programs and studies are conducted in the Mediterranean by ichthyologists and biologists working for marine biology institutes, natural history museums and universities. The reader can find an updated and complete list of the institutes where research on sharks of the Mediterranean are conducted as of this writing, including the species on which these studies are focused. The names of the institutes and the researchers that are involved, and their contact addresses are shown below.

Algeria

Faculté des Sciences Biologiques, Université des Sciences et Techniques Houari Boumediene
Address: USTHB BP 32, 16111 El Alia, Alger, Algérie
E-mail: fhemida@usthb.dz, hemidafarid@yahoo.fr
Researchers: Farid Hemida
Species studied: all species of the Algerian waters

Croatia

Department of Marine Studies, University of Split
Address: Livanjska 5 / III, 21000 Split, Croatia
Website: http://more.unist.hr/
E-mail: soldo@unist.hr
Researchers: Alen Soldo, Ivan Jardas
Species studied: all species of the Adriatic Sea and particularly the great white shark (*Carcharodon carcharias*) and basking shark (*Cetorhinus maximus*)

France

Ailerons
Address: Campus de l'Université de Montpellier II, place Eugène Bataillon, 34090 Montpellier
Website: http://asso-ailerons.fr
E-mail : contact@asso-ailerons.fr
Researchers: Matthieu Lapinski, Mickaël Diter, Nicolas Ziani
Species studied: all species occurring along the Mediterranean French coast

APECS
Address: 13, rue J.-Fr. Tartu BP 51151, 29111 Brest Cedex, France
Website: www.asso-apecs.org

E-mail: asso@asso-apecs.org
Researchers: Hélène Gadenne, Agathe Lefranc, Eric Stephan

Laboratoire d'ichtyologie, Université Montpellier II, Sciences et Techniques du Languedoc
Address: case 102, 34095 Montpellier cedex 05, France
Researchers: Christian Capapé, Jean-Pierre Quignard
Species studied: all species of the Tunisian and French waters

Stellaris
Address: avenue du Palais de la mer 30240 Le Grau-du-Roi, France
Website: www.stellaris-asso.org
E-mail: contact@stellaris-asso.org
Researchers: Jean-Marc Groul, François Poisson, Sarah Muttoni
Shark species studied: all species of the Gulfe du Lion

Italy

Aquastudio Research Institute
via Trapani 6, IT-98121 Messina, Italy
E-mail: aquauno@tin.it
Researchers: Antonio Di Natale, Antonio Celona
Shark species studied: fishery of all species of the Italian waters

Dipartimento di Scienze Della Terra, Universita' Di Parma
Address: Parco Area delle Scienze 157/A , 43100 Parma, Italy
Researchers: Franco Cigala Fulgosi
Shark species studied: rare species of the italian waters and shark fossils

Dipartimento di Scienze Della Vita, Seconda Universitá Di Napoli
via Vivaldi 43, 81100 Caserta, Italy
E-mail: lucia.rocco@unina2.it
Researchers: Lucia Rocco, Vincenzo Stingo, Domenico Costagliola, Innocenza Liguori
Shark species studied: genetic of the nursehound (*Scyliorhinus stellaris*), small-spotted catshark (*Scyliorhinus canicula*) and starry smooth-hound (*Mustelus asterias*).

FAO
Address: viale delle Terme di Caracalla, IT-00100 Roma, Italy
Website: http://www.fao.org/fi
E-mail: FI-Inquiries@fao.org
Researchers: Stefania Vannuccini
Shark species studied: fishery of all species

Italian Great White Shark Data Bank
Address: Adresse : 12 Solent Court, 136 Runciman Drive, 7975 Simon's Town, South Africa
Website: www.alessandrodemaddalena.com
E-mail: alessandrodemaddalena@gmail.com

Researchers: Alessandro De Maddalena
Shark species studied: great white shark (*Carcharodon carcharias*) in the Mediterranean Sea

NECTON
Address: via Celona 11, I-98165 Ganzirri (Messina), Italy
Website: http://www.necton.it/
E-mail: celona.necton@email.it
Researchers: Antonio Celona
Shark species studied: all species of the Sicilian waters

Malta

Conservation Research, Department of Biology, University of Malta
Address: Msida, MSD 06, Malta
E-mail: avel@cis.um.edu.mt
Researchers: Adriana Vella, Jesmond Dalli
Shark species studied: all species of the Maltese waters

Sharklab
Address: 404 Sqaq Il Forn, Hamrun, HMR 1961, Malta
Website: http://www.sharklab-malta.org
E-mail: info@sharklab-malta.org

Slovenia

Marine Biological Station, National Institute of Biology
Address: Fornace 41, SI-6330 Piran, Slovenia
E-mail: Lipej@mbss.org
Researchers: Lovrenc Lipej, Tihomir Makovec, Bojan Marceta
Shark species studied: all species of the Adriatic Sea

Piran Aquarium
Address: Kidričevo nabrežje, SI-6330, Piran, Slovenia
E-mail: akvarij.piran@guest.arnes.si
Researchers: Valter Ziza
Shark species studied: all species of the Adriatic Sea

Spain

Associación Iberica De Tiburones y Rayas (Aityr)
Address: Apartado de Correos 7.052, 28080 Madrid, Spain
Web site: http://www.aityr.com
E-mail: aityr@aityr.com
Shark species studied: all species of the Spanish waters

Grupo de Investigación Ictiológica de Los Tiburones (Giit)

Address: Ctra. Nacional VI, km 82, n° 13, 40150 Villacastín (Segovia), Spain
E-mail: ja.moreno.giit@teleline.es
Shark species studied: all species of the Spanish waters

Laboratorio de Vertebrats, Secció Ictiologia, Museo de Ciencias Naturales, Museo de Zoologia
Address: apartat de Correus 593, E-08080 Barcelona, Spain
E-mail: jbarrull@pie.xtec.es
Researchers: Joan Barrull, Isabel Mate, Manel Bueno
Shark species studied: all species of the Catalan Sea and particularly the great white shark (*Carcharodon carcharias*) and basking shark (*Cetorhinus maximus*)

L'elasmogrup
Address: c/ San Valewro 8 pta 6, E-46005 Valencia, Spain
Website: www.facebook.com/pages/LElasmogrup/155964927938413
E-mail: javier.guallart@uv.es
Researchers: Javier Guallart, Pablo García-Salinas, Arantxa Catalán-Arnandis
Shark species studied: species caught in commercial fisheries, particularly deepsea species

Turkey

Ichthyological Research Society
Address: Atatürk Mahallesi, Mentesoglu Cad. Idil apt., No 3, D 4, Ümraniye, 81230 Istanbul, Turkey
E-mail: hakankabasakal@hotmail.com
Researchers: Hakan Kabasakal
Shark species studied: all species of the Turkish waters and Aegean Sea

How to Collaborate on the Research

Everyone can contribute to the research of sharks in the Mediterranean waters. Reporting sightings and captures of sharks is the best way to contribute. The data collected will be archived in an existing research database. The report will be used again as new research projects are started focused on species that are not the subject of any current study. Note that information on captures and sightings of all shark species are of interest, not just those for large species.

To help the data collection, the following form is included here. The information in the form needs to be as accurate and complete as possible. However, do not hesitate to send incomplete forms. For anglers that capture a shark, we strongly recommend releasing the shark after capture. In this, these wonderful animals will live to fight another day. For catch and release cases, it is not important that the form be filled out completely.

In order to make the contribution as useful as possible, measure the total length in a straight line, from the tip of the snout to the tip of the upper lobe of caudal fin. If

Small-spotted catshark (*Scyliorhinus canicula*) (photo by Sarah Muttoni).

A bluntnose sixgill shark (*Hexanchus griseus*) photographed in the Eastern Mediterranean Sea at 750 m depth (photo by E. Gilat and A. Gelman).

there is no way to accurately measure the specimen, an estimate of length is acceptable. Note that there are creative ways to capture the length. Pace the number of steps, heal to toe, that cover the length. Repeat the same pacing when a measuring instrument is available. Alternately, a cord or string can be used to span the length. The cord length can be measured later.

The weight is considered less important and the best weight is for the whole shark.

The weight of a dressed shark is also valuable, but the extent of the dressing (gutted, beheaded, finned or other) needs to be specified. Like the length measurement, the weight can be estimated if a scale is not available.

Remember that the sex of the specimen is easily recognizable by observing the underside of the shark, at the level of the pelvic fins (the pair fins located in the pelvic region), where males have two claspers (copulatory organs) in shape of cylindrical appendages.

Try to take a photo of the shark as it will be very useful for allowing us to identify the species for our archives. When you shoot a photo of the shark, try to take it of the whole specimen, from its side; additional photos of details, especially the underside of the head and the teeth are also suggested.

The form for reporting sightings or captures of sharks in the Mediterranean Sea is shown below.

Logo of the Mediterranean Shark Research Group (by Juan Antonio Moreno).

Mediterranean Shark Research Group

Form for Reporting Sightings or Captures of Sharks in the Mediterranean Sea

Shark species: _____

On which characteristics do you recognized the species? _____

_____

Type of record (capture, underwater encounter, sighting or attack):

_____

Date: _____

Time: _____

Location (if possible, indicate even the exact position): _____

_____

Position (latitude and longitude): _____

Sea depth: _____

Distance from the coast: _____

Weather: _____

State of the sea: _____

Activity of the observer at the time of the encounter: _____

_____

Total length (in a straight line from the snout to the tip of the upper lobe of caudal fin): _____

Weight (specify if whole or gutted): _____

Sex (on their underside males have two cylindrical appendages at the pelvic fin base): _____

Stomach contents: _____

Comments on the behavior of the specimen: _____

If it's a pregnant female add: _____

    Number of embryos: _____

    Total length of embryos: _____

    Weight of embryos: _____

    Sex of embryos: _____

Presence of other animals in the immediate area: _____

_____

Other details and comments: _____

_____

Enclose a photo of the specimen. _____

Names of the eyewitness / fisherman / diver: _____

_____

_____

Data of the compiler

Name: _____

Address: _____

Telephone: _____

E-mail: _____

Do you authorize the publication of these data and pictures? _____

Please send this form to the following address:
Dott. Alessandro De Maddalena
e-mail: alessandrodemaddalena@gmail.com
website: www.alessandrodemaddalena.com
Facebook: www.facebook.com/alessandro.demaddalena.1

Classification of Sharks Living in the Mediterranean Sea

In this section, 50 species of sharks that inhabit the Mediterranean Sea are described. They are classified in 5 orders, 17 families and 27 Genera. The list includes the rarest species, even those for which just one or two specimens have been recorded in these waters. The list does not include the species without at least one confirmed record. The whale shark (*Rhincodon typus*) and the barbeled houndshark (*Leptocharias smithii*) have been reported, but there is no confirming evidence.

Order Hexanchiformes

Family Hexanchidae

Genus Heptranchias
    Heptranchias perlo–Sharpnose sevengill shark
Genus Hexanchus
    Hexanchus griseus–Bluntnose sixgill shark
    Hexanchus nakamurai–Bigeyed sixgill shark

Order Squaliformes

Family Echinorhinidae

Genus Echinorhinus
    Echinorhinus brucus–Bramble shark

Family Squalidae

Genus Squalus
    Squalus acanthias–Piked dogfish
    Squalus blainvillei–Longnose spurdog
    Squalus megalops–Shortnose spurdog

Family Centrophoridae

Genus Centrophorus
  Centrophorus granulosus–Gulper shark

Family Etmopteridae

Genus Etmopterus
  Etmopterus spinax–Velvet belly

Family Somniosidae

Genus Centroscymnus
  Centroscymnus coelolepis—Portuguese dogfish
Genus Somniosus
  Somniosus rostratus–Little sleeper shark

Family Oxynotidae

Genus Oxynotus
  Oxynotus centrina -Angular roughshark

Family Dalatiidae

Genus Dalatias
  Dalatias licha–Kitefin shark

Order Squatiniformes

Family Squatinidae

Genus Squatina
  Squatina aculeata–Sawback angelshark
  Squatina oculata–Smoothback angelshark
  Squatina squatina—Common angelshark

Order Lamniformes

Family Odontaspididae

Genus Carcharias
  Carcharias taurus–Sandtiger shark
Genus Odontaspis
  Odontaspis ferox–Smalltooth sand tiger

Family Alopiidae

Genus Alopias
  Alopias superciliosus—Bigeye thresher
  Alopias vulpinus—Common thresher shark

Family Cetorhinidae

Genus Cetorhinus
  Cetorhinus maximus–Basking shark

Family Lamnidae

Genus Carcharodon
  Carcharodon carcharias–Great white shark
Genus Isurus
  Isurus oxyrinchus–Shortfin mako
  Isurus paucus–Longfin mako
Genus Lamna
  Lamna nasus–Porbeagle

Order Carcharhiniformes

Family Scyliorhinidae

Genus Galeus
  Galeus melastomus–Blackmouth catshark
Genus Scyliorhinus
  Scyliorhinus canicula–Small-spotted catshark
  Scyliorhinus stellaris–Nursehound

Family Triakidae

Genus Galeorhinus
  Galeorhinus galeus–Tope shark
Genus Mustelus
  Mustelus asterias–Starry smooth-hound
  Mustelus mustelus–Common smooth-hound
  Mustelus mediterraneus–Blackspotted smooth-hound

Family Carcharhinidae

Genus Carcharhinus
  Carcharhinus acarenatus—Strait shark
  Carcharhinus altimus—Bignose shark

Carcharhinus amboinensis—Pigeye shark
Carcharhinus brachyurus—Copper shark
Carcharhinus brevipinna—Spinner shark
Carcharhinus falciformis—Silky shark
Carcharhinus limbatus–Blacktip shark
Carcharhinus longimanus–Oceanic whitetip shark
Carcharhinus melanopterus—Blacktip reef shark
Carcharhinus obscurus—Dusky shark
Carcharhinus plumbeus–Sandbar shark
Genus Galeocerdo
    Galeocerdo cuvier—Tiger shark
Genus Prionace
    Prionace glauca–Blue shark
Genus Rhizoprionodon
    Rhizoprionodon acutus—Milk shark

Family Sphyrnidae

Genus Sphyrna
    Sphyrna lewini—Scalloped hammerhead
    Sphyrna mokarran—Great hammerhead
    Sphyrna tudes–Golden hammerhead
    Sphyrna zygaena–Smooth hammerhead

Species Identification

Introduction to Species Identification

Some species inhabiting the Mediterranean, such as the bigeyed thresher (*Alopias superciliosus*) and the basking shark (*Cetorhinus maximus*) are very easy to identify even by a casual observer. For other species, like the whaler sharks (*Carcharhinus sp.*), the identification is complicated, because these sharks show several similarities to other sharks and many details need to be considered to identify the right species. Moreover, the morphology of a shark can show variability within a species, especially with age. Even species which are easy to identify as adults, such as the sandbar shark (*Carcharhinus plumbeus*), can be hard to identify for very young individuals. In fact, the new-born sandbar sharks often have lower first dorsal fin, smaller pectoral fins and longer snout than the adult specimens.

What is needed to identify a shark? Important characteristics are size (the shark may be a juvenile of a large species), body shape, length and shape of the snout, absence or presence and size of spiracles, size and color of the eyes, number and size and position of gill slits. In some cases, teeth can be prominent and visible exteriorly, and their shape may be visible. Shape and position of fins is one of the most important diagnostic characteristics. In some species, a dorsal fin or the anal fin can be absent. Even coloration can help in species identification, especially when the shark shows a pattern. Juveniles can show differences in coloration, particularly in the tips and posterior margins of the fins that can be lighter or darker than in adults. Dead specimens loose brightness of color that is present when alive. If the dead specimen needs to be identified, teeth shape and dental formula that may lead to a positive identification.

Key to the Species

In order to systematically identify the species of a given animal group, scientific books include keys to identification. The reader has to answer to a series of questions related to the external morphology of the specimen. Each reply narrows the possibilities and is followed by another question that eventually leads to the identification. Unfortunately, keys can be long and based on characteristics not easily observed. Consequently, we have prepared a key to identification that is as simple as possible.

To identify the species, use the tables as follows:
(a) identify the right Order among the 5 listed;
(b) inside the Order, choose a family;
(c) inside the family, identify the right species.

A glossary is provided to clarify some of the terms used in the key and detailed descriptions of these sharks.

ORDER HEXANCHIFORMES	**6 or 7 gill slits, 1 dorsal fin, anal fin**
Family Hexanchidae	same characteristics as the order
Heptranchias perlo–Sharpnose sevengill shark	7 gill slits
Hexanchus griseus–Bluntnose sixgill shark	6 gill slits, caudal peduncle short
Hexanchus nakamurai–Bigeyed sixgill shark	6 gill slits, caudal peduncle long
ORDER SQUALIFORMES	**No anal fin, body not ray-like, 2 dorsal fins, 5 gill slits**
(a) Family Echinorhinidae	dorsal fins located far back on shark (the origin of the first dorsal over the pelvic fins)
Echinorhinus brucus–Bramble shark	same characteristics as the family
(b) Family Squalidae	dorsal fin spines, no caudal fin terminal lobe
Squalus acanthias–Piked dogfish	dorsal fin spines, small caudal keels, first dorsal fin origin posterior to pectoral fin free rear tip, white spotted coloration
Squalus blainvillei–Longnose spurdog	dorsal fin spines, small caudal keels, head massive, first dorsal fin origin over pectoral fin inner margin, pectoral fin free rear tips rounded, no white spots on body nor black fin apex
Squalus megalops–Shortnose spurdog	dorsal fin spines, small caudal keels, head massive, first dorsal fin origin over pectoral fin inner margin, pectoral fin free rear tips pointed, dorsal and caudal fin apex black, no white spots on body
(c) Family Centrophoridae	dorsal fin spines, pectoral fin free rear tips very long and pointed
Centrophorus granulosus–Gulper shark	same characteristics as the family
(d) Family Etmopteridae	dorsal fin spines, all fins small, a black pattern on the ventral surfaces with perfectly sharp boundary
Etmopterus spinax–Velvet belly	same characteristics as the family

(e) Family Somniosidae	pectoral fins small, dorsal fins small and of similar size, dorsal fin spines very small or absent
Centroscymnus coelolepis—Portuguese dogfish	dorsal fin spines very short, pectoral fins small
Somniosus rostratus–Little sleeper shark	no dorsal fin spines, small caudal keels, caudal fin almost symmetrical
(f) Family Oxynotidae	dorsal fins enormous, dorsal fin spines
Oxynotus centrina -Angular roughshark	same characteristics as the family
(g) Family Dalatiidae	no dorsal fin spines, pectoral fins small, pelvic fins large
Dalatias licha–Kitefin shark	same characteristics as the family
ORDER SQUATINIFORMES	**no anal fin, body ray-like, 2 dorsal fins, 5 gill slits**
Family Squatinidae	same characteristics as the Order
Squatina aculeata–Sawback angelshark	trunk narrow (the shark total length is 5.4 to 6 times the distance between pectoral fin axils), large dermal denticles on midline of back, small dark and white spots
Squatina oculata–Smoothback angelshark	trunk quite narrow (the shark total length is 4.9 to 5.9 times the distance between pectoral fin axils), no large dermal denticles on midline of back, ocelli (white spots having dark margins) and dark and light spots
Squatina squatina—Common angelshark	trunk wide (the shark total length is 3.6 to 4 times the distance between pectoral fin axils), no large dermal denticles on midline of back, 1–3 straight dark bands on the pectoral fins and small white and dark spots
ORDER LAMNIFORMES	**snout conical, anal fin, 2 dorsal fins, 5 gill slits**
(a) Family Odontaspididae	teeth protruding from the mouth in lower jaw, first dorsal fin slightly larger to second dorsal and anal fin
Carcharias taurus–Sandtiger shark	snout moderately long, eyes small and 2 cusplets in each tooth
Odontaspis ferox–Smalltooth sand tiger	snout long, eyes large and 4 or more cusplets in each tooth
(b) Family Alopiidae	caudal fin upper lobe extremely long (about as long as the rest of the body)
Alopias superciliosus—Bigeye thresher	eyes enormous (extending up to the dorsal

	surface of the head), a very deep groove on sides of the head
Alopias vulpinus—Common thresher shark	eyes large but not extending up to the dorsal surface of the head, no deep grooves on sides of the head
(c) Family Cetorhinidae	**very long gill slits (almost encircling the head), very small teeth, wide caudal keels, second dorsal and anal fin small**
Cetorhinus maximus–Basking shark	same characteristics as the family
(d) Family Lamnidae	**caudal fin almost symmetrical, teeth protruding from the mouth in lower jaw, wide caudal keels, second dorsal and anal fin very small**
Carcharodon carcharias–Great white shark	body massive, pectoral fins long, snout large, mouth wide, teeth large, triangular and with serrated edges
Isurus oxyrinchus–Shortfin mako	body strongly spindle-shaped, pectoral fins relatively short, snout narrow, teeth long and narrow with cutting edges, iridescent blue color, undersurface of head white
Isurus paucus—Longfin mako	body strongly spindle-shaped, pectoral fins long, snout short, teeth long and narrow with cutting edges, eyes large, secondary caudal keels on the sides of the caudal fin, undersurface of head dark
Lamna nasus—Porbeagle	body stout, pectoral fins relatively short, first dorsal fin very large and with a white patch on the free rear tip, teeth short and with 2 small cusplets, secondary caudal keels on the sides of the caudal fin
ORDER CARCHARHINIFORMES	**snout dorso-ventrally depressed, anal fin, 2 dorsal fins, 5 gill slits**
(a) Family Scyliorhinidae	**dorsal fins located far back on shark (the first dorsal origin posterior to the pelvic fin origin)**
Galeus melastomus–Blackmouth catshark	anal fin very long, snout long, characteristic pattern of regular small and large light spots
Scyliorhinus canicula–Small-spotted catshark	anal fin relatively long, snout short, body very slender, numerous small simple white and dark spots and bands
Scyliorhinus stellaris—Nursehound	anal fin relatively long, snout short, body slender but with the dorsal part pronounced, large black spots (some are united forming ring-like patches similar to those of a leopard)
(b) Family Triakidae	**dorsal fins not located far back on shark (the origin of the first dorsal very distant from the pelvic fins), caudal fin terminal**

	lobe large to enormous, eyes located dorsally, underside of head strongly flattened, snout long, upper labial folds short to long, no nasal barbels
Galeorhinus galeus–Tope shark	caudal fin terminal lobe enormous, first dorsal fin large, second dorsal small
Mustelus asterias–Starry smooth-hound	caudal fin terminal lobe large, first dorsal fin large (its origin over the pectoral fin base or the inner margin), second dorsal slightly smaller, upper labial folds conspicuously longer than lower folds, internarial space is 1.2 to 1.3 times the nostril width, often with white spots
Mustelus mustelus–Common smooth-hound	caudal fin terminal lobe large, first dorsal fin large (its origin over the pectoral fin free rear tip), second dorsal slightly smaller, upper labial folds slightly longer than lower folds, internarial space is 1.5 to 2.0 times the nostril width, usually no spots
Mustelus mediterraneus–Blackspotted smooth-hound	caudal fin terminal lobe large, first dorsal fin large (its origin over the pectoral fin free rear tip), second dorsal slightly smaller, dorsal fin posterior margins prominently fringed, upper labial folds slightly longer than lower folds, internarial space is 1.1 to 1.3 times the nostril width, usually with black spots
(c) Family Carcharhinidae	**dorsal fins not located far back on shark (the origin of the first dorsal very distant from the pelvic fins), the second dorsal much smaller than the first dorsal, eyes located exactly laterally on the head, underside of head not strongly flattened, no nasal barbels**
Carcharhinus acarenatus—Strait shark	no spiracles, characteristic upper labial fold Y-shaped, first dorsal fin relatively large (its origin immediately posterior to the pectoral fin free rear tip), pectoral fins moderately long, no interdorsal ridge
Carcharhinus altimus—Bignose shark	no spiracles, anal fin posterior margin deeply concave, first dorsal fin relatively large and usually tall (its origin over the pectoral fin inner margin), usually with the anterior margin with an angle, pectoral fins long and wide, high interdorsal ridge
Carcharhinus amboinensis—Pigeye shark	no spiracles, body massive, snout short, anal fin posterior margin deeply concave, first dorsal fin relatively large, pointed and erect (its origin over the axil or the pectoral fin inner margin), no interdorsal ridge

Carcharhinus brachyurus—Copper shark	no spiracles, anal fin posterior margin deeply concave, first dorsal fin relatively large (its origin immediately posterior to the pectoral fin free rear tip), pectoral fins long, interdorsal ridge present or absent
Carcharhinus brevipinna—Spinner shark	no spiracles, pectoral fins short, first dorsal fin relatively small (its origin posterior to or over the pectoral fin free rear tip), no interdorsal ridge
Carcharhinus falciformis—Silky shark	no spiracles, anal fin posterior margin deeply concave, pectoral fins relatively short, first dorsal fin usually low (its origin posterior to the pectoral fin free rear tip), second dorsal and anal fin free rear tips long and narrow, pelvic fins very small, high interdorsal ridge
Carcharhinus limbatus–Blacktip shark	pectoral fins moderately long, perfectly falcate, first dorsal fin pointed, erect, tall (its origin over the pectoral fin inner margin), no interdorsal ridge, fin apex and posterior margins with a well evident small black area
Carcharhinus longimanus–Oceanic whitetip shark	no spiracles, first dorsal fin very large and tall, with wide apex, pectoral fins very long and with wide apex, interdorsal ridge present or absent, a conspicuous irregular white patch on first dorsal, pectoral, pelvic and caudal fin apex
Carcharhinus melanopterus—Blacktip reef shark	no spiracles, first dorsal fin moderately large (its origin over the pectoral fin inner margin), pectoral fins relatively short, no interdorsal ridge, all fins with an irregular black patch at their apex, that is very wide on the first dorsal fin and caudal fin lower lobe
Carcharhinus obscurus—Dusky shark	no spiracles, anal fin posterior margin deeply concave, first dorsal fin relatively large (its origin over the pectoral fin inner margin), pectoral fins moderately long, interdorsal ridge, body rather stout
Carcharhinus plumbeus–Sandbar shark	no spiracles, anal fin posterior margin deeply concave, first dorsal fin large to enormous and very tall (its origin over the pectoral fin base or its axil), pectoral fins long and wide, interdorsal ridge, body rather stout
Galeocerdo cuvier—Tiger shark	spiracles small, snout short with an almost straight anterior margin, upper labial folds very long, caudal fin upper lobe long and narrow, anal and pelvic fins falcate, small caudal keels, usually with dark vertical bands

Prionace glauca – Blue shark	no spiracles, snout very long and narrow, pectoral fins very long and narrow, small caudal keels, eyes large, color bright blue
Rhizoprionodon acutus — Milk shark	no spiracles, anal fin with elongated pre-anal ridges, eyes large, snout long, pectoral fins short
(d) Family Sphyrnidae	**very wide hammer-shaped head (dorso-ventrally compressed and greatly laterally expanded)**
Sphyrna lewini — Scalloped hammerhead	hammer anterior margin curved with a median notch and its posterior margin concave, second dorsal fin small, anal fin larger
Sphyrna mokarran — Great hammerhead	hammer anterior margin almost straight with a median notch and its posterior margin slightly concave, first dorsal, pectoral, anal and caudal fins strongly falcate, second dorsal fin tall and large about as the anal fin
Sphyrna tudes – Golden hammerhead	hammer anterior margin curved with a median notch and its posterior margin about straight, anal fin much longer than second dorsal
Sphyrna zygaena – Smooth hammerhead	hammer anterior margin curved without a median notch and its posterior margin concave, second dorsal fin small, anal fin about as large as the second dorsal

Bluntnose sixgill shark (*Hexanchus griseus*) (photo by Greg Amptman).

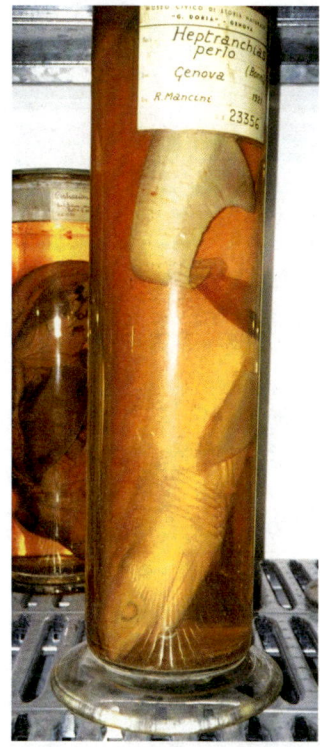

A sharpnose sevengill shark (*Heptranchias perlo*) preserved in the Museo civico di Storia Naturale "Giacomo Doria" in Genoa, Italy (photo by Alessandro De Maddalena, courtesy Museo Civico di Storia Naturale "Giacomo Doria," Genoa).

Bigeyed sixgill shark (*Hexanchus nakamurai*) (photo by Katie Grudecki).

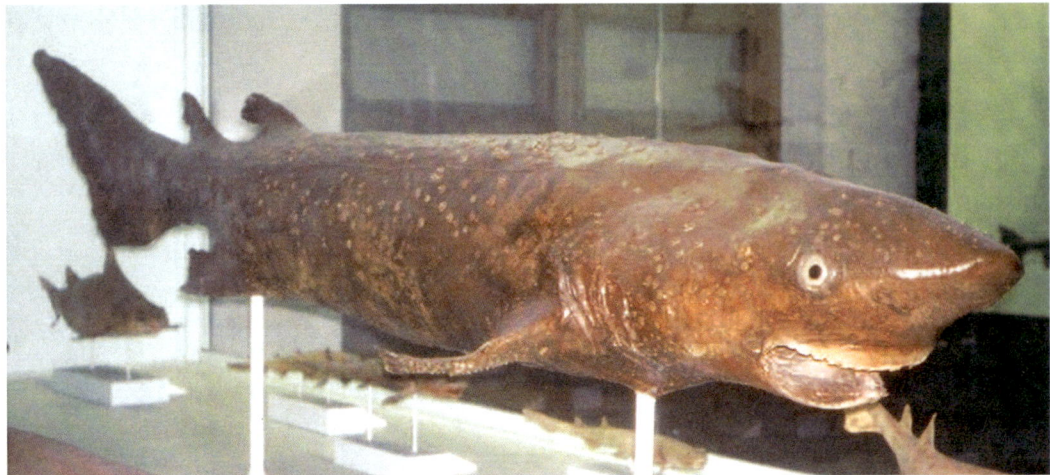

A 230 cm female bramble shark (*Echinorhinus brucus*) caught off Noli, Italy, Ligurian Sea, preserved in the Museo civico di Storia Naturale "Giacomo Doria" in Genoa, Italy (photo by Alessandro De Maddalena, courtesy Museo Civico di Storia Naturale "Giacomo Doria," Genoa).

Piked dogfish (*Squalus acanthias*) (photo by Erling Svensen).

Shortnose spurdog (*Squalus megalops*) (photo by Thomas Gloerfelt-Tarp).

An 89 cm male gulper shark (*Centrophorus granulosus*) caught off Viareggio, Italy, Ligurian Sea, on 23 May 2001 (photo by Alessandro De Maddalena).

Velvet belly (*Etmopterus spinax*) (photo by Erling Svensen).

A Portuguese dogfish (*Centroscymnus coelolepis*) (photo by Pedro Miguel Niny Cambraia Duarte © ImagDOP).

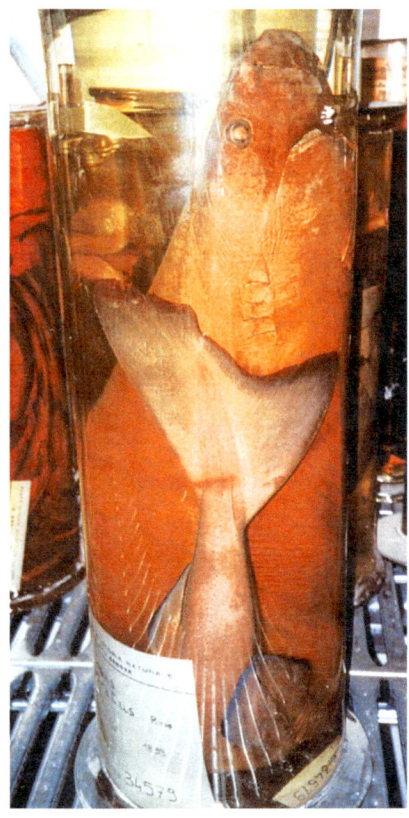

A 103 cm female kitefin shark (*Dalatias licha*) caught off Viareggio, Italy, Ligurian Sea, on 24 May 2000 (photo by Alessandro De Maddalena).

A little sleeper shark (*Somniosus rostratus*) preserved in the Museo civico di Storia Naturale "Giacomo Doria" in Genoa, Italy (photo by Alessandro De Maddalena, courtesy Museo civico di Storia Naturale "Giacomo Doria," Genoa).

Angular roughshark (*Oxynotus centrina*) in Catalan waters, Spain (photo by Javier Guallart / L'Elasmogrup).

An embryo sawback angelshark (*Squatina aculeata*) from Nice, France, Ligurian Sea, preserved in the Národní muzeum in Prague (photo by Radek Šanda, courtesy Národní muzeum, Prague).

A smoothback angelshark (*Squatina oculata*) at the fish market of Istanbul, Turkey, in spring 2002 (photo by Viktor Goushterov).

A common angelshark (*Squatina squatina*) (photo by Manuela Domingues / Alianza Tiburones de Canarias).

A sandtiger shark (*Carcharias taurus*) (photo by Nicolas Barraqué).

A smalltooth sand tiger (*Odontaspis ferox*) (photo by Clay Bryce).

A bigeye thresher (*Alopias superciliosus*) (photo by Seinen Chow / National Research Institute of Fisheries Science, Yokohama, Kanagawa, Japan).

Common thresher shark (*Alopias vulpinus*) (photo by Nicolas Barraqué).

An estimated 8 meter basking shark (*Cetorhinus maximus*) encountered in January 2011 in the Tavolara Marine Protected Area, Sardinia, Italy (photo by Egidio Trainito).

A great white shark (*Carcharodon carcharias*) (photo by Claudio Perotti).

A shortfin mako (*Isurus oxyrinchus*) (photo by Walter Heim).

A longfin mako (*Isurus paucus*) (photo by Miguel Berrios / NOAA Fisheries, Pacific Islands Region Observer Program).

A porbeagle (*Lamna nasus*) (photo by Gilles Di Raimondo).

A blackmouth catshark (*Galeus melastomus*) (photo by Erling Svensen).

Small-spotted catshark (*Scyliorhinus canicula*) (photo by Patrick Louisy).

A nursehound (*Scyliorhinus stellaris*) (photo by Dominique Barray).

A tope shark (*Galeorhinus galeus*) (photo by Erling Svensen).

A starry smooth-hound (*Mustelus asterias*) (photo by Erling Svensen).

A common smooth-hound (*Mustelus mustelus*) (photo by Patrick Louisy).

Ventral view of the head of a 56 cm female blackspotted smooth-hound (*Mustelus mediterraneus*) caught in Italian waters (photo by Roberto Farkas).

Spanish researcher Juan Antonio Moreno preparing a taxidermied specimen of strait shark (*Carcharhinus acarenatus*), the species he described in 1981 (photo by Juan Antonio Moreno).

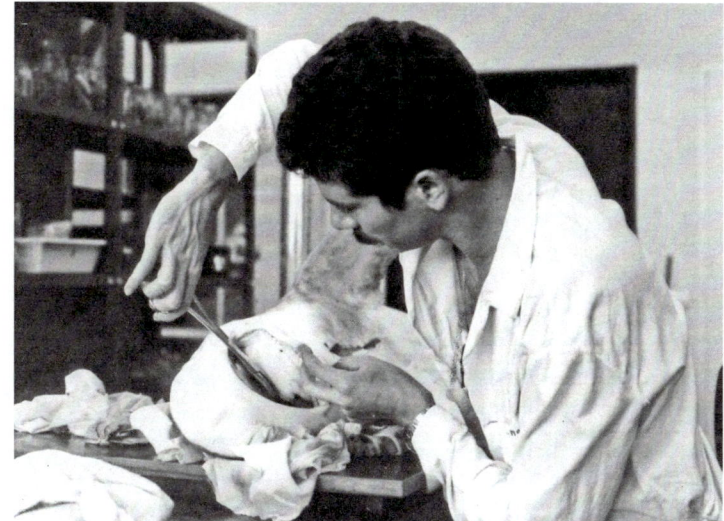

A bignose shark (*Carcharhinus altimus*) (photo by Keith Sainsbury / CSIRO).

Pigeye shark (*Carcharhinus amboinensis*) (photo by John E. Randall).

A copper shark (*Carcharhinus brachyurus*) (photo by Claus Qvist Jessen).

A spinner shark (*Carcharhinus brevipinna*) (photo by John E. Randall).

A blacktip shark (*Carcharhinus limbatus*) (photo by Dominique Barray).

An oceanic whitetip shark (*Carcharhinus longimanus*) (photo by Christine Gstoettner).

A silky shark (*Carcharhinus falciformis*) (photo by Nicolas Barraqué).

A blacktip reef shark (*Carcharhinus melanopterus*) (photo by Philippe Joachim).

A dusky shark (*Carcharhinus obscurus*) (photo by John E. Randall).

A female longnose spurdog (*Squalus blainvillei*) caught off the Sardinia coast, Italy, on 5 June 2000 (photo by Alessandro De Maddalena).

A sandbar shark (*Carcharhinus plumbeus*) (photo by Nicolas Barraqué).

A tiger shark (*Galeocerdo cuvier*) (photo by Gilles Di Raimondo).

A blue shark (*Prionace glauca*) (photo by Stéphane Moity-Banchard).

A milk shark (*Rhizoprionodon acutus*) (photo by Pedro Miguel Niny Cambraia Duarte © ImagDOP).

A scalloped hammerhead (*Sphyrna lewini*) (photo by Nicolas Barraqué).

A great hammerhead (*Sphyrna mokarran*) (photo by Cinémarine).

A smooth hammerhead (*Sphyrna zygaena*) (photo by Alessandro De Maddalena).

Species Profiles

The arrangement of species is presented
in the same order used by Campagno (1984).

About This Section

This part of the book gives detailed and up to date information on all shark species recorded in the Mediterranean Sea. For each species, the following information and pictures are included.

Common name and Latin name, followed by the name of the naturalist that initially described the species and the year in which the description was published are shown first. Illustrations include drawings of lateral or side view, ventral or bottom view of the head, upper and lower teeth, and ventral view of the pectoral fin. A photo or illustration is also included. Classification (Order, family, genus) and common names in other languages (French, Spanish, Italian and German) are provided. For immediate identification, there are aspects of morphology, coloration, teeth shape and dental formula (teeth in the right side of the upper jaw—teeth in the left side of the upper jaw / teeth in the right side of the lower jaw—teeth in the left side of the lower jaw). Size information covers maximum size (usually the total length in a straight line from the snout to the tip of the upper lobe of caudal fin), size at birth (total length) and size at maturity (total length; for male and female). Reproductive information includes embryonic development (oviparous, aplacental viviparous, placental viviparous), gestation, litter size (minimum and maximum) and spawning areas in the Mediterranean. Along with maximum size, maximum age for the shark is provided. Diet is defined by the prey species consumed and is presented as taxonomic classes. Habitat (sea region and depth range), geographical distribution in the Mediterranean Sea and geographical distribution in the rest of the world are addressed. Known behavior is described as well as potential danger to man (not dangerous, potentially dangerous, dangerous or highly dangerous). Fishery importance in the Mediterranean (none, scarce, some, certain, notable importance), status in the Mediterranean (very rare, rare, uncommon, relatively common, common, very common) and kind of presence in the Mediterranean (stable, occasional) is covered. For each species, information on notable Mediterranean specimens, such as the largest shark, the smallest free-swimming shark, the largest litter, the few specimens recorded that are very rare and the deepest dive. Similar species that are difficult to identify are addressed.

Main references are provided for the Mediterranean sharks, as well as non-Mediterranean related references. The name of the author and year of publication is

This 589 cm female great white shark captured off Maguelone, France, on 13 October 1956 is preserved as the largest cast in the world, which was reconstructed directly from a whole specimen and is in the Musée cantonal de Zoologie in Lausanne, Switzerland (without a catalogue number) (photograph by Michel Krafft, courtesy Musée cantonal de Zoologie, Lausanne).

provided where cited. The full reference is in the bibliography at the end of the book. The term "pers. comm." indicates a personal communication received by the authors.

Sharpnose sevengill shark
Heptranchias perlo (Bonnaterre, 1788)

Classification: Order Hexanchiformes, family Hexanchidae, genus *Heptranchias*.
Common names in other languages: French: requin perlon; Spanish: boquidulce; Italian: notidano cinereo; German: spitzkopf-siebenkiemerhai.
Distinctive characteristics for immediate identification: 7 pairs of gill slits and a unique dorsal fin.
Morphology: 7 pairs of long gill slits, all located anterior to the pectoral fin origin. Body slender. The first gill slits are conspicuously longer than the others. A unique relatively small dorsal fin, located far back on the shark, with its origin over the posterior part of the pelvic fins. Caudal fin upper lobe long and with a large terminal lobe, lower lobe short. Pectoral fins relatively short. Caudal peduncle long. Head narrow and pointed. Eyes large. Mouth long. Spiracles small.

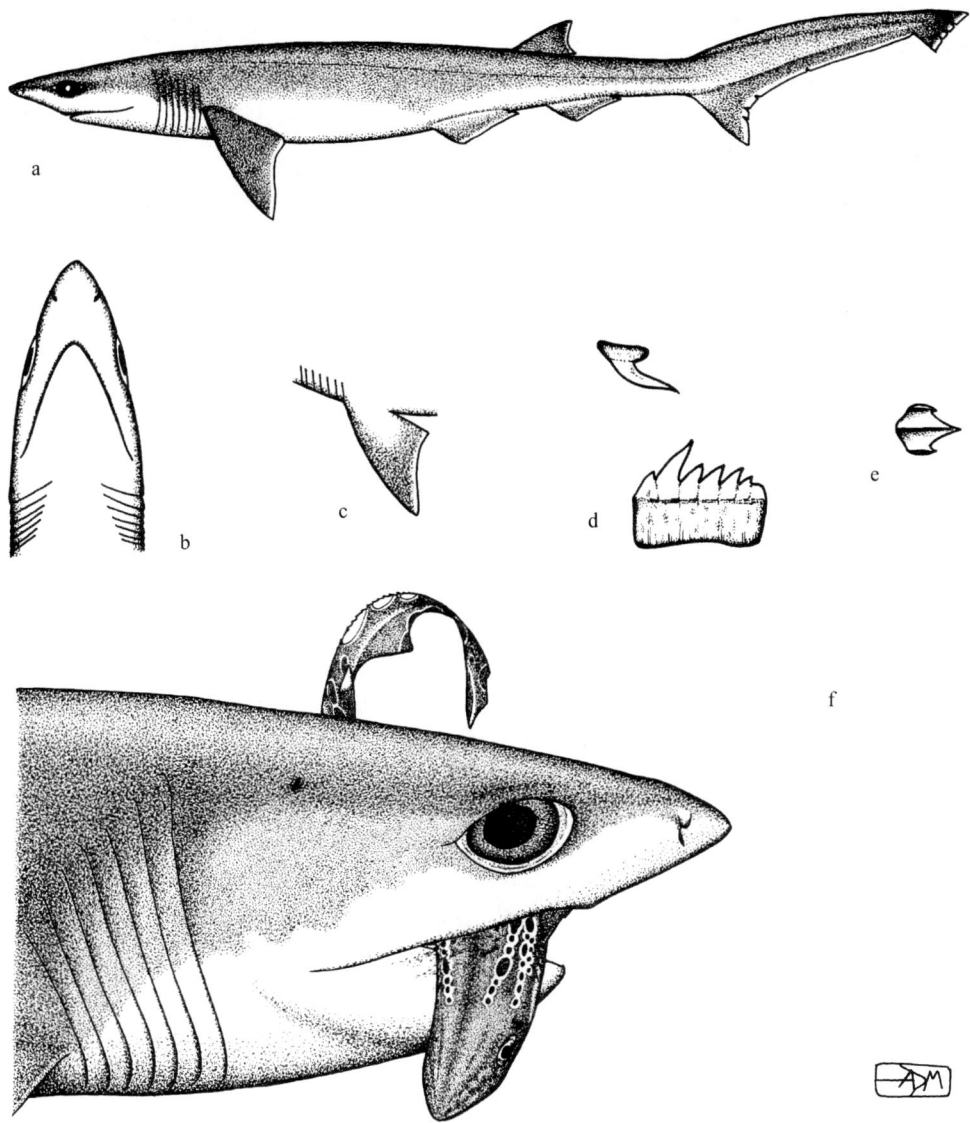

Sharpnose sevengill shark (*Heptranchias perlo*): (a) lateral view, (b) ventral view of the head, (c) ventral view of the pectoral fin, (d) upper and lower teeth, (e) placoid scale, (f) a specimen with a captured blackmouth catshark (*Galeus melastomus*).

Coloration: dorsal surfaces grey-brownish, ventral surfaces whitish. Fin posterior margins white. Eyes fluorescent green. In juveniles, dorsal fin and caudal fin upper lobe have black apex.

Teeth shape: upper teeth narrow and pointed with one cusp, with or without 1–5 small cusplets depending by the position in the jaw. Lower teeth much larger, comblike, with one cusp and 8–9 cusplets.

Dental formula: 9 to 13–9 to 13 / 5–1–5.

Maximum size: 137 cm.

Size at birth: about 26 cm.
Size at maturity: 85 cm (male) and 89–93 cm (female).
Embryonic development: aplacental viviparous.
Gestation: unknown.
Litter size: 9–20 young.
Reproduction in the Mediterranean: reproduces in the Mediterranean, data indicates parturition must occur in the Sicilian Channel.
Maximum age: unknown.
Diet: bony fishes, elasmobranchs, cephalopods, crustaceans.
Habitat: benthic, mainly in deep water, on the continental and insular shelves and upper slopes, at depths ranging from the surface to at least 1000 m.
Geographical distribution in the Mediterranean Sea: all Mediterranean.
Geographical distribution in the rest of the world: Atlantic, Pacific and Indian Oceans.
Behavior: active and fast, occur individually or in large groups.
Dangerousness for man: not dangerous.
Importance for fishery in the Mediterranean: scarce importance.
Status in the Mediterranean: generally uncommon.
Kind of presence in the Mediterranean: stable.
Specimens of particular interest recorded in the Mediterranean: one of the largest specimens ever recorded was a 135 cm female caught in the Adriatic Sea in August 1926 (preserved in the Museo civico di Storia Naturale di Venezia).
Species with which can be confused: none.
Main references for the Mediterranean: Lo Bianca (1909), Tortonese (1956), Capapé (1980), Cadenat & Blache (1981), Bauchot (1987), Vanni (1992), Moreno (1995), De Maddalena et al. (2002), Barrull & Mate (2002), Lipej et al. (2004).
Other selected non Mediterranean related references: Bigelow & Schroeder (1948), Bass et al. (1973–1976), Castro (1983), Compagno (1984), Last & Stevens (1994).

Bluntnose sixgill shark
Hexanchus griseus (Bonnaterre, 1788)

Classification: Order Hexanchiformes, family Hexanchidae, genus *Hexanchus*.
Common names in other languages: French: requin griset; Spanish: cañabota; Italian: notidano grigio, capopiatto; German: sechskiemerhai.
Distinctive characteristics for immediate identification: 6 pairs of gill slits, a unique dorsal fin, short caudal peduncle (its length equal or slightly longer than the dorsal fin base), large size (from 65 cm up to over 500 cm).
Morphology: 6 pairs of long gill slits, all located anterior to the pectoral fin anterior margin. The first gill slits are longer than the others. A unique dorsal fin, located far back on the shark, with its origin over the posterior part of the pelvic fins, moderately large. Pectoral fins moderately long and wide. Caudal fin upper lobe long to very long, lower lobe short. Caudal peduncle short, its length equal or slightly longer than the dorsal fin base. Body massive, head wide and rounded in dorso-ventral view. Mouth very wide and long. Eyes relatively large. Spiracles small.

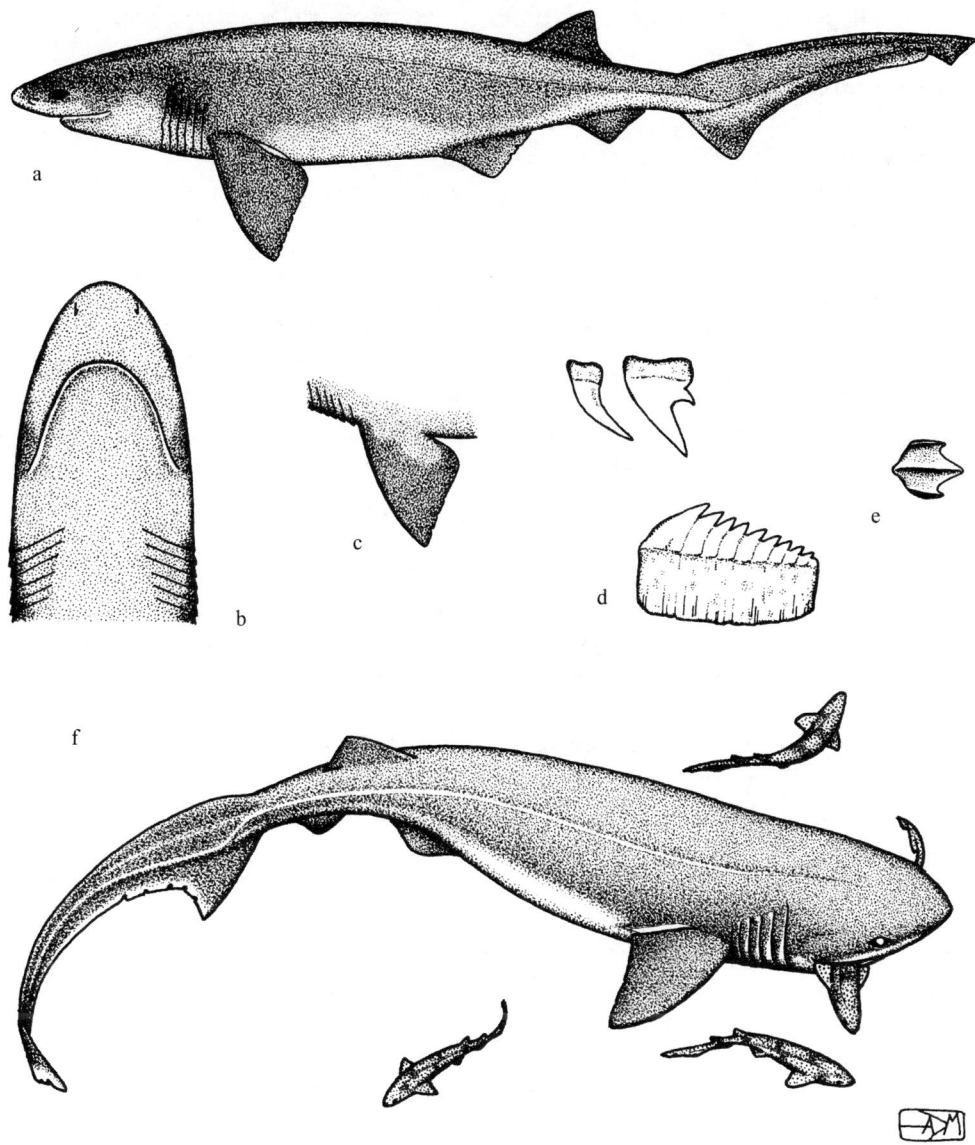

Bluntnose sixgill shark (*Hexanchus griseus*): (a) lateral view, (b) ventral view of the head, (c) ventral view of the pectoral fin, (d) upper and lower teeth, (e) placoid scale, (f) a bluntnose sixgill attacking a group of small-spotted catsharks (*Scyliorhinus canicula*).

Coloration: dorsal surfaces light grey, dark grey, black, brownish or yellow ochre, and lighter along the lateral line; ventral surfaces slightly lighter than the dorsal surfaces or whitish, except the gill slits region that shows an irregular dark coloration similar to that of the dorsal surfaces. Sometimes the fin posterior margins are white. A white area at the pectoral fin axil. The pectoral fin ventral surface has the same dark coloration as the dorsal surface, except at the base, that is grey-whitish. Eyes fluorescent green. Coloration lighter in juveniles.

Teeth shape: upper teeth narrow and pointed with one cusp, with or without 1–3 cus-

plets depending by the tooth position; lower teeth much larger, comblike, with up to 11 cusplets.
Dental formula: 9 to 10–9 to 10 / 6–1–6.
Maximum size: at least 482 cm, but it is estimated to exceed 500 cm.
Size at birth: 56–70 cm.
Size at maturity: 320–350 cm (male) and 396 cm (female).
Embryonic development: aplacental viviparous.
Gestation: unknown.
Litter size: 22–108 young.
Reproduction in the Mediterranean: reproduces in the Mediterranean.
Maximum age: unknown.
Diet: cartilaginous fishes, bony fishes, cephalopods, gastropods, crustaceans, marine mammals, sea urchins, carcasses.
Habitat: primarily in deep waters, benthic, on continental and insular shelves and upper slopes, at depths ranging from the surface to at least 2500 m. Juveniles occur in shallower waters than adults.
Geographical distribution in the Mediterranean Sea: all Mediterranean.
Geographical distribution in the rest of the world: Atlantic, Pacific and Indian Oceans.
Behavior: slow, nocturnal, solitary or in pairs, can approach divers closely (without showing any aggressive behavior), usually shows little resistance even when hooked.
Dangerousness for man: not dangerous.
Importance for fishery in the Mediterranean: some importance.
Status in the Mediterranean: common.
Kind of presence in the Mediterranean: stable.
Specimens of particular interest recorded in the Mediterranean: perhaps the largest specimen ever reported was caught in the Messina Strait, Italy, and examined by Dr. Luigi Piscitelli in December 2000, estimated at 500–600 cm.
Species with which can be confused: the bigeyed sixgill shark (*Hexanchus nakamurai*), but this species has a longer caudal peduncle (much longer than the dorsal fin base) and it is much smaller (the maximum length is 180 cm).
Main references for the Mediterranean: Arcidiacono (1931), Tortonese (1956), Cadenat & Blache (1981), Gilat & Gelman (1984), Bauchot (1987), Vanni (1992), Moreno (1995), Barrull *et al.* (1999), Barrull & Mate (2000), Barrull & Mate (2002), Capapé *et al.* (2003), Cugini & De Maddalena (2003), Celona *et al.* (2003), Capapé *et al.* (2004), Lipej *et al.* (2004).
Other selected non–Mediterranean related references: Bigelow & Schroeder (1948), Bass *et al.* (1973–1976), Castro (1983), Compagno (1984), Ebert (1994), Last & Stevens (1994).

Bigeyed sixgill shark
Hexanchus nakamurai Teng, 1962

Classification: Order Hexanchiformes, family Hexanchidae, genus *Hexanchus*.
Common names in other languages: French: requin vache; Spanish: cañabota oji-

Bigeyed sixgill shark (*Hexanchus nakamurai*): (a) lateral view, (b) ventral view of the head, (c) ventral view of the pectoral fin, (d) upper and lower teeth, (e) pregnant female.

grande; Italian: notidano dagli occhi grandi; German: großaugen-sechskiemer-hai.

Distinctive characteristics for immediate identification: 6 pairs of gill slits, a unique dorsal fin, long caudal peduncle (much longer than the dorsal fin base), small size (from 43 cm to 180 cm).

Morphology: 6 pairs of long gill slits, all located anterior to the pectoral fin anterior margin. The first gill slits are longer than the others. A unique dorsal fin, located far back on the shark, with its origin over the posterior part of the pelvic fins, relatively small. Pectoral fins moderately long and wide. Caudal fin upper lobe long, lower lobe short. Caudal peduncle long, much longer than the dorsal fin base. Body slender. Snout narrow. Head wide and rounded in dorso-ventral view. Mouth very wide and long. Eyes large. Spiracles small.

Coloration: dorsal surfaces grey-brown; ventral surfaces whitish. Fin posterior margins white. In juveniles the caudal fin upper lobe has black apex. Eyes fluorescent green.

Teeth shape: upper teeth narrow and pointed with one cusp, with or without 1–4 very small cusplets depending by the tooth position; lower teeth much larger, comblike, with one cusp and up to 11 cusplets.

Dental formula: 9–9 / 5–1–5.

Maximum size: 180 cm.

Size at birth: 43 cm.

Size at maturity: 123–157 cm (male) and 142–178 cm (female).

Embryonic development: aplacental viviparous.

Gestation: unknown.

Litter size: 13–26 young.

Reproduction in the Mediterranean: does not reproduce in the Mediterranean.

Maximum age: unknown.

Diet: fishes and invertebrates.

Habitat: benthic, mainly in deep waters, on continental and insular shelves, at depths ranging from surface to at least 711 m.

Geographical distribution in the Mediterranean Sea: unknown.

Geographical distribution in the rest of the world: Atlantic, Pacific and Indian Oceans.

Behavior: unknown.

Dangerousness for man: not dangerous.

Importance for fishery in the Mediterranean: no importance.

Status in the Mediterranean: very rare.

Kind of presence in the Mediterranean: unknown.

Specimens of particular interest recorded in the Mediterranean: only three specimens have been recorded from the Mediterranean Sea including a 98 cm female caught, capture location and date unknown (preserved in the Museo di Storia Naturale dell'Università di Firenze, Sezione di Zoologia "La Specola"), an 82 cm female, capture location and date unknown (preserved in the Národní muzeum in Prague), and a 106 cm male caught near Western Crete, Greece, Aegean Sea, on 18 May 2001.

Species with which can be confused: the bluntnose sixgill shark (*Hexanchus griseus*), but this species has a shorter caudal peduncle (equal or slightly longer than the dorsal fin base) and it is much larger (maximum length exceeds 500 cm).

Main references for the Mediterranean: Tortonese (1985), Vanni (1992), Barrull & Mate (2002), Megalofonou *et al.* (2003), Šanda & De Maddalena (2003).

Other selected non–Mediterranean related references: Bass *et al.* (1973–1976), Castro (1983), Compagno (1984), Clark & Kristof (1991), Last & Stevens (1994).

Bramble shark

Echinorhinus brucus (Bonnaterre, 1788)

Classification: Order Squaliformes, family Echinorhinidae, genus *Echinorhinus*.
Common names in other languages: French: requin bouclé; Spanish: tiburón de clavos; Italian: ronco spinoso, echinorino; German: nagelhai.
Distinctive characteristics for immediate identification: no anal fin, dorsal fins located far back on shark (the origin of the first dorsal over pelvic fins), dermal denticles large and pointed, thorn like.

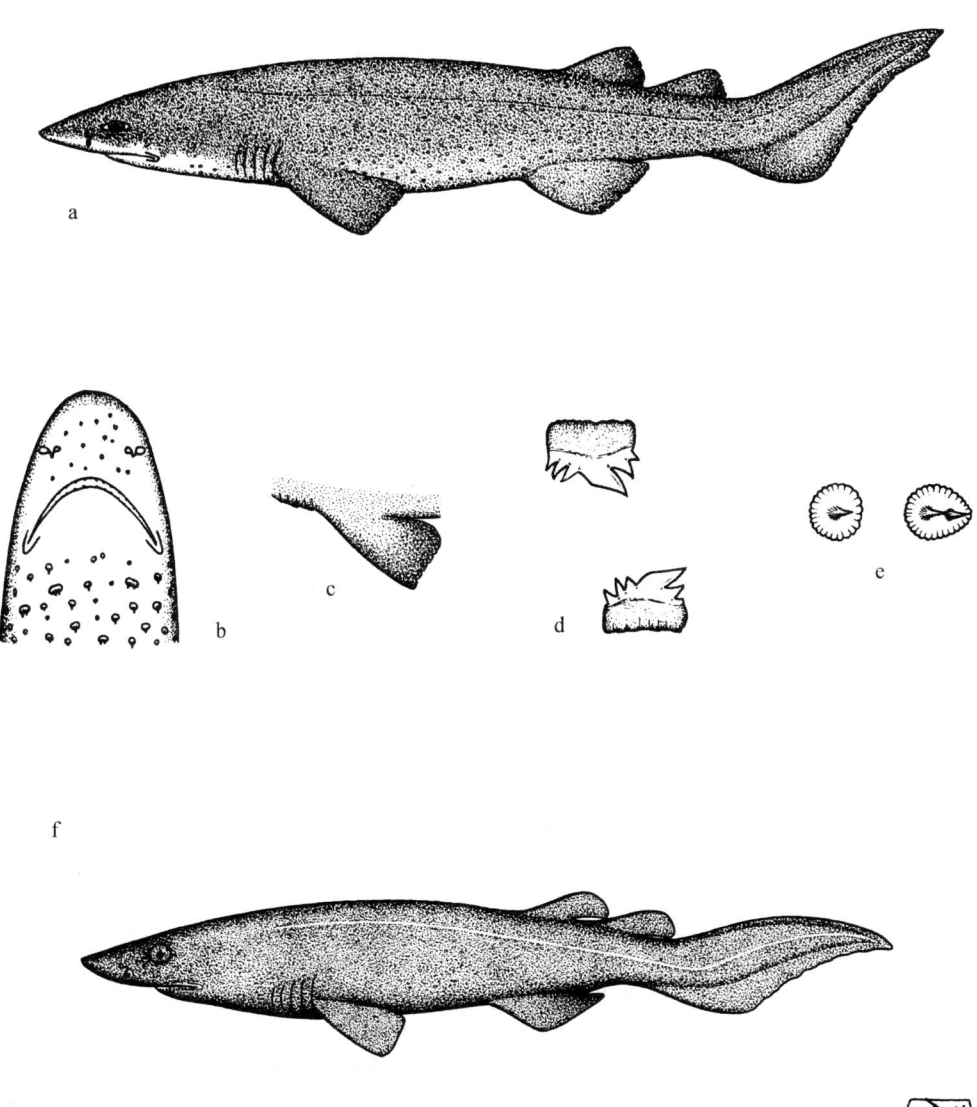

Bramble shark (*Echinorhinus brucus*): (a) lateral view, (b) ventral view of the head, (c) ventral view of the pectoral fin, (d) upper and lower teeth, (e) placoid scale, (f) embryo.

Morphology: no anal fin. Dorsal fins located far back on shark, the origin of the first dorsal over pelvic fins. First dorsal fin slightly larger than second dorsal. Pelvic fins large. Pectoral fins short. Caudal fin upper lobe large, lower lobe short. Caudal fin lacking posterior notch. Fin posterior margins frayed. Body massive and stout. Caudal peduncle large. Dermal denticles very large and pointed, thorn like, both individual and fused in multiples, measuring up to 2.5 cm and widely spaced. Eyes large. Nostrils wide. Spiracles small. 5 pairs of relatively small gill slits, all located anterior to pectoral fin origin, the first gill slits shorter than the others.
Coloration: dorsal surfaces grey-brown tending to reddish-purplish, sometimes with black spots; ventral surfaces lighter or whitish. Dermal denticles whitish.
Teeth shape: upper teeth small, with a low oblique cusp and 2–4 cusplets; lower teeth similar.
Dental formula: 10 to 12–10 to 12 / 11 to 14–11 to 14.
Maximum size: 310 cm.
Size at birth: 29–90 cm.
Size at maturity: 150–174 cm (male) and 213–231 cm (female).
Embryonic development: aplacental viviparous.
Gestation: unknown.
Litter size: 15–24 young.
Reproduction in the Mediterranean: reproduces in the Mediterranean; data indicates parturition may occur in the Ligurian and Tyrrhenian Seas.
Maximum age: unknown.
Diet: small sharks, bony fishes, crabs.
Habitat: benthic, mainly in deep waters, on continental and insular shelves and upper slopes, at depths ranging from 20 m to at least 900 m.
Geographical distribution in the Mediterranean Sea: Central and Western Mediterranean.
Geographical distribution in the rest of the world: Atlantic, Pacific and Indian Oceans.
Behavior: slow, solitary, timid.
Dangerousness for man: not dangerous.
Importance for fishery in the Mediterranean: no importance
Status in the Mediterranean: very rare.
Kind of presence in the Mediterranean: stable.
Specimens of particular interest recorded in the Mediterranean: two gravid females were recorded including a female caught in the Messina Strait, Italy, on 22 July 1937, and an estimated 250 cm female carrying at least 13 embryos caught off Capo Bianco, Elba Island, Italy, Thyrrhenian Sea, around 1985. Three of the largest specimens ever reported were captured in these waters including a 296 cm female caught off Nice, France, Ligurian Sea, in 1856, a 258 cm male caught off Nice, France, before 1879 (preserved in the Museo di Scienze Naturali dell'Università di Pavia, is the largest of any Mediterranean specimen presently preserved), and a 254 cm female caught off Anaba (Algeria) on 2 April 2000.
Species with which can be confused: none.
Main references for the Mediterranean: Risso (1810), Doderlein (1881), Trois (1876), Ninni (1904), Lo Bianco (1909), Vinciguerra (1923), Borri (1934), Cipria (1937),

Tortonese (1938), Tortonese (1956), Granier (1964), Boero & Carli (1979), Cadenat & Blache (1981), Bauchot (1987), Sarà & Sarà (1990), Vanni (1992), Mizzan (1994), Moreno (1995), Barrull & Mate (2002), Hemida & Capapé (2002), De Maddalena & Zuffa (2003), Šanda & De Maddalena (2003), Lipej et al. (2004).

Other selected non–Mediterranean related references: Bigelow & Schroeder (1948), Castro (1983), Compagno (1984), Last & Stevens (1994).

Piked dogfish or spiny dogfish
Squalus acanthias Smith & Radcliffe, 1912

Classification: Order Squaliformes, family Squalidae, genus *Squalus*.
Common names in other languages: French: aiguillat commun; Spanish: mielga; Italian: spinarolo; German: dornhai.
Distinctive characteristics for immediate identification: no anal fin, dorsal fin spines short to moderately long, small caudal keels, first dorsal fin origin posterior to pectoral fin free rear tip, white spotted coloration.
Morphology: no anal fin. Fin spines on both dorsal fins, the first spine short, the second spine slightly longer. First dorsal fin moderately large, second dorsal smaller; first dorsal fin origin posterior to pectoral fin free rear tip. Pectoral fins moderately wide. No caudal fin subterminal notch. Caudal fin upper lobe moderately long, lower lobe short. Small caudal keels. Snout long. Mouth almost straight in ventral view. Long labial folds. Eyes large. Spiracles large. 5 pairs of short gill slits, all located anterior to the pectoral fin origin.
Coloration: dorsal surfaces grey-bluish or brown with some small white spots; ventral surfaces white. Pectoral, pelvic, caudal fins with posterior margin light; first dorsal fin apex dark. The pectoral fin ventral surface is grey like the dorsal surface, faded at the base with the posterior margin white. In the adult the white spots can be faded and sometimes absent.
Teeth shape: upper teeth with one cusp, small, oblique, almost horizontal, with cutting edges, the teeth are interlocked forming a cutting wall; lower teeth similar.
Dental formula: 12 to 14–12 to 14 / 11 to 12 -11 to 12.
Maximum size: 160 cm.
Size at birth: 20–33 cm.
Size at maturity: 56–72 cm (male) and 60–95 cm (female).
Embryonic development: aplacental viviparous.
Gestation: 18–24 months.
Litter size: 1–20 young.
Reproduction in the Mediterranean: reproduces in the Mediterranean, data indicates parturition must occur in the Golfe du Lion, France and the Catalan Sea, Spain.
Maximum age: at least 40 years and possibly up to 100 years.
Diet: bony fishes, sharks, cephalopods, crustaceans, polychaetes, sea cucumbers, ctenophores, hydrozoans, jellyfishes.
Habitat: pelagic, on continental and insular shelves and upper slopes, at depths ranging

Piked dogfish or spiny dogfish

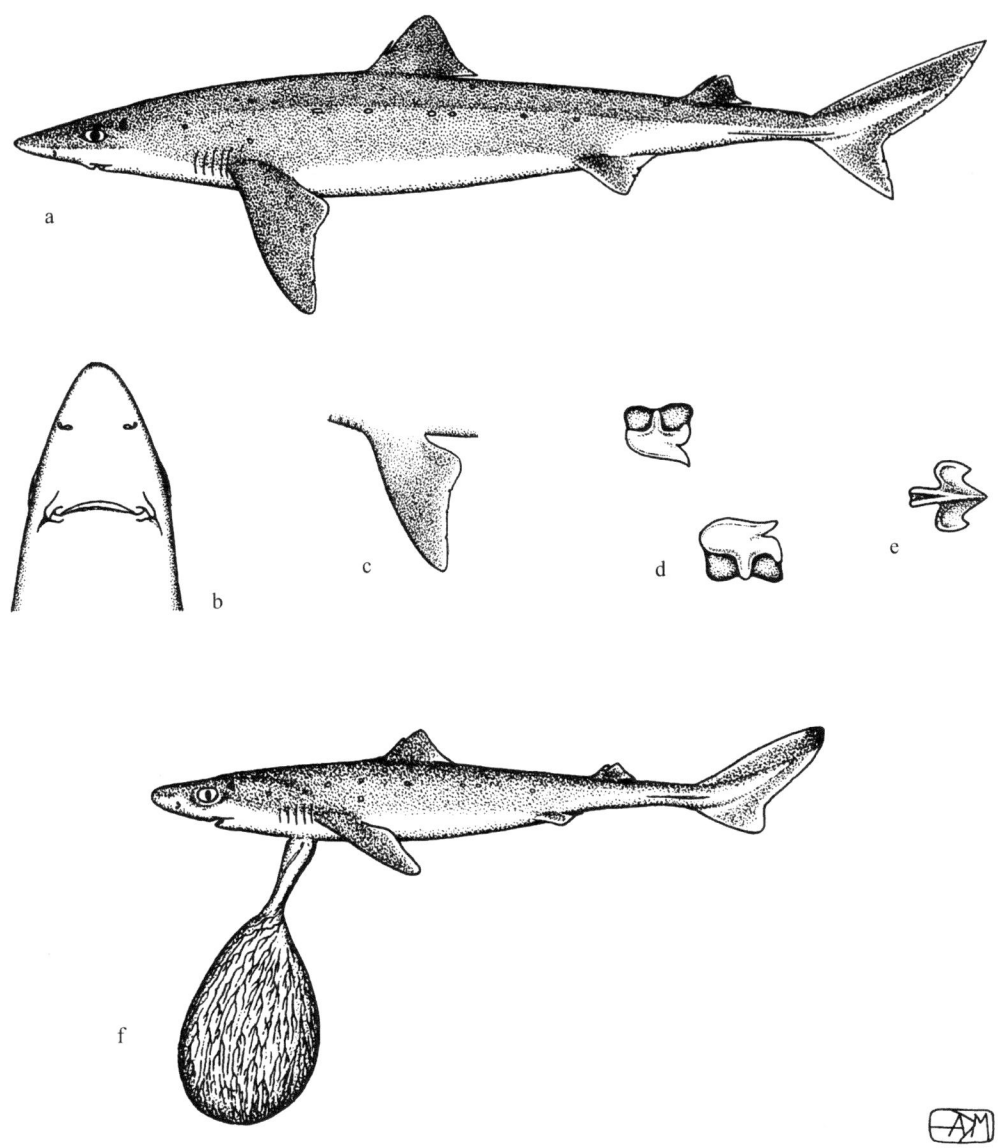

Piked dogfish (*Squalus acanthias*): (a) lateral view, (b) ventral view of the head, (c) ventral view of the pectoral fin, (d) upper and lower teeth, (e) placoid scale, (f) embryo with yolk-sac.

from the surface to at least 900 m. Males occur in shallower waters than females; pregnant females can give birth in shallow waters.

Geographical distribution in the Mediterranean Sea: All Mediterranean.
Geographical distribution in the rest of the world: Atlantic and Pacific Oceans.
Behavior: active and slow, solitary or in enormous groups, migratory, timid, can segregate by sex and size, use the dorsal fin spines as a defensive weapon.
Dangerousness for man: not dangerous.
Importance for fishery in the Mediterranean: notable importance.

Status in the Mediterranean: common.
Kind of presence in the Mediterranean: stable.
Specimens of particular interest recorded in the Mediterranean: the largest specimen recorded in the area was 106 cm long.
Species with which can be confused: the longnose spurdog (*Squalus blainvillei*) and the shortnose spurdog (*Squalus megalops*), but both these species have a larger head and lack white spots.
Main references for the Mediterranean: Roule (1912), Lozano Cabo (1945), Tortonese (1956), Jardas (1972), Cadenat & Blache (1981), Bauchot (1987), Vanni (1992), Moreno (1995), Barrull *et al.* (1999), Capapé *et al.* (2000), Barrull & Mate (2002), Lipej *et al.* (2004).
Other selected non–Mediterranean related references: Bigelow & Schroeder (1948), Bigelow & Schroeder (1957), Bass *et al.* (1973–1976), Castro (1983), Compagno (1984), Ebert *et al.* (1992), Last & Stevens (1994), Jones & Ugland (2001), Alonso *et al.* (2002), Soldat (2002), McFarlane & King (2003).

Longnose spurdog
Squalus blainvillei (Risso, 1826)

Classification: Order Squaliformes, family Squalidae, genus *Squalus*.
Common names in other languages: French: aiguillat coq, aiguillat galludo; Spanish: galludo; Italian: spinarolo bruno; German: langnasen-dornhai.
Distinctive characteristics for immediate identification: no anal fin, dorsal fin spines relatively short to long, small caudal keels, head massive, first dorsal fin origin over pectoral fin inner margin, pectoral fin free rear tips rounded, no white spots on body, no black fin apex.
Morphology: no anal fin. Relatively short to long fin spines on both dorsal fins, usually the second longer than the first. First dorsal fin moderately large, second dorsal smaller; first dorsal fin origin over pectoral fin inner margin. Pectoral fins moderately wide, their free rear tips rounded. No caudal fin subterminal notch. Caudal fin upper lobe moderately long, lower lobe short. Small caudal keels. Head massive. Snout long. Mouth almost straight in ventral view. Labial folds long. Eyes large. Spiracles large. 5 pairs of short gill slits, all located anterior to the pectoral fin origin.
Coloration: dorsal surfaces grey to brown; ventral surfaces white. Pectoral, pelvic and caudal fins with posterior margin light. Dorsal fins apex dark. The pectoral fin ventral surface is grey like the dorsal surface, whitish at the base with the posterior margin white.
Teeth shape: upper teeth with one cusp, small, oblique, almost horizontal, with cutting edges, the teeth are interlocked forming a cutting wall; lower teeth similar.
Dental formula: 12 to 13–12 to 13 / 10 to 13–10 to 13.
Maximum size: 96 cm.
Size at birth: 20–23 cm.
Size at maturity: 51 cm (male) and 51–65 cm (female).

Longnose spurdog

Longnose spurdog (*Squalus blainvillei*): (a) lateral view, (b) ventral view of the head, (c) ventral view of the pectoral fin, (d) upper and lower teeth, (e) placoid scale, (f) spurdogs swimming in school.

Embryonic development: aplacental viviparous.
Gestation: 9–12 months.
Litter size: 2–4 young.
Reproduction in the Mediterranean: reproduces in the Mediterranean.
Maximum age: unknown.
Diet: bony fishes, sharks, crustaceans, cephalopods, polychaetes.
Habitat: pelagic, on continental shelves and upper slopes, at depths ranging from 15 to at least 700 m.

Geographical distribution in the Mediterranean Sea: all Mediterranean.
Geographical distribution in the rest of the world: Eastern Atlantic, Western Pacific Oceans.
Behavior: active and slow, solitary or in enormous groups, migratory, timid, can segregate by sex and size, use the dorsal fin spines as a defensive weapon.
Dangerousness for man: not dangerous.
Importance for fishery in the Mediterranean: certain importance.
Status in the Mediterranean: relatively common.
Kind of presence in the Mediterranean: stable.
Specimens of particular interest recorded in the Mediterranean: one of the largest specimens was a 79 cm female caught off Sardegna, Italy, on 6 June 2000.
Species with which can be confused: the piked dogfish (*Squalus acanthias*) and the shortnose spurdog (*Squalus megalops*); but *S. acanthias* has a smaller head and a white spotted coloration, while *S. megalops* has dorsal and caudal fin black apex and pectoral fin rear tip is pointed.
Main references for the Mediterranean: Ranzi (1932–1934), Lozano Cabo (1945), Tortonese (1956), Quignard (1971), Capapé (1974a), Capapé & Pantoustier (1975), Cadenat & Blache (1981), Bauchot (1987), Vanni (1992), Moreno (1995), Barrull *et al.* (1999), Capapé *et al.* (2000), De Maddalena & Piscitelli (2001), Barrull & Mate (2002), Kabasakal (2002b), Lipej *et al.* (2004).
Other selected non–Mediterranean related references: Poll (1951), Bigelow & Schroeder (1957), Castro (1983), Compagno (1984), Last & Stevens (1994).

Shortnose spurdog
Squalus megalops (Macleay, 1881)

Classification: Order Squaliformes, family Squalidae, genus *Squalus*.
Common names in other languages: French: aiguillat nez court; Spanish: galludo ñato; Italian: spinarolo dalla testa grande; German: kurznasen-dornhai.
Distinctive characteristics for immediate identification: no anal fin, dorsal fin spines relatively short to long, small caudal keels, head massive, first dorsal fin origin over pectoral fin inner margin, pectoral fin free rear tips pointed, dorsal and caudal fin apex black, no white spots on body.
Morphology: no anal fin. Relatively short to long fin spines on both dorsal fins, usually the second longer than the first. First dorsal fin moderately large, second dorsal smaller; first dorsal fin origin over pectoral fin inner margin. Pectoral fins moderately wide, with free rear tips pointed. No caudal fin subterminal notch. Caudal fin upper lobe moderately long, lower lobe short. Small caudal keels. Head massive. Snout long. Mouth almost straight in ventral view. Long labial folds. Eyes large. Spiracles large. 5 pairs of short gill slits, all located anterior to the pectoral fin origin.
Coloration: dorsal surfaces grey to brown; ventral surfaces white. Dorsal and caudal fins with posterior margin light and their apex and anterior margins black. Rare cases of albino specimens.

Shortnose spurdog (*Squalus megalops*): (a) lateral view, (b) ventral view of the head, (c) ventral view of the pectoral fin, (d) upper and lower teeth, (e) placoid scale, (f) a spurdog tries to escape an attack from a porbeagle (*Lamna nasus*).

Teeth shape: upper teeth with one cusp, small, oblique, almost horizontal, with cutting edges, the teeth are interlocked forming a cutting wall; lower teeth similar.
Dental formula: 11 to 13–11 to 13 / 11 to 13–11 to 13.
Maximum size: 71 cm.
Size at birth: about 20 cm.
Size at maturity: 40–42 cm (male) and 53–57 cm (female).
Embryonic development: aplacental viviparous.

Gestation: about 24 months.
Litter size: 2–4 young.
Reproduction in the Mediterranean: does not reproduce in the Mediterranean.
Maximum age: unknown.
Diet: bony fishes, elasmobranchs, crustaceans, cephalopods, polychaetes.
Habitat: pelagic, on outer continental shelves and upper slopes, at depths ranging from 50 to at least 730 m.
Geographical distribution in the Mediterranean Sea: Western Mediterranean.
Geographical distribution in the rest of the world: Eastern Atlantic, Western Pacific and Indian Oceans.
Behavior: active and slow, solitary or in enormous groups, migratory, timid, can segregate by sex and size, use the dorsal fin spines as a defensive weapon.
Dangerousness for man: not dangerous.
Importance for fishery in the Mediterranean: unknown, probably of no importance.
Status in the Mediterranean: very rare.
Kind of presence in the Mediterranean: occasional (the specimens recorded must have entered the Mediterranean Sea from the Eastern Atlantic Ocean through the Gibraltar Strait).
Specimens of particular interest recorded in the Mediterranean: only two specimens, preserved in the Musée Océanographique de Monaco, have been recorded: a 20 cm male captured off Melilla, Morocco, Alboran Sea, on 18 June 1894 and a 56 cm female caught off Formentera, Balearic Islands, Spain on 29 August 1900.
Can be confused with: the piked dogfish (*Squalus acanthias*) and the longnose spurdog (*Squalus blainvillei*); but *S. acanthias* has a smaller head and a white spotted coloration, while *S. blainvillei* has pectoral fin free rear tips rounded and lack dorsal and caudal fin black apex.
Main references for the Mediterranean: Bruni & Würtz (2002).
Other selected general references: Bass *et al.* (1973–1976), Compagno (1984), Ebert *et al.* (1992), Last & Stevens (1994), Šanda & De Maddalena (2003).

Gulper shark
Centrophorus granulosus (Bloch & Schneider, 1801)

Classification: Order Squaliformes, family Centrophoridae, genus *Centrophorus*.
Common names in other languages: French: squale-chagrin commun; Spanish: quelvacho; Italian: centroforo; German: schlinghai.
Distinctive characteristics for immediate identification: no anal fin, pectoral fin free rear tips very long and pointed, dorsal fin spines.
Morphology: no anal fin. Fin spines on both dorsal fins: the first short, the second slightly longer. Pectoral fins short, with free rear tip pointed and very long. First dorsal low, its base longer than second dorsal base, but the second dorsal can be higher than the first dorsal; first dorsal fin origin over the pectoral fin inner margin. Caudal fin upper lobe moderately long, lower lobe short; caudal fin terminal lobe large. Snout long. Mouth almost straight in ventral view, with long lower labial

Gulper shark

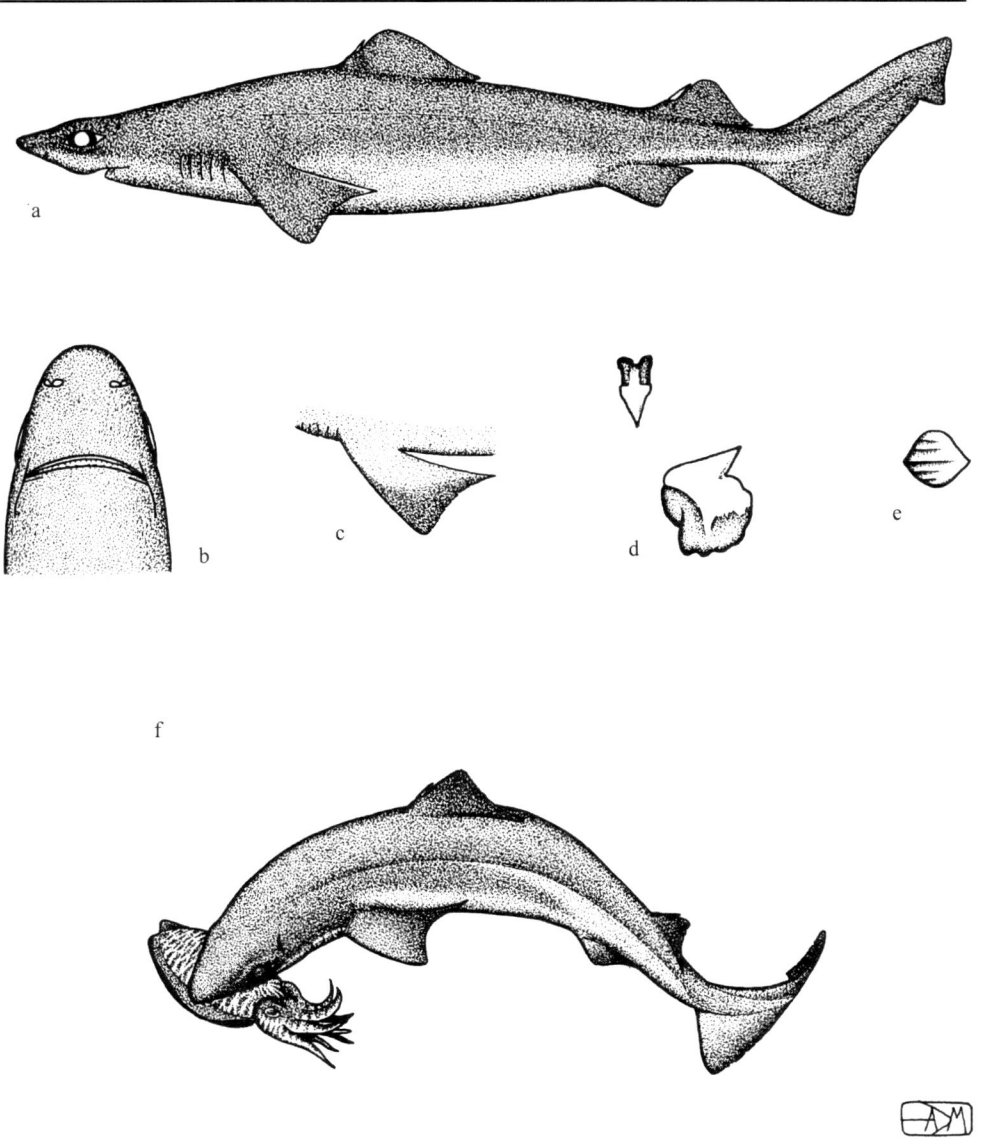

Gulper shark (*Centrophorus granulosus*): (a) lateral view, (b) ventral view of the head, (c) ventral view of the pectoral fin, (d) upper and lower teeth, (e) placoid scale, (f) a gulper shark has captured a common cuttlefish (*Sepia officinalis*).

folds. Nostrils large. Eyes large. Spiracles large. 5 pairs of relatively small gill slits, all located anterior to the pectoral fin origin.

Coloration: dorsal surfaces grey-brown; ventral surfaces lighter. Fin posterior margins can be lighter. Eyes greenish.

Teeth shape: upper teeth with one cusp, small, low and vertical; lower teeth larger, with one oblique cusp having cutting or finely serrated edges.

Dental formula: 16 to 21–0 to 1–16 to 21 / 13 to 16–0 to 1–13 to 16.

Maximum size: 160 cm.

Size at birth: 32–46 cm.
Size at maturity: 80–85 cm (male) and 89–100 cm (female).
Embryonic development: aplacental viviparous.
Gestation: possibly 2–3 years.
Litter size: 1 young.
Reproduction in the Mediterranean: reproduces in the Mediterranean.
Maximum age: at least 18 years.
Diet: bony fishes, elasmobranchs, cephalopods, crustaceans, carcasses.
Habitat: mainly benthic, in deep waters, on continental and insular shelves and upper slopes, at depths ranging from 100 m to at least 1490 m.
Geographical distribution in the Mediterranean Sea: all Mediterranean.
Geographical distribution in the rest of the world: Atlantic, Pacific and Indian Oceans.
Behavior: solitary and possibly in large groups, can segregate by size (even bathymetrically) and possibly by sex.
Dangerousness for man: not dangerous.
Importance for fishery in the Mediterranean: scarce importance.
Status in the Mediterranean: relatively common.
Kind of presence in the Mediterranean: stable.
Specimens of particular interest recorded in the Mediterranean: the largest specimen recorded in this area is a 104 cm female caught off Roses, Spain, Catalan Sea, on 30 December 1995 (preserved in the Museo El Cau del Taurò de L'Arboç).
Species with which can be confused: none.
Main references for the Mediterranean: Ranzi (1932–1934), Tortonese (1956), Cadenat & Blache (1981), Gilat & Gelman (1984), Capapé (1985), Golani (1986–1987), Bauchot (1987), Vanni (1992), Moreno (1995), Barrull et al. (1999), Golani & Pisanty (2000), Barrull & Mate (2002), Lipej et al. (2004).
Other selected non–Mediterranean related references: Bigelow & Schroeder (1957), Castro (1983), Compagno (1984), Last & Stevens (1994).

Velvet belly
Etmopterus spinax (Linnaeus, 1758)

Classification: Order Squaliformes, family Etmopteridae, genus *Etmopterus*.
Common names in other languages: French: sagre commun; Spanish: negrito; Italian: moretto; German: samtbauchhai.
Distinctive characteristics for immediate identification: no anal fin, dorsal fin spines (the second long), all fins small, a black pattern on the ventral surfaces with a sharp boundary.
Morphology: no anal fin. Body slender. Fin spines on both dorsal fins, the second spine much longer than the first. All fins small with their posterior margins often strongly frayed. First dorsal fin origin over or posterior to pectoral fin free rear tip. Second dorsal fin larger than first dorsal and falcate. Minute photophores on the ventral and lateral surfaces. Mouth almost straight in ventral view. Eyes large. Nostrils

large. Spiracles large. 5 pairs of short gill slits, all located anterior to the pectoral fin origin.

Coloration: dorsal surfaces brown; ventral surfaces with a wide black pattern and sharp boundaries that extends from the lower surface of the snout to the pelvic region and also on part of caudal peduncle, pelvic fins, caudal fin upper and lower apex, anterior margin and free rear tip of dorsal fins. A narrow light stripe on sides of the head behind the mouth. Fin posterior margins white. The pectoral fin ventral

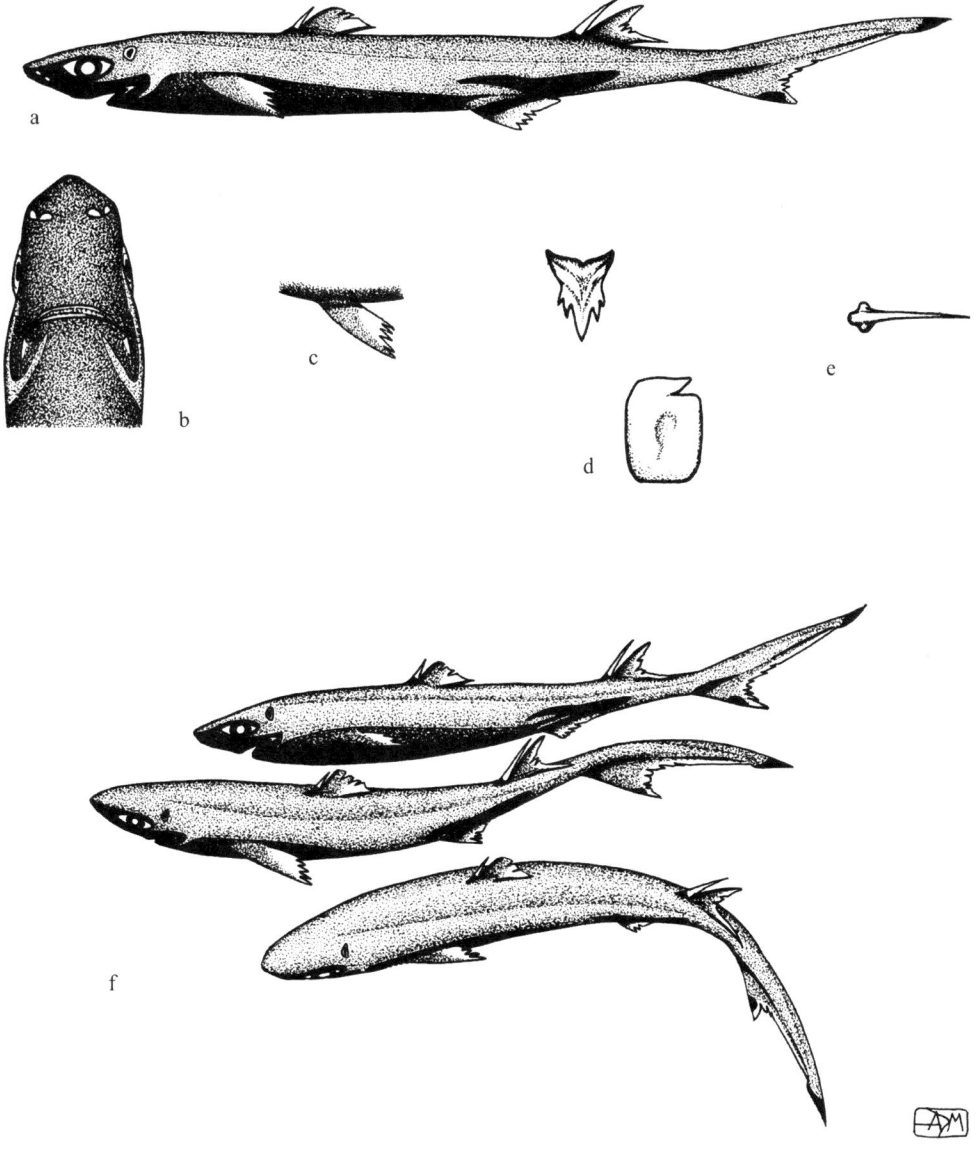

Velvet belly (*Etmopterus spinax*): (a) lateral view, (b) ventral view of the head, (c) ventral view of the pectoral fin, (d) upper and lower teeth, (e) placoid scale, (f) velvet bellies often swim in a group.

surface is partially grey-brown, with the posterior margin and inner margin white, and a black band at the base.
- **Teeth shape:** upper teeth small, with one cusp and 2 or more minute cusplets; lower teeth larger, with one cusp, oblique, almost horizontal, with cutting edges. In newborn specimens the cusplets of the upper teeth are much smaller than in adults.
- **Dental formula:** 13 to 16–13 to 16 / 18 to 20–18 to 20.
- **Maximum size:** at least 83 cm and perhaps up to 115 cm.
- **Size at birth:** 10–11 cm.
- **Size at maturity:** 28 cm (male) and 34–36 cm (female).
- **Embryonic development:** aplacental viviparous.
- **Gestation:** unknown.
- **Litter size:** 5–20 young.
- **Reproduction in the Mediterranean:** reproduces in the Mediterranean; data indicates parturition must occur in the Ligurian Sea.
- **Maximum age:** at least 7 years.
- **Diet:** bony fishes, sharks, squids, crustaceans, polychaetes.
- **Habitat:** Mainly in deep waters, on outer continental shelves and upper slopes, at depths ranging from 70 m to at least 2000 m. It seems that juveniles stay in shallower waters than adults.
- **Geographical distribution in the Mediterranean Sea:** all Mediterranean.
- **Geographical distribution in the rest of the world:** Eastern Atlantic Ocean.
- **Behavior:** probably nocturnal, occur in large groups, can segregate by size (even bathymetrically), possibly can cooperatively catch their prey.
- **Dangerousness for man:** not dangerous.
- **Importance for fishery in the Mediterranean:** no importance.
- **Status in the Mediterranean:** very common.
- **Kind of presence in the Mediterranean:** stable.
- **Specimens of particular interest recorded in the Mediterranean:** the largest specimen recorded in this area is a 54.7 cm female caught off Barcelona, Catalan Sea, Spain, in 2000.
- **Species with which can be confused:** none.
- **Main references for the Mediterranean:** Tortonese (1956), Vacchi & Relini Orsi (1979), Macpherson (1980), Cadenat & Blache (1981), Bauchot (1987), Vanni (1992), Bello (1998), Barrull *et al.* (1999), Kabasakal & Ünsal (1999), Sion *et al.* (2000), De Maddalena & Piscitelli (2001), Barrull & Mate (2002), Bruni & Würtz (2002), Lipej *et al.* (2004).
- **Other selected non–Mediterranean related references:** Bigelow & Schroeder (1957), Compagno (1984), Shestopal *et al.* (2002).

Portuguese dogfish
Centroscymnus coelolepis (Bocage & Capello, 1864)

Classification: Order Squaliformes, family Somniosidae, genus *Centroscymnus*.

Common names in other languages: French: pailona commun; Spanish: pailona; Italian: centroscimno; German: portugiesenhai.

Distinctive characteristics for immediate identification: no anal fin, dorsal fin spines very short, pectoral fins small.

Morphology: no anal fin. Very short fin spines on both dorsal fins. First dorsal fin small, with the origin posterior to pectoral fin free rear tips or over the pectoral fin inner margin. Second dorsal fin slightly larger than first dorsal. Pectoral fins short. Upper caudal fin lobe moderately long, lower lobe short; large caudal fin terminal lobe. Lower labial folds long. Eyes large. Spiracles large. 5 pairs of short gill slits, all located anterior to pectoral fin origin.

Coloration: dorsal surfaces dark golden brown or blackish with iridescence; ventral surfaces similar.

Teeth shape: upper teeth with one cusp, small, narrow and pointed; lower teeth larger, with one cusp almost horizontal, with cutting edges.

Dental formula: 29 to 35–29 to 35 / 19 to 21–19 to 21.

Maximum size: 122 cm.

Size at birth: 19–30 cm.

Size at maturity: 82 cm (male) and 97 cm (female).

Embryonic development: aplacental viviparous.

Gestation: about 26 months.

Litter size: 5–17 young.

Reproduction in the Mediterranean: reproduces in the Mediterranean.

Maximum age: unknown.

Diet: bony fishes, sharks, crustaceans, cephalopods, gastropods, foraminifera, cetaceans, carcasses.

Habitat: mainly benthic, in deep waters, on continental slopes, at depths ranging from 270 m to at least 3700 m.

Geographical distribution in the Mediterranean Sea: Western and Central Mediterranean.

Geographical distribution in the rest of the world: Atlantic and Pacific Oceans.

Behavior: unknown.

Dangerousness for man: not dangerous.

Importance for fishery in the Mediterranean: probably scarce importance.

Status in the Mediterranean: relatively common.

Kind of presence in the Mediterranean: stable.

Specimens of particular interest recorded in the Mediterranean: a 52 cm female was caught at 2718 m depth off Balearic Islands, Spain on 8 September 1909: this is the greatest depth recorded for a shark in the Mediterranean. A 20 cm male caught in the Catalan Sea, Spain on 30 July 1987 (preserved in the Museu de Zoologia de Barcelona), is the smallest free-swimming specimen ever recorded. The largest specimen recorded in the area was a 100 cm female probably caught off Toulon, France; another large specimen was a 76.5 cm male caught in the Catalan Sea, Spain in 1983 (preserved in the Museu de Zoologia de Barcelona).

Species with which can be confused: the kitefin shark (*Dalatias licha*), but this species lacks the dorsal fin spines.

Main references for the Mediterranean: Roule (1912), Tortonese (1956), Torchio & Michelangeli (1971), Capapé (1977), Cadenat & Blache (1981), Bauchot (1987), Carrassón *et al.* (1992), Vanni (1992), Moreno (1995), Barrull *et al.* (1999), Barrull & Mate (2002), Bruni & Würtz (2002).

Other selected non–Mediterranean related references: Bigelow & Schroeder (1948), Bigelow & Schroeder (1957), Castro (1983), Compagno (1984), Ebert *et al.* (1992), Last & Stevens (1994), Girard & Du Buit (1999).

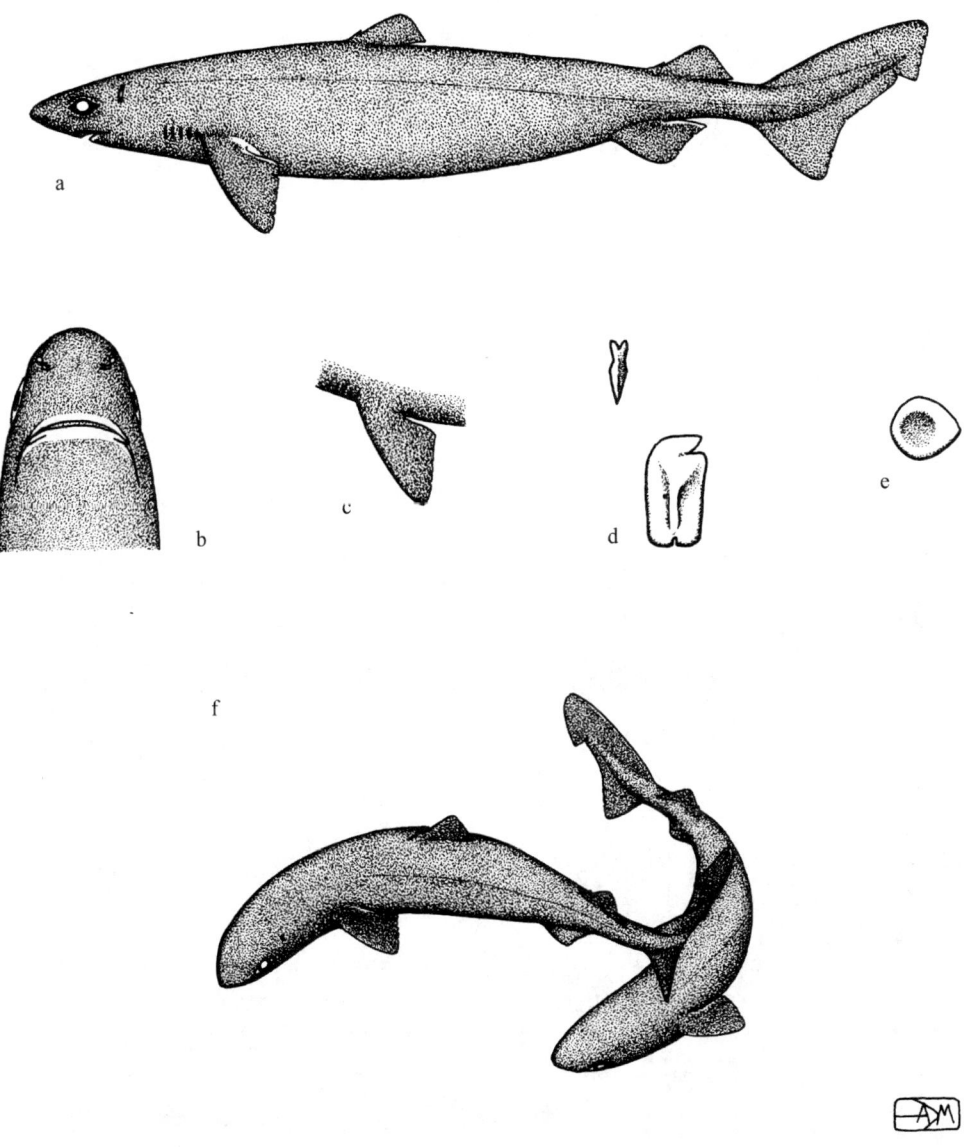

Portuguese dogfish (*Centroscymnus coelolepis*): (a) lateral view, (b) ventral view of the head, (c) ventral view of the pectoral fin, (d) upper and lower teeth, (e) placoid scale, (f) two dogfish swimming.

Little sleeper shark

Somniosus rostratus (Risso, 1826)

Classification: Order Squaliformes, family Somniosidae, genus *Somniosus*.
Common names in other languages: French: laimargue de la Méditerranée; Spanish: dormilón; Italian: lemargo; German: kleiner schlafhai.

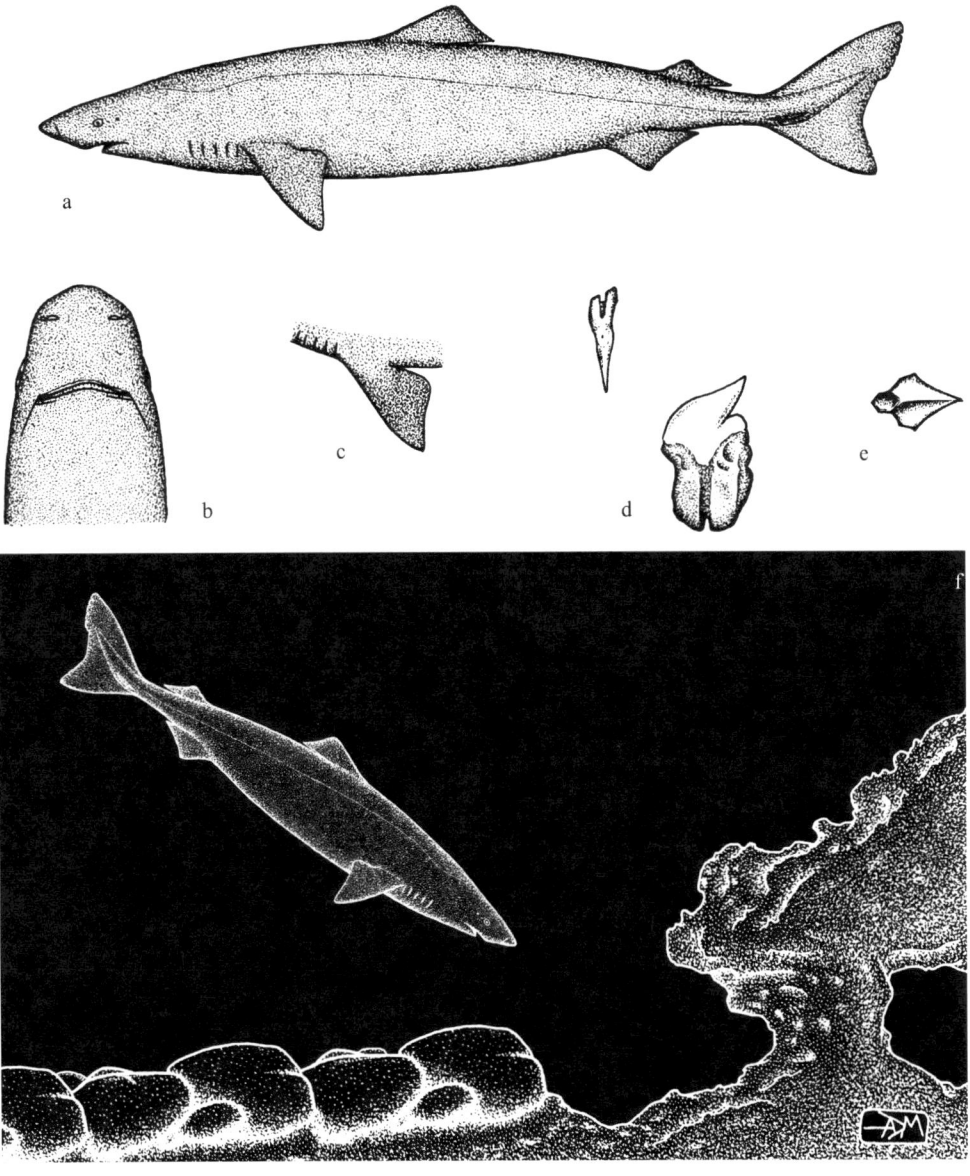

Little sleeper shark (*Somniosus rostratus*): (a) lateral view, (b) ventral view of the head, (c) ventral view of the pectoral fin, (d) upper and lower teeth, (e) placoid scale, (f) a little sleeper shark dives to a great depth.

Little sleeper shark

Distinctive characteristics for immediate identification: no anal fin, no dorsal fin spines, small caudal keel, caudal fin almost symmetrical.

Morphology: no anal fin. Pectoral fins short. Dorsal fins low, the first dorsal slightly larger than second dorsal, its origin posterior to the pectoral fin free rear tip. Caudal fin upper lobe moderately long, lower lobe almost large as the upper lobe. Small caudal keels, located on the sides of the caudal fin, immediately below the caudal peduncle. Mouth almost straight in ventral view; lower labial folds long. Spiracles small. 5 pairs of short gill slits, all located anterior to the pectoral fin origin and in a lower position.

Coloration: dorsal surfaces light brown; ventral surfaces similar.

Teeth shape: upper teeth with one small vertical cusp; lower teeth larger, with one cusp, oblique, with cutting edges.

Dental formula: 29 to 32–29 to 32 / 16 to 17–1—16 to 18.

Maximum size: 140 cm.

Size at birth: 21–28 cm.

Size at maturity: 71 cm (male) and 82–134 cm (female).

Embryonic development: aplacental viviparous.

Gestation: unknown.

Litter size: 8–17 young.

Reproduction in the Mediterranean: reproduces in the Mediterranean; data indicates parturition must occur in the Ligurian Sea and Catalan Sea.

Maximum age: unknown.

Diet: bony fishes, cephalopods.

Habitat: mainly benthic, in deep waters, on outer continental shelves and upper slopes, at depths ranging from 200 to at least 1975 m.

Geographical distribution in the Mediterranean Sea: all Mediterranean.

Geographical distribution in the rest of the world: Eastern Atlantic and Western Pacific Oceans.

Behavior: solitary.

Dangerousness for man: not dangerous.

Importance for fishery in the Mediterranean: no importance.

Status in the Mediterranean: very rare.

Kind of presence in the Mediterranean: stable.

Specimens of particular interest recorded in the Mediterranean: a pregnant female caught off Genoa carried 17 embryos measuring from 10 to 11 cm: this is the largest litter recorded. A 68 cm male was caught off Barcelona, Catalan Sea, Spain on 2 August 1987 at 1975 m depth (preserved in the Museu de Zoologia de Barcelona): this is the greatest depth ever recorded for this species.

Species with which can be confused: none.

Main references for the Mediterranean: Sicher (1898), Tortonese (1956), Cadenat & Blache (1981), Bauchot (1987), Vanni (1992), Cigala Fulgosi & Gandolfi (1983), Barrull & Mate (1995), Barrull et al. (1999), Barrull & Mate (2001), Barrull & Mate (2002), Šanda & De Maddalena (2003).

Other selected non–Mediterranean related references: Bigelow & Schroeder (1957), Compagno (1984).

Angular roughshark
Oxynotus centrina (Linnaeus, 1758)

Classification: Order Squaliformes, family Oxynotidae, genus *Oxynotus*.

Common names in other languages: French: centrine commune; Spanish: tiburón cerdo; Italian: pesce porco; German: meersau.

Distinctive characteristics for immediate identification: no anal fin, body very stout, dorsal fins very high and wide.

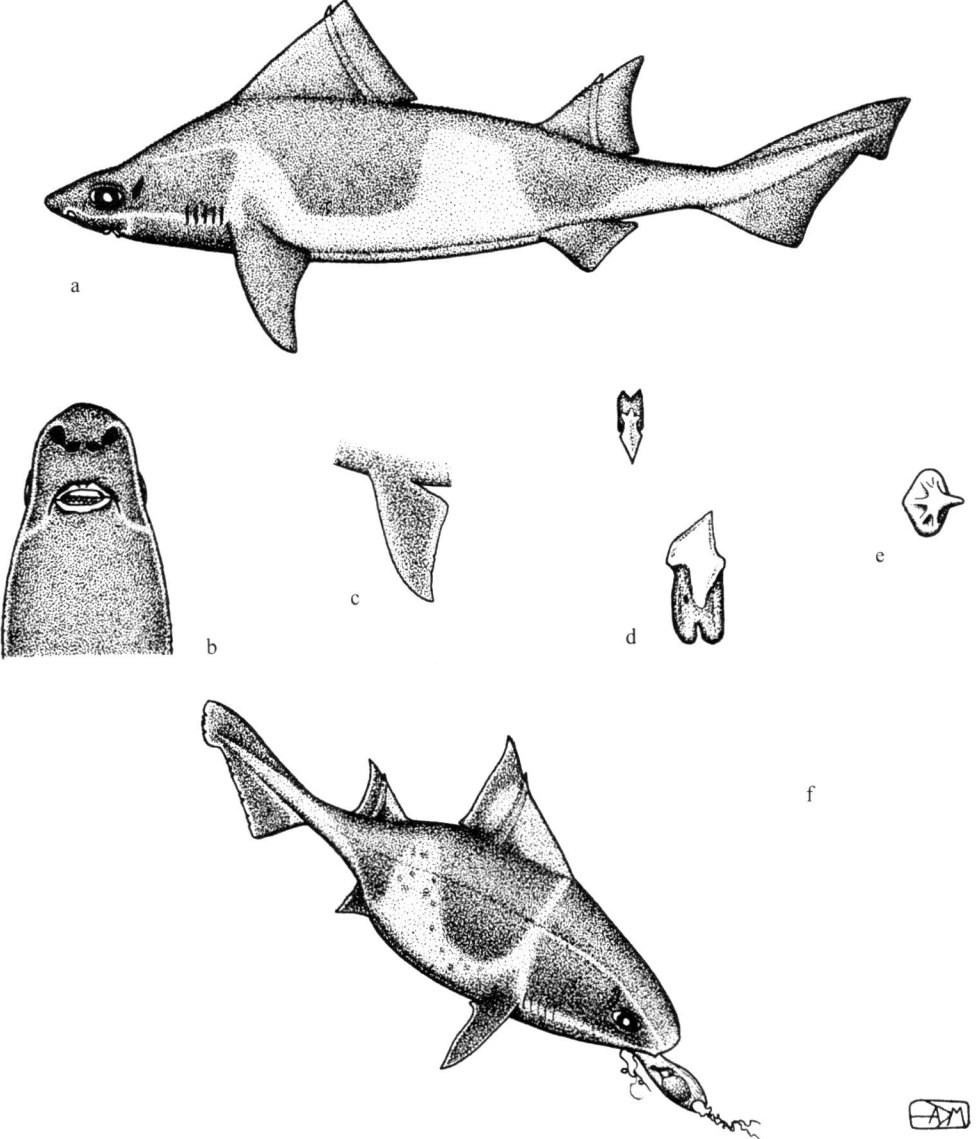

Angular roughshark (*Oxynotus centrina*): (a) lateral view, (b) ventral view of the head, (c) ventral view of the pectoral fin, (d) upper and lower teeth, (e) placoid scale, (f) an angular roughshark preying on the egg-case of a small-spotted catshark (*Scyliorhinus canicula*).

Morphology: no anal fin. Dorsal fins very high and wide; first dorsal fin origin over pectoral fin origin. Fin spines on both dorsal fins. Pectoral fins short. Caudal fin upper lobe moderately long, lower lobe short; no caudal fin posterior notch. Body stout, with the dorsal part highly pronounced. Ventral ridges. Dermal denticles large. Snout short. Mouth very small with enlarged labial parts. Nostrils large. Eyes large. Spiracles large. 5 pairs of short gill slits, all located anterior to the pectoral fin origin.

Coloration: dorsal surfaces grey-brown or blackish with a lighter pattern on part of head, sides, caudal peduncle and caudal fin; ventral surfaces partially lighter.

Teeth shape: upper teeth with one cusp, small and lanceolate; lower teeth larger, with one cusp, vertical or oblique depending on the position in the jaw, with serrated edges.

Dental formula: 5–1–5 / 4 to 5–1–4 to 5.

Maximum size: 150 cm.

Size at birth: 21–24 cm.

Size at maturity: 60 cm (male) and 66–75 cm (female).

Embryonic development: aplacental viviparous.

Gestation: unknown.

Litter size: 7–23 young.

Reproduction in the Mediterranean: reproduces in the Mediterranean; data indicates parturition must occur in the Catalan Sea, Spain.

Maximum age: unknown.

Diet: bony fishes, small-spotted catshark eggs, crustaceans, polychaetes.

Habitat: benthic, on continental shelves and upper slope, at depths ranging from 50 m to at least 725 m.

Geographical distribution in the Mediterranean Sea: all Mediterranean.

Geographical distribution in the rest of the world: Eastern Atlantic Ocean.

Behavior: slow, nocturnal, solitary or in pairs, timid, possibly segregate by sex.

Dangerousness for man: not dangerous.

Importance for fishery in the Mediterranean: no importance.

Status in the Mediterranean: uncommon.

Kind of presence in the Mediterranean: stable.

Specimens of particular interest recorded in the Mediterranean: a 73 cm pregnant females carrying 9 near-term embryos was caught off Barcelona, Spain, Catalan Sea, in March 1998.

Species with which can be confused: none.

Main references for the Mediterranean: Tortonese (1956), Capapé (1977), Cadenat & Blache (1981), Bauchot (1987), Vanni (1992), Moreno (1995), Mizzan (1996), Barrull et al. (1999), Capapé et al. (1999), Barrull & Mate (2001), Barrull & Mate (2002), Bruni & Würtz (2002), Lipej et al. (2004).

Other selected non–Mediterranean related references: Bigelow & Schroeder (1948), Poll (1951), Bigelow & Schroeder (1957), Bass et al. (1973–1976), Compagno (1984).

Kitefin shark

Dalatias licha (Bonnaterre, 1788)

Classification: Order Squaliformes, family Dalatiidae, genus *Dalatias*.
Common names in other languages: French: squale licha; Spanish: negra; Italian: scimnorino; German: schokoladenhai.
Distinctive characteristics for immediate identification: no anal fin, no dorsal fin spines, pectoral fins small, pelvic fins large.
Morphology: no anal fin. Body cylindrical and slender. Pelvic fins large. First dorsal fin small, with its origin posterior to pectoral fin free rear tip. Second dorsal fin larger than first dorsal. Pectoral fins short. Upper caudal fin lobe moderately long, lower

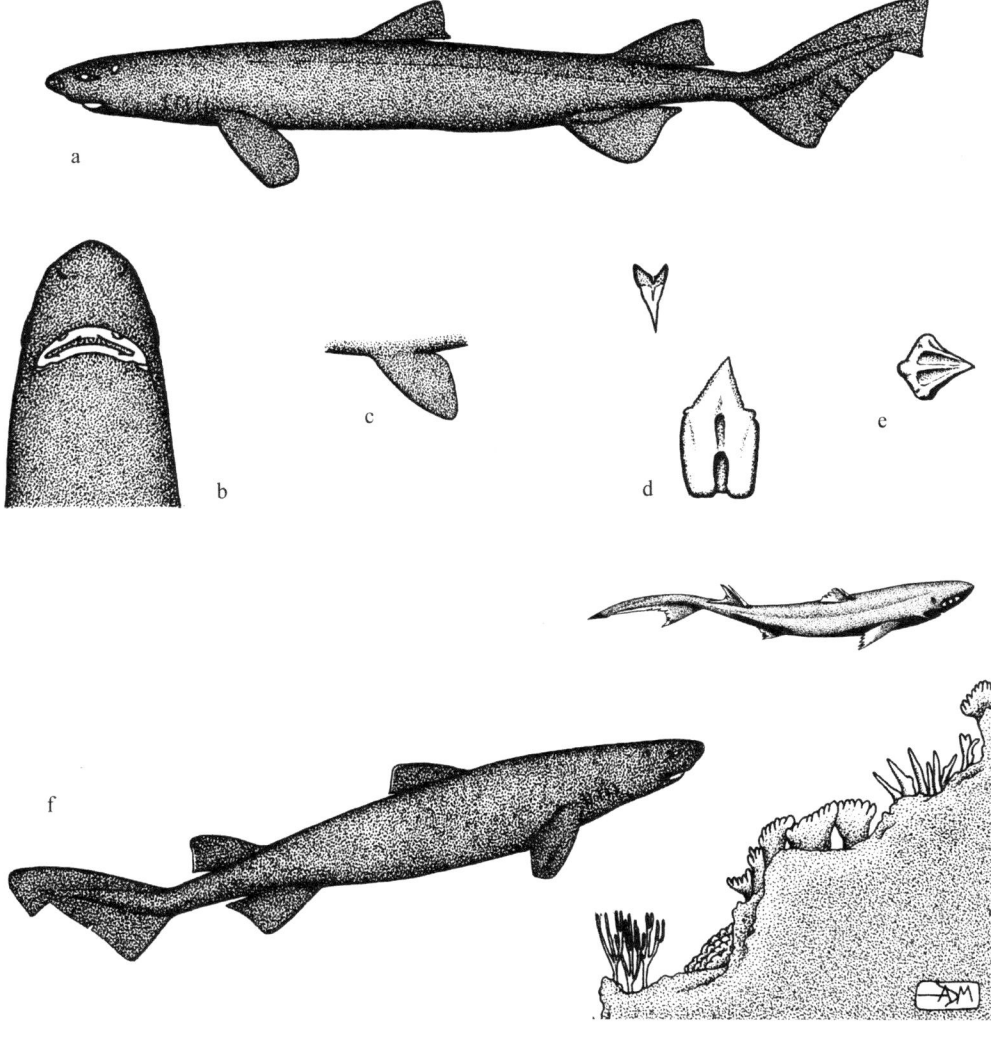

Kitefin shark (*Dalatias licha*): (a) lateral view, (b) ventral view of the head, (c) ventral view of the pectoral fin, (d) upper and lower teeth, (e) placoid scale, (f) a kitefin shark pursuing a velvet belly (*Etmopterus spinax*).

lobe short; caudal fin terminal lobe large; caudal fin posterior margin frayed and without posterior notch. Snout short. Mouth almost straight in ventral view. Eyes large. Nostrils large. Spiracles large. 5 pairs of short gill slits all located anterior to the pectoral fin origin.

Coloration: dorsal surfaces black or brown, sometimes purplish; ventral surfaces similar. Area around the mouth white. The pectoral fin ventral surface has dark coloration similar to the dorsal surface. The juveniles can show fin posterior margins white.

Teeth shape: upper teeth with one cusp, small, narrow, pointed, curved; lower teeth larger, with one cusp, triangular, with serrated edges: these teeth are interlocked forming a cutting wall.

Dental formula: 8 to 9–1–7 to 9 / 8 to 9–1–8 to 9.

Maximum size: 182 cm.

Size at birth: 30–37 cm.

Size at maturity: 77–121 cm (male) and 115–159 cm (female).

Embryonic development: aplacental viviparous.

Gestation: unknown.

Litter size: 3–16 young.

Reproduction in the Mediterranean: reproduces in the Mediterranean; data indicates parturition must occur in the Aegean Sea.

Maximum age: unknown.

Diet: bony fishes, sharks, cephalopods, crustaceans, polychaetes, siphonophores, ophiuroids, carcasses.

Habitat: pelagic, in deep waters, on outer continental and insular shelves and upper slopes, at depths ranging from 40 m to at least 1800 m.

Geographical distribution in the Mediterranean Sea: all Mediterranean.

Geographical distribution in the rest of the world: Atlantic, Pacific and Indian Oceans.

Behavior: active, solitary, timid.

Dangerousness for man: not dangerous.

Importance for fishery in the Mediterranean: scarce importance.

Status in the Mediterranean: relatively common.

Kind of presence in the Mediterranean: stable.

Specimens of particular interest recorded in the Mediterranean: the largest specimens recorded in the Mediterranean, both 113 cm long, were two females caught off Monaco in 1998 (preserved in the Musée Océanographique de Monaco) and off Blanes, Catalan Sea, Spain, in 1920 (preserved in the Museu de Zoologia de Barcelona).

Species with which can be confused: the Portuguese dogfish (*Centroscymnus coelolepis*), but this species has dorsal fin spines.

Main references for the Mediterranean: Tortonese (1956), Macpherson (1980), Cadenat & Blache (1981), Matallanas (1982), Golani (1986–1987), Bauchot (1987), Vanni (1992), Moreno (1995), Barrull *et al.* (1999), Barrull & Mate (2002), Bruni & Würtz (2002), Kabasakal & Kabasakal (2002), Piscitelli & De Maddalena (2003), Lipej *et al.* (2004).

Other selected non-Mediterranean related references: Bigelow & Schroeder (1948), Bigelow & Schroeder (1957), Bass *et al.* (1973–1976), Castro (1983), Compagno (1984), Last & Stevens (1994).

Sawback angelshark
Squatina aculeata Dumeril, 1829

Classification: Order Squatiniformes, family Squatinidae, genus *Squatina*.
Common names in other languages: French: ange de mer épineux; Spanish: angelote espinoso; Italian: pesce angelo aculeato, squadro aculeato; German: sägerücken-engelshai.
Distinctive characteristics for immediate identification: body ray-like, trunk narrow (the shark total length is 5.4 to 6 times the distance between pectoral fin axils), large dermal denticles on midline of back and caudal peduncle, on the snout and above the eyes, numerous small dark and white spots.
Morphology: body ray-like: strongly dorso-ventrally flattened (depressed), with very wide head and very wide pectoral and pelvic fins. No anal fin. Dorsal fins way back on shark. First dorsal fin origin over the pelvic fin free rear tip. Caudal fin lower lobe larger than upper lobe. Caudal keels. Trunk narrow (the shark total length is 5.4 to 6 times the distance between pectoral fin axils). Large dermal denticles on midline of back and caudal peduncle and also on the snout and above the eyes. Mouth terminal and very wide. Eyes located on dorsal surface of the head. Nasal barbels complex and very fringed. Large spiracles. 5 pairs of gill slits, not visible when the shark rests on the sea bottom.
Coloration: dorsal surfaces grey to brown light with numerous small dark and white spots; ventral surfaces white.
Teeth shape: upper teeth with one cusp, small and pointed; lower teeth similar.
Dental formula: 9 to 11–9 to 11 / 9 to 11–9 to 11.
Maximum size: 188 cm.
Size at birth: 25–30 cm.
Size at maturity: about 125 cm (male) and about 125 cm (female).
Embryonic development: aplacental viviparous.
Gestation: unknown.
Litter size: unknown.
Reproduction in the Mediterranean: reproduces in the Medeterranean.
Maximum age: unknown.
Diet: bony fishes, cartilaginous fishes, crustaceans, cephalopods.
Habitat: Benthic, on continental shelves and upper slopes, at depths ranging from 30 m to at least 500 m.
Geographical distribution in the Mediterranean Sea: all Mediterranean.
Geographical distribution in the rest of the world: Eastern Atlantic Ocean.
Behavior: torpid and slow, nocturnal, solitary, timid, lies buried in the sand waiting for a prey.
Dangerousness for man: not dangerous.

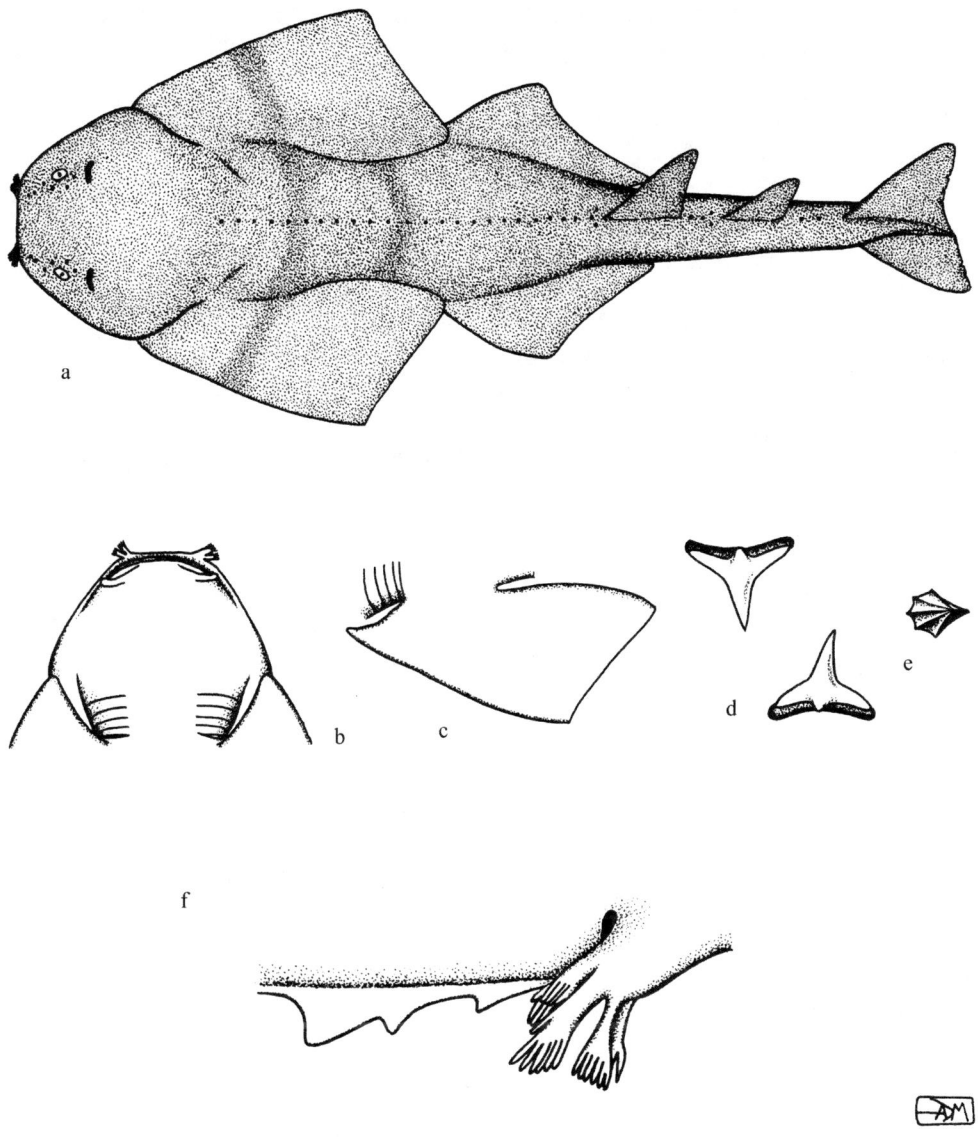

Sawback angelshark (*Squatina aculeata*): (a) lateral view, (b) ventral view of the head, (c) ventral view of the pectoral fin, (d) upper and lower teeth, (e) placoid scale, (f) right nostril.

Importance for fishery in the Mediterranean: scarce importance.
Status in the Mediterranean: rare.
Kind of presence in the Mediterranean: stable.
Specimens of particular interest recorded in the Mediterranean: the largest specimen recorded in this area is a 125 cm female caught off Roses, Catalan Sea, Spain.
Species with which can be confused: the smoothback angelshark (*Squatina oculata*) and the common angelshark (*Squatina squatina*); but both these species lack the large dermal denticles on midline of back, caudal peduncle, snout and above the eyes.
Main references for the Mediterranean: Tortonese (1956), Quignard & Capapé (1971),

Capapé (1974a), Cadenat & Blache (1981), Bauchot (1987), Moreno (1995), Golani (1996), Barrull *et al.* (1999), Barrull & Mate (2002), Basusta (2002), Šanda & De Maddalena (2003).

Other selected non–Mediterranean related references: Compagno (1984).

Smoothback angelshark
Squatina oculata Bonaparte, 1840

Classification: Order Squatiniformes, family Squatinidae, genus *Squatina*.
Common names in other languages: French: ange de mer ocellé, ange de mer de Bonaparte; Spanish: pez ángel; Italian: pesce angelo ocellato, squadro ocellato; German: weichrückiger engelshai.
Distinctive characteristics for immediate identification: body ray-like, trunk quite narrow (the shark total length is 4.9 to 5.9 times the distance between pectoral fin axils), no large dermal denticles on midline of back, ocelli (white spots having black or dark margins) and normal dark and light spots.
Morphology: body ray-like: strongly dorso-ventrally flattened (depressed), with very wide head and very wide pectoral and pelvic fins. No anal fin. Dorsal fins way back on shark. First dorsal fin origin posterior to the pelvic fin free rear tip. Caudal fin lower lobe larger than upper lobe. Caudal keels. Trunk relatively narrow (the shark total length is 4.9 to 5.9 times the distance between pectoral fin axils). Mouth terminal and very wide. Eyes located on dorsal surface of the head. Nasal barbels quite simple and moderately fringed. Large spiracles. 5 pairs of gill slits, not visible when the shark rests on the sea bottom.
Coloration: dorsal surfaces brown-grey light or reddish with characteristic ocelli (white spots having black or dark margins) and normal dark and light spots; ventral surfaces white.
Teeth shape: upper teeth with one cusp, small and pointed; lower teeth similar.
Dental formula: 7 to 9 -7 to 9 / 7 to 9–7 to 9.
Maximum size: 160 cm.
Size at birth: 24–27 cm.
Size at maturity: 71–93 cm (male) and 100–121 cm (female).
Embryonic development: aplacental viviparous.
Gestation: unknown.
Litter size: 6–17 young.
Reproduction in the Mediterranean: reproduces in the Mediterranean.
Maximum age: unknown.
Diet: bony fishes, crustaceans, cephalopods.
Habitat: benthic, on continental shelves and upper slopes, at depths ranging from 20 m to at least 550 m.
Geographical distribution in the Mediterranean Sea: all Mediterranean.
Geographical distribution in the rest of the world: Eastern Atlantic Ocean.
Behavior: torpid and slow, nocturnal, solitary, timid, lets divers approach closely, lies buried in the sand waiting for a prey.

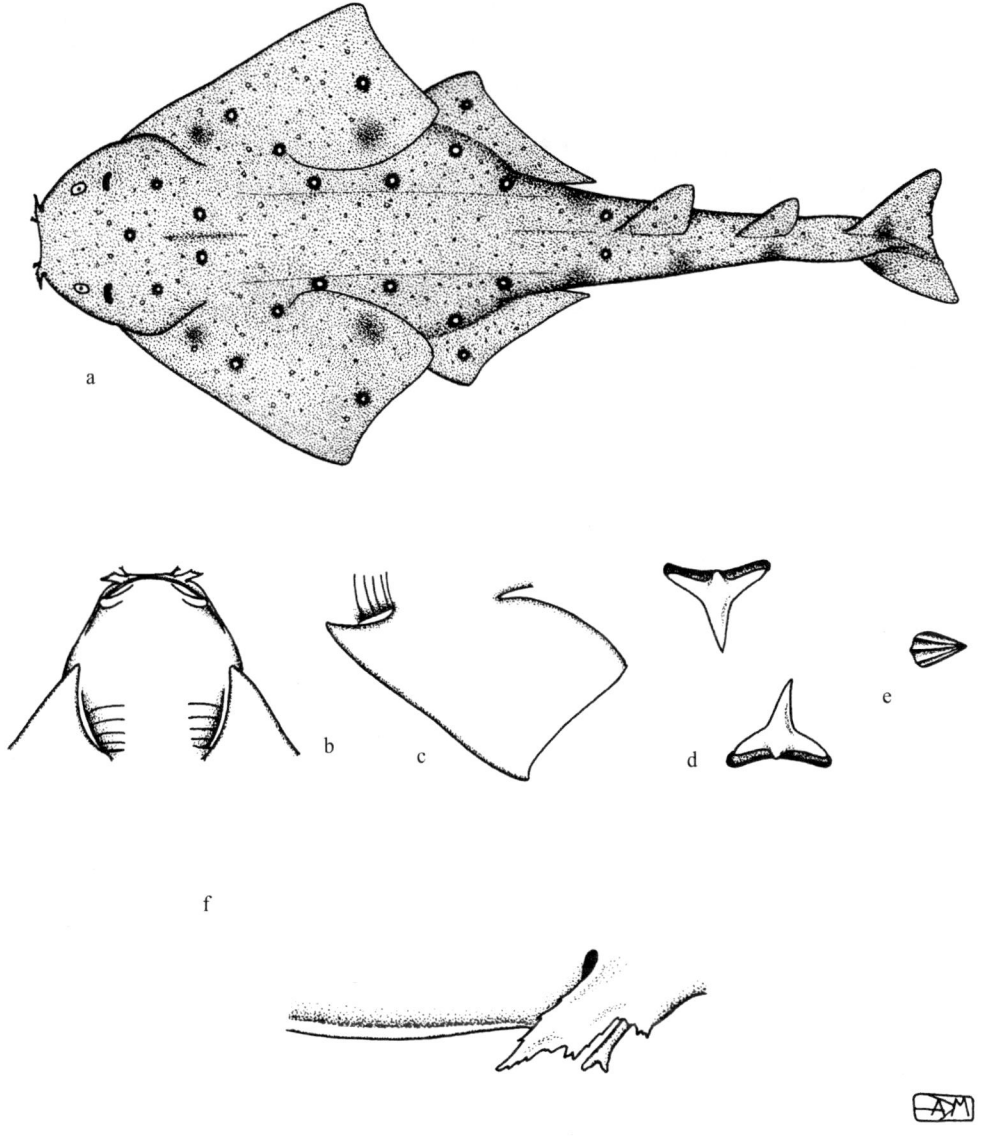

Smoothback angelshark (*Squatina oculata*): (a) lateral view, (b) ventral view of the head, (c) ventral view of the pectoral fin, (d) upper and lower teeth, (e) placoid scale, (f) right nostril.

Dangerousness for man: not dangerous.
Importance for fishery in the Mediterranean: scarce importance.
Status in the Mediterranean: uncommon.
Kind of presence in the Mediterranean: stable.
Specimens of particular interest recorded in the Mediterranean: one of the largest specimens, a 140 cm male was caught off Toulon, France.
Species with which can be confused: the sawback angelshark (*Squatina aculeata*) and the common angelshark (*Squatina squatina*); but *S. aculeata* has a trunk narrower (the shark total length is 5.4 to 6 times the distance between pectoral fin axils) and

also large dermal denticles on midline of back, and *S. squatina* has a trunk wider (the shark total length is 3.6 to 4 times the distance between pectoral fin axils).

Main references for the Mediterranean: Tortonese (1956), Capapé (1974a), Capapé (1977), Cadenat & Blache (1981), Bauchot (1987), Capapé *et al.* (1990), Vanni (1992), Moreno (1995), Golani (1996), Barrull & Mate (2002), Lipej *et al.* (2004).

Other selected non–Mediterranean related references: Poll (1951), Compagno (1984).

Common angelshark
Squatina squatina (Linnaeus, 1758)

Classification: Order Squatiniformes, family Squatinidae, genus *Squatina*.
Common names in other languages: French: ange de mer commun; Spanish: angelote; Italian: pesce angelo comune, squadro comune; German: engelshai.
Distinctive characteristics for immediate identification: body ray-like, trunk wide (the shark total length is 3.6 to 4 times the distance between pectoral fin axils), no large dermal denticles on midline of back, a straight dark band on the pectoral fins and small white and dark spots.
Morphology: body ray-like: strongly dorso-ventrally flattened (depressed), with very wide head and very wide pectoral and pelvic fins. No anal fin. Dorsal fins way back on shark. First dorsal fin origin over the pelvic fin free rear tip. Caudal fin lower lobe larger than upper lobe. Caudal keels. Trunk wide (the shark total length is 3.6 to 4 times the distance between pectoral fin axils). Mouth terminal and very wide. Eyes located on dorsal surface of the head. Nasal barbels not fringed. Large spiracles. 5 pairs of gill slits, not visible when the shark rests on the sea bottom.
Coloration: dorsal surfaces brown-grey light or dark with 1 to 3 straight dark bands on the pectoral fins, small white and dark spots and dark patches; ventral surfaces white.
Teeth shape: upper teeth with one cusp, small and pointed; lower teeth similar.
Dental formula: 9 to 11–9 to 11 / 9 to 11–9 to 11.
Maximum size: 244 cm.
Size at birth: 24–30 cm.
Size at maturity: 80–132 cm (male) and 128–169 cm (female).
Embryonic development: aplacental viviparous.
Gestation: about 10 months.
Litter size: 7–25 young.
Reproduction in the Mediterranean: reproduces in the Mediterranean; data indicates parturition must occur off the French coast.
Maximum age: unknown.
Diet: bony fishes, elasmobranchs, crustaceans and cephalopods.
Habitat: benthic, on continental shelves, at depths ranging from the surface to at least 300 m. Juveniles are found very close inshore and possibly pregnant females give birth in shallow waters.
Geographical distribution in the Mediterranean Sea: all Mediterranean.

Common angelshark

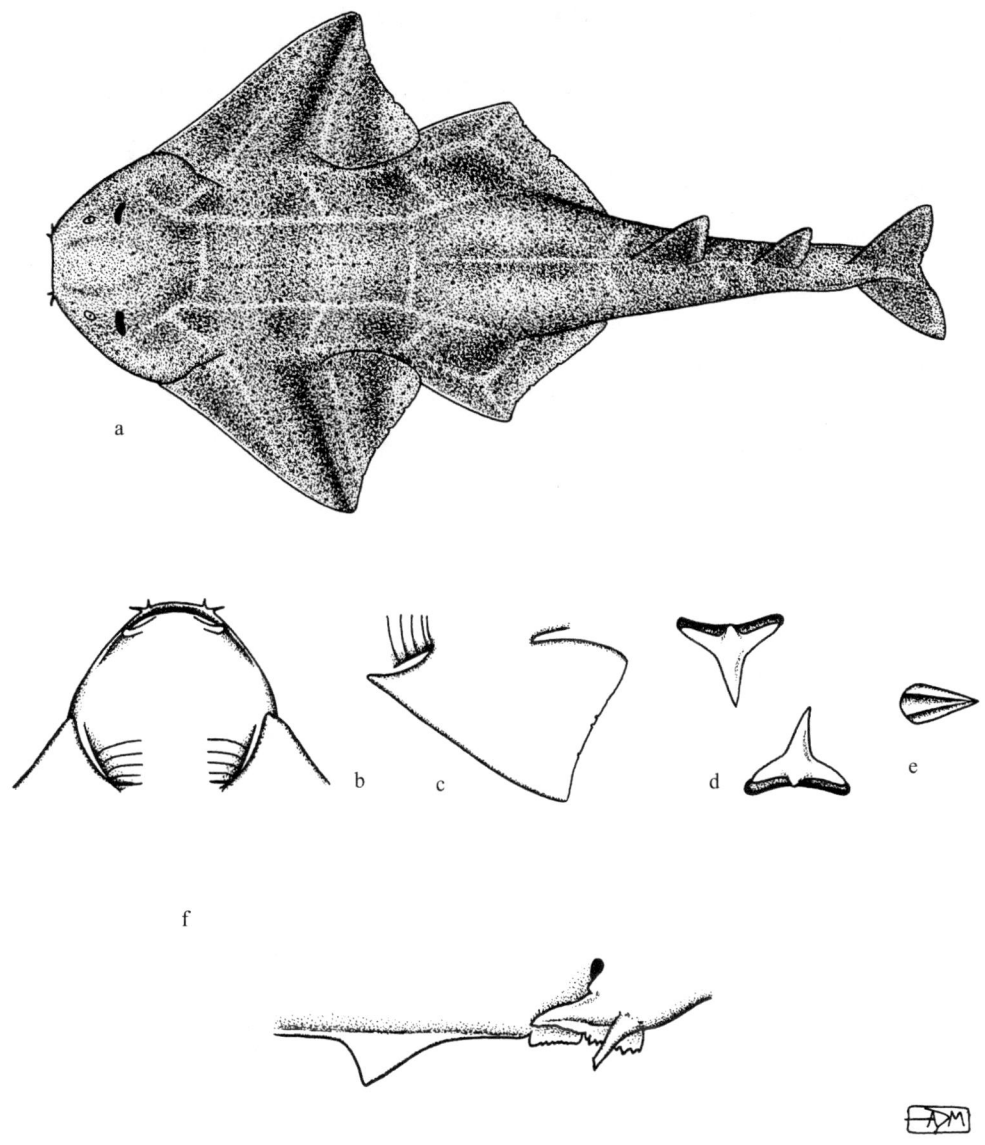

Common angelshark (*Squatina squatina*): (a) lateral view, (b) ventral view of the head, (c) ventral view of the pectoral fin, (d) upper and lower teeth, (e) placoid scale, (f) right nostril.

Geographical distribution in the rest of the world: Eastern Atlantic Ocean.
Behavior: torpid and slow, nocturnal, solitary, migratory, timid, lies buried in the sand waiting for a prey.
Dangerousness for man: not dangerous.
Importance for fishery in the Mediterranean: scarce importance.
Status in the Mediterranean: uncommon.
Kind of presence in the Mediterranean: stable.
Specimens of particular interest recorded in the Mediterranean: the largest specimen recorded in this area is a 162 cm female caught off Villefranche-sur-mer,

France, Ligurian Sea, in 1910 (preserved in the Musée Océanographique de Monaco).

Species with which can be confused: the sawback angelshark (*Squatina aculeata*) and smoothback angelshark (*Squatina oculata*); but both these species have a narrower trunk (the *S. aculeata* total length is 5.4 to 6 times the distance between pectoral fin axils, while the *S. oculata* total length is 4.9 to 5.9 times the distance between pectoral fin axils). Moreover, *S. aculeata* has large dermal denticles on midline of back.

Main references for the Mediterranean: Tortonese (1956), Capapé (1974a), Capapé (1977), Cadenat & Blache (1981), Bauchot (1987), Capapé *et al.* (1990), Vanni (1992), Moreno (1995), Mizzan (1996), Barrull & Mate (2002), Lipej *et al.* (2004).

Other selected non–Mediterranean related references: Bigelow & Schroeder (1948), Compagno (1984).

Sandtiger shark
Carcharias taurus (Rafinesque, 1810)

Classification: Order Lamniformes, family Odontaspididae, genus *Carcharias*.
Common names in other languages: French: requin taureau; Spanish: tiburón toro; Italian: squalo toro; German: sandtigerhai.
Distinctive characteristics for immediate identification: anal fin present, second dorsal fin slightly smaller than first dorsal and about as large as the anal fin, snout conical and moderately long, long gill slits, teeth protruding from the mouth in lower jaw and having one narrow pointed cusp and 2 small cusplets.
Morphology: snout conical, large and moderately long. First dorsal fin large, its origin posterior to pectoral fin free rear tip. Second dorsal fin almost as large as first dorsal. Anal fin about large as the second dorsal. Pectoral fins wide but relatively short. Caudal fin upper lobe long, lower lobe short. Body massive, with the dorsal part pronounced. Caudal peduncle large and short. Eyes small. Spiracles very small. 5 pairs of long gill slits, all located anterior to the pectoral fin anterior margin.
Coloration: dorsal surfaces grey-brown with iridescence and yellowish, brownish or reddish spots; ventral surfaces whitish. Sometimes fin posterior margins and apex dark. The pectoral fin ventral surface is partially whitish and partially grey-brown with indented margins forming patches, darker at the apex and part of the posterior margin.
Teeth shape: upper teeth with the cusp long, narrow, slightly curved and 2 minute cusplets; lower teeth similar. Teeth of the lower jaw protrude from the mouth and visible even when its mouth is closed.
Dental formula: 22 to 24–22 to 24 / 20 to 23–20 to 23.
Maximum size: 380 cm.
Size at birth: 89–105 cm.
Size at maturity: 193 cm (male) and about 218–235 cm (female).
Embryonic development: aplacental viviparous (embryos nourishment by oophagy and embryophagy).

Sandtiger shark

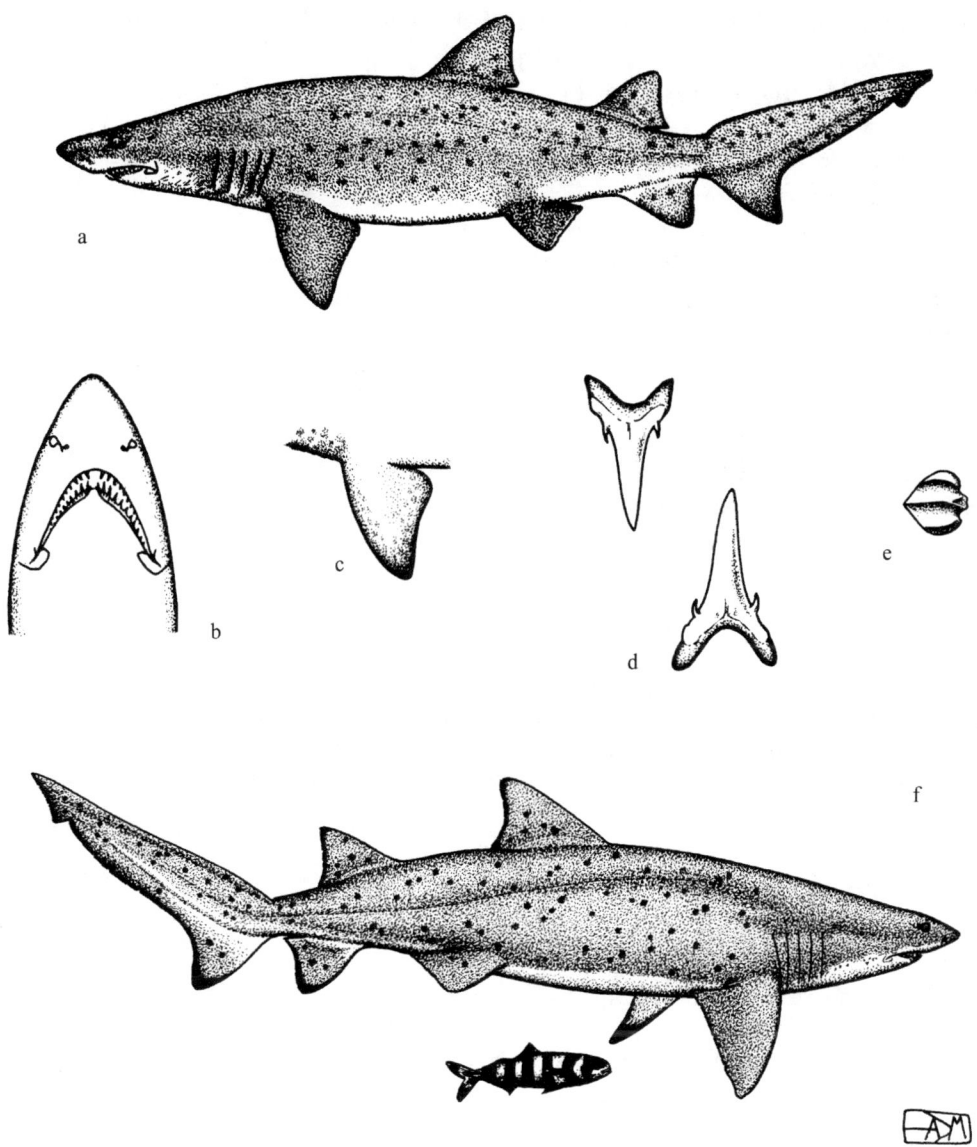

Sandtiger shark (*Carcharias taurus*): (a) lateral view, (b) ventral view of the head, (c) ventral view of the pectoral fin, (d) upper and lower teeth, (e) placoid scale, (f) a sandtiger swims accompanied by a pilot fish (*Naucrates ductor*).

Gestation: 8–9 months.
Litter size: 2 young.
Reproduction in the Mediterranean: reproduces in the Mediterranean.
Maximum age: unknown.
Diet: bony fishes, elasmobranchs, cephalopods, crustaceans.
Habitat: pelagic, on continental shelves, at depths ranging from the surface to at least 270 m.
Geographical distribution in the Mediterranean Sea: all Mediterranean.

Geographical distribution in the rest of the world: Atlantic, Pacific and Indian Oceans.

Behavior: slow and torpid, primarily nocturnal, solitary or in small groups, migratory, can approach divers closely (without showing any aggressive behavior), can segregate by sex and size, can cooperatively catch their prey, can swallow air at the surface and hold it in the stomach to float.

Dangerousness for man: not dangerous.

Importance for fishery in the Mediterranean: no importance.

Status in the Mediterranean: very rare.

Kind of presence in the Mediterranean: stable.

Specimens of particular interest recorded in the Mediterranean: the largest specimen was about 380 cm long and was caught off the Island of Molat, Croatia, Adriatic Sea, in September 1999; another large specimen, about 300 cm long, was caught on 1 October 1999 off Limassol, Cyprus.

Species with which can be confused: the smalltooth sand tiger (*Odontaspis ferox*), but this species has a longer snout, larger eyes and 4 or more cusplets in each tooth.

Main references for the Mediterranean: Tortonese (1956), Granier (1964), Quignard & Capapé (1972b), Cadenat & Blache (1981), Bauchot (1987), Vanni (1992), Moreno (1995), Golani (1996), Barrull & Mate (2002), Lipej et al. (2004).

Other selected non–Mediterranean related references: Bigelow & Schroeder (1948), Springer (1948), Lineweaver & Backus (1970), Bass et al. (1973–1976), Castro (1983), Gilmore et al. (1983), Compagno (1984), Randall (1986), Last & Stevens (1994), Lucifora et al. (2002).

Smalltooth sand tiger
Odontaspis ferox (Risso, 1810)

Classification: Order Lamniformes, family Odontaspididae, genus *Odontaspis*.

Common names in other languages: French: requin féroce; Spanish: solrayo; Italian: cagnaccio; German: schildzahnhai.

Distinctive characteristics for immediate identification: anal fin present, second dorsal fin slightly smaller than first dorsal and about large as anal fin, snout conical and long, long gill slits, teeth protruding from the mouth in lower jaw and having one narrow pointed cusp and 4 or more small cusplets.

Morphology: snout conical, large and long. First dorsal fin large, origin over the pectoral fin free rear tip or the inner margin. Second dorsal almost as large as first dorsal. Anal fin about as large as the second dorsal. Pectoral fins wide but relatively short. Caudal fin upper lobe long, lower lobe short. Body massive, with the dorsal part pronounced. Caudal peduncle large and short. Eyes moderately large. Spiracles very small. 5 pairs of long gill slits, all located anterior to the pectoral fin anterior margin.

Coloration: dorsal surfaces grey-brown with iridescence and sometimes reddish spots; ventral surfaces whitish. Juveniles have dark fin apex.

Teeth shape: upper teeth with the cusp long, narrow, slightly curved and 4 or more

Smalltooth sand tiger

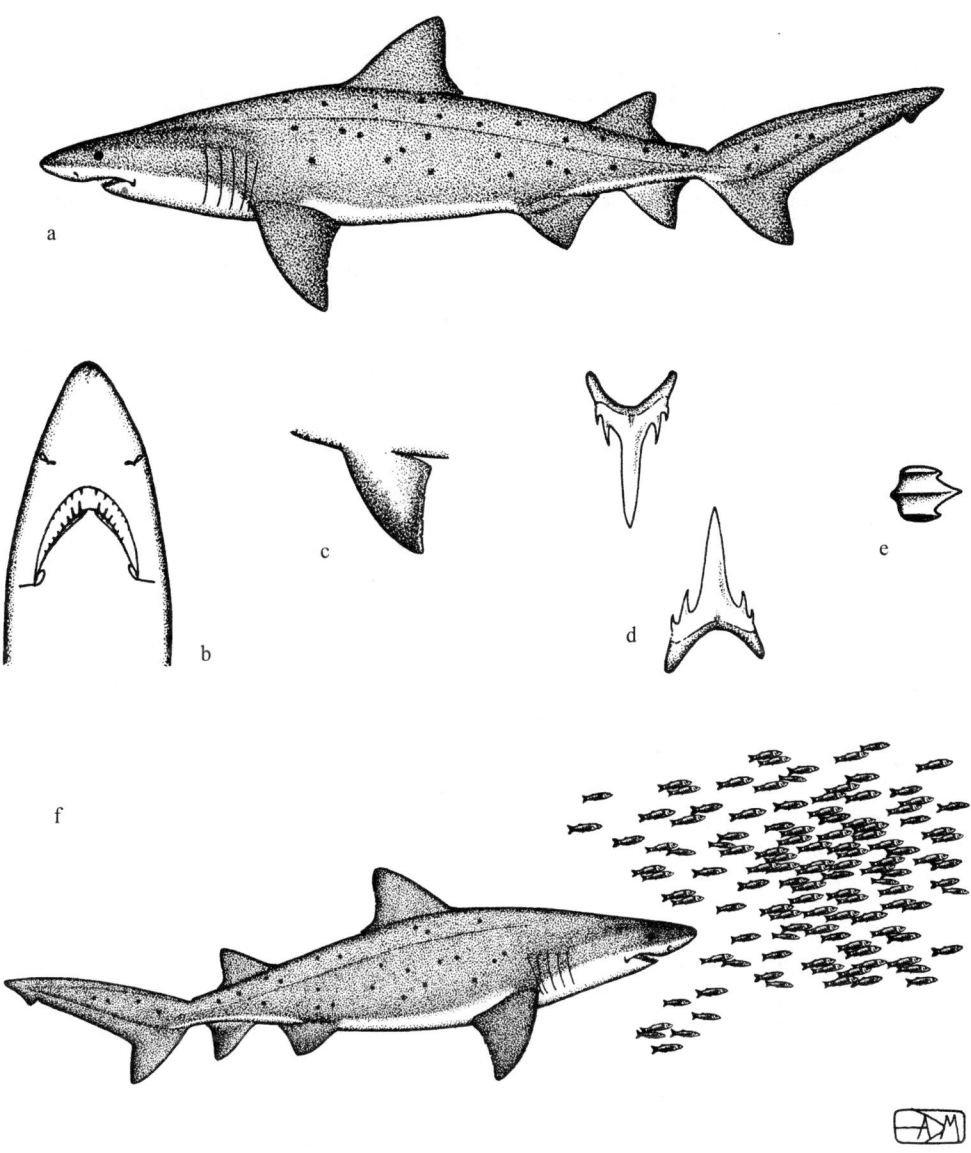

Smalltooth sand tiger (*Odontaspis ferox*): (a) lateral view, (b) ventral view of the head, (c) ventral view of the pectoral fin, (d) upper and lower teeth, (e) placoid scale, (f) a smalltooth sandtiger catching small schooling fish.

minute cusplets; lower teeth similar. Teeth of the lower jaw protruding from the mouth and visible even when the shark has its mouth closed.

Dental formula: 23 to 27–1 -23 to 27 / 18 to 24–1–18 to 24.
Maximum size: 410 cm.
Size at birth: about 105 cm.
Size at maturity: 275 cm (male) and 350 cm (female).
Embryonic development: aplacental viviparous (embryos nourishment probably by oophagy and embryophagy).

Gestation: unknown.
Litter size: 2 young.
Reproduction in the Mediterranean: reproduces in the Mediterranean.
Maximum age: unknown.
Diet: small bony fishes, squids and crustaceans.
Habitat: pelagic, on continental and insular shelves and upper slopes, at depths ranging from 10 m to at least 420 m.
Geographical distribution in the Mediterranean Sea: all Mediterranean.
Geographical distribution in the rest of the world: Atlantic, Pacific and Indian Oceans.
Behavior: slow and torpid, solitary or in small groups, can approach divers closely (without showing any aggressive behavior), can segregate by size.
Dangerousness for man: not dangerous.
Importance for fishery in the Mediterranean: no importance.
Status in the Mediterranean: very rare.
Kind of presence in the Mediterranean: stable.
Specimens of particular interest recorded in the Mediterranean: the largest specimen ever reported was a 410 cm female caught on 6 May 1985 off Scherchi shoal, Sicily, Italy. Other very large specimens were captured in these waters include a 371 cm female caught off Annaba, Algeria in May-June 1998, and a 360 cm female caught in the Gulf of Genoa, Italy (preserved in the Museo civico di Storia Naturale "Giacomo Doria" in Genoa). Small groups of these sharks have been repeatedly observed and approached by divers off Beirut, Lebanon.
Species with which can be confused: the sandtiger shark (*Carcharias taurus*), but this species has a shorter snout, smaller eyes and 2 cusplets in each tooth.
Main references for the Mediterranean: Tortonese (1956), Capapé (1975b), Cadenat & Blache (1981), Bauchot (1987), Vanni (1992), Moreno (1995), Vacchi & Serena (1997), Barrull & Mate (2002), Lipej *et al.* (2004).
Other selected non–Mediterranean related references: Bass *et al.* (1973–1976), Castro (1983), Compagno (1984), Last & Stevens (1994).

Bigeye thresher
Alopias superciliosus (Lowe, 1839)

Classification: Order Lamniformes, family Alopiidae, genus *Alopias*.
Common names in other languages: French: renard à gros yeux; Spanish: zorro negro; Italian: pesce volpe dagli occhi grandi; German: großaugen-fuchshai.
Distinctive characteristics for immediate identification: caudal fin upper lobe extremely long (about as long as the rest of the body), eyes enormous (extending up to the dorsal surface of the head), a deep groove on side of the head.
Morphology: caudal fin upper lobe extremely long, about as long as the rest of the body, lower lobe relatively short. Eyes enormous, extending up to the dorsal surface of the head. Dorsal part pronounced. Two deep grooves originating on the dorsal part of the head extending to above the gill region and form a sort of highly pronounced "step" on the head (V-shaped viewed from above). Snout conical. Pectoral

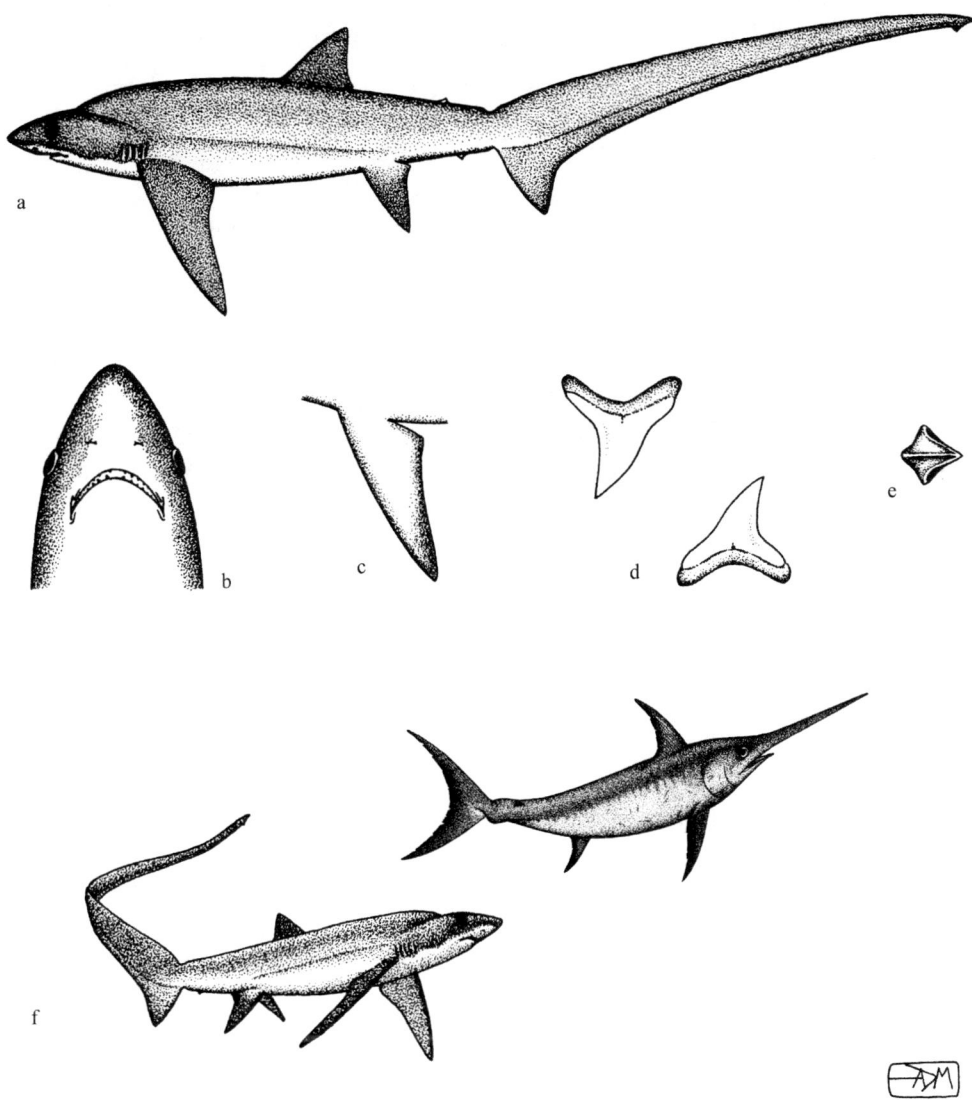

Bigeye thresher (*Alopias superciliosus*): (a) lateral view, (b) ventral view of the head, (c) ventral view of the pectoral fin, (d) upper and lower teeth, (e) placoid scale, (f) a bigeye thresher pursuing a swordfish (*Xiphias gladius*).

and pelvic fins long. First dorsal fin relatively large, its origin posterior to pectoral fin free rear tip. Second dorsal and anal fins very small. Caudal peduncle large. Mouth relatively small. Spiracles very small. 5 pairs of short gill slits, the 4th and 5th located over the pectoral fin base.

Coloration: dorsal surfaces dark grey-purplish or black, with iridescence on the sides; ventral surfaces white.

Teeth shape: upper teeth with one cusp, pointed and oblique, with cutting edges; lower teeth similar.

Dental formula: 11 to 12–11 to 12 / 10 to 12–10 to 12.

Maximum size: 461 cm.
Size at birth: 135–140 cm.
Size at maturity: 270–287 cm (male) and 332–341 cm (female).
Embryonic development: aplacental viviparous (embryos nourished by oophagy).
Gestation: about 12 months.
Litter size: 2–4 young.
Reproduction in the Mediterranean: reproduces in the Mediterranean; data indicates parturition must occur in the Eastern Mediterranean.
Maximum age: at least 20 years.
Diet: bony fishes, squids, crustaceans.
Habitat: pelagic, on continental shelves, at depths ranging from surface to at least 835 m.
Geographical distribution in the Mediterranean Sea: all Mediterranean.
Geographical distribution in the rest of the world: Atlantic, Pacific and Indian Oceans.
Behavior: particularly active and fast (thanks to their heat-retaining systems), solitary or in groups, timid, uses its long caudal fin upper lobe to slash the water in order to herd and disorient schooling fish on which they prey.
Dangerousness for man: not dangerous.
Importance for fishery in the Mediterranean: some importance.
Status in the Mediterranean: relatively common.
Kind of presence in the Mediterranean: stable.
Specimens of particular interest recorded in the Mediterranean: one of the largest specimens, a 438 cm female, was caught off Islas Chafarinas, Spain. A 400 cm female stranded in November 1994 at Tavolara Island had a 15 cm long swordfish bill embedded in the head. Two new-born were reported from Israel waters: a 88 cm female caught off Ashdod on 30 May 1986 and a 86 cm female caught off Tel Aviv on 15 May 1991 (both preserved at the Hebrew University in Jerusalem).
Species with which can be confused: the common thresher (*Alopias vulpinus*), but this species has smaller eyes that do not extend up to the dorsal surface of the head and no deep groove on sides of the head.
Main references for the Mediterranean: Cadenat & Blache (1981), Cigala Fulgosi (1983b), Bauchot (1987), Tortonese (1987), Moreno & Moron (1992b), Golani (1996), Moreno (1995), Buencuerpo *et al.* (1998), Vacchi & Serena (2000), Barrull & Mate (2002), de la Serna *et al.* (2002).
Other selected non–Mediterranean related references: Bigelow & Schroeder (1948), Bass *et al.* (1973–1976), Castro (1983), Compagno (1984), Last & Stevens (1994), Chen *et al.* (1997), Liu *et al.* (1998).

Common thresher shark
Alopias vulpinus (Bonnaterre, 1788)

Classification: Order Lamniformes, family Alopiidae, genus *Alopias*.
Common names in other languages: French: renard, renard de mer; Spanish: zorro; Italian: pesce volpe; German: gewöhnlicher fuchshai.
Distinctive characteristics for immediate identification: caudal fin upper lobe extremely

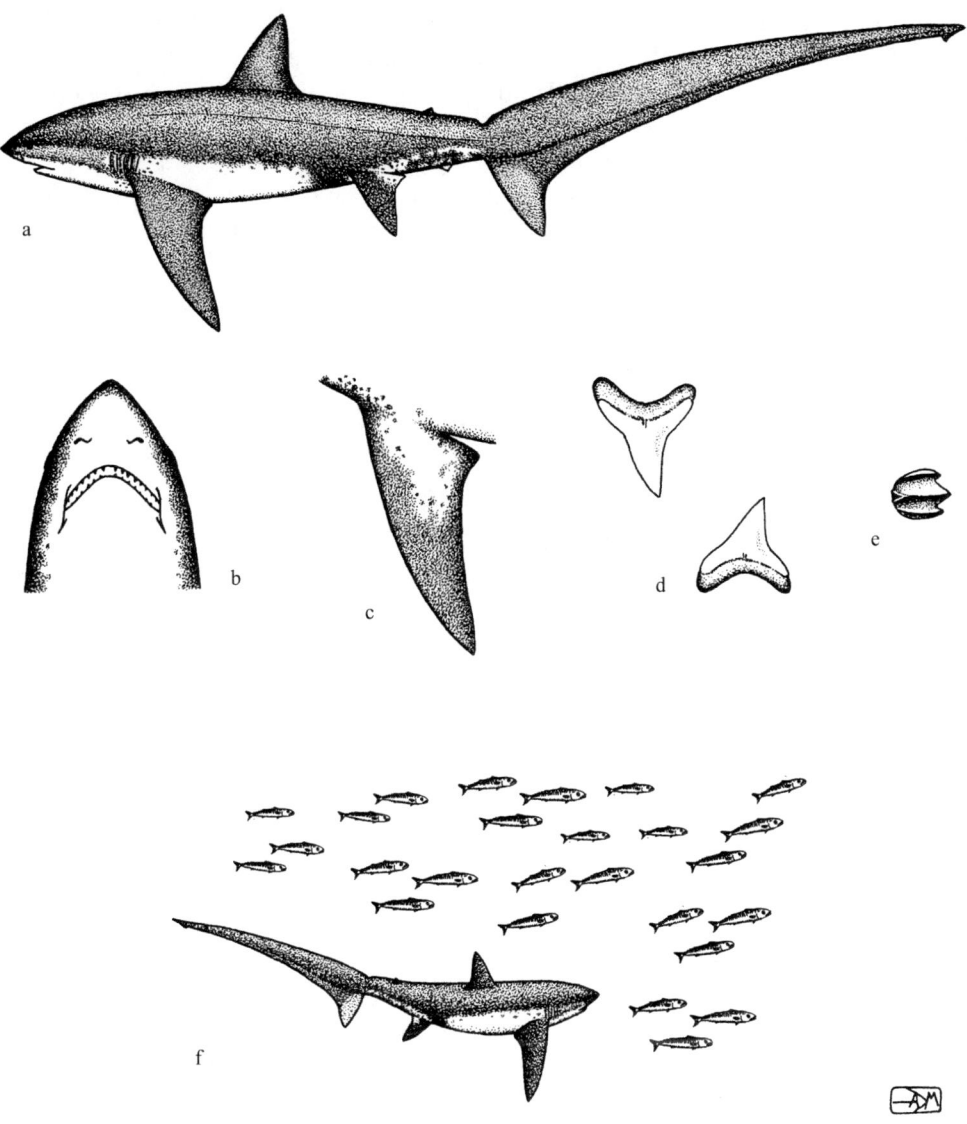

Common thresher shark (*Alopias vulpinus*): (a) lateral view, (b) ventral view of the head, (c) ventral view of the pectoral fin, (d) upper and lower teeth, (e) placoid scale, (f) a common thresher herds a school of small fish.

long (about as long as the rest of the body), eyes large but not extending up to the dorsal surface of the head, no deep groove on sides of the head.

Morphology: caudal fin upper lobe extremely long, about as long as the rest of the body, lower lobe relatively short. Eyes large, but not extending up to the dorsal surface of the head. Dorsal part pronounced. Snout conical. Pectoral and pelvic fins long. First dorsal fin large, its origin posterior to the pectoral fin free rear tip. Second dorsal and anal fins very small. Caudal peduncle large. Mouth relatively small. Spiracles very small. 5 pairs of short gill slits, the 4th and 5th located over the pectoral fin base.

Coloration: dorsal surfaces dark grey-bluish, with iridescence on the sides; ventral surfaces white except on the pelvic region and caudal peduncle where the dark coloration extend forming an irregular indented pattern with patches and small spots. Boundary separating dorsal from ventral coloration sharp on the head. The pectoral fin ventral surface has extended dark coloration like the dorsal surface and with indented margins forming irregular patches and a white V-shaped area at the base.

Teeth shape: upper teeth with one cusp, pointed and oblique, with cutting edges; lower teeth similar.

Dental formula: 19 to 26–0 to 1–19 to 26 / 21 to 24–0 to 1–21 to 24.

Maximum size: at least 549 cm.

Size at birth: 114–155 cm.

Size at maturity: 320 cm (male) and 375 cm (female).

Embryonic development: aplacental viviparous (embryos nourished by oophagy).

Gestation: unknown.

Litter size: 2–7 young.

Reproduction in the Mediterranean: reproduces in the Mediterranean; data indicates parturition must occur in the Gulfe du Lion, France and in Spanish waters.

Maximum age: at least 19 years.

Diet: bony fishes, cephalopods, crustaceans.

Habitat: pelagic, on continental shelves, at depths ranging from the surface to at least 350 m. Juveniles occur in shallower waters than adults.

Geographical distribution in the Mediterranean Sea: all Mediterranean.

Geographical distribution in the rest of the world: Atlantic, Pacific and Indian Oceans.

Behavior: particularly active and fast (thanks to their heat-retaining systems), solitary or in groups, timid, can leap out of the water, can segregate by sex, uses its long caudal fin upper lobe to slash the water in order to herd and disorient schooling fish on which they prey.

Dangerousness for man: not dangerous.

Importance for fishery in the Mediterranean: certain importance.

Status in the Mediterranean: relatively common.

Kind of presence in the Mediterranean: stable.

Specimens of particular interest recorded in the Mediterranean: one of the largest specimens was caught off Giulianova, Italy, Adriatic Sea, in 1987 and was about 600 cm long. A 470 cm pregnant female caught off Sète, Golfe du Lion, France carried 4 embryos measuring from 150 to 155 cm (this is the largest size recorded for an embryo).

Species with which can be confused: the bigeye thresher (*Alopias superciliosus*), but this species has larger eyes that extend up to the dorsal surface of the head, and a deep groove on sides of the head.

Main references for the Mediterranean: Tortonese (1956), Capapé (1977), Cadenat & Blache (1981), Bauchot (1987), Moreno (1989), Vanni (1992), Moreno (1995), Buencuerpo *et al.* (1998), Barrull *et al.* (1999), Barrull & Mate (2002), de la Serna *et al.* (2002), Lipej *et al.* (2004).

Other selected non–Mediterranean related references: Bigelow & Schroeder (1948),

Gubanov (1972), Bass *et al.* (1973–1976), Castro (1983), Compagno (1984), Last & Stevens (1994), Preti *et al.* (2001).

Basking shark
Cetorhinus maximus (Gunnerus, 1765)

Classification: Order Lamniformes, family Cetorhinidae, genus *Cetorhinus*.

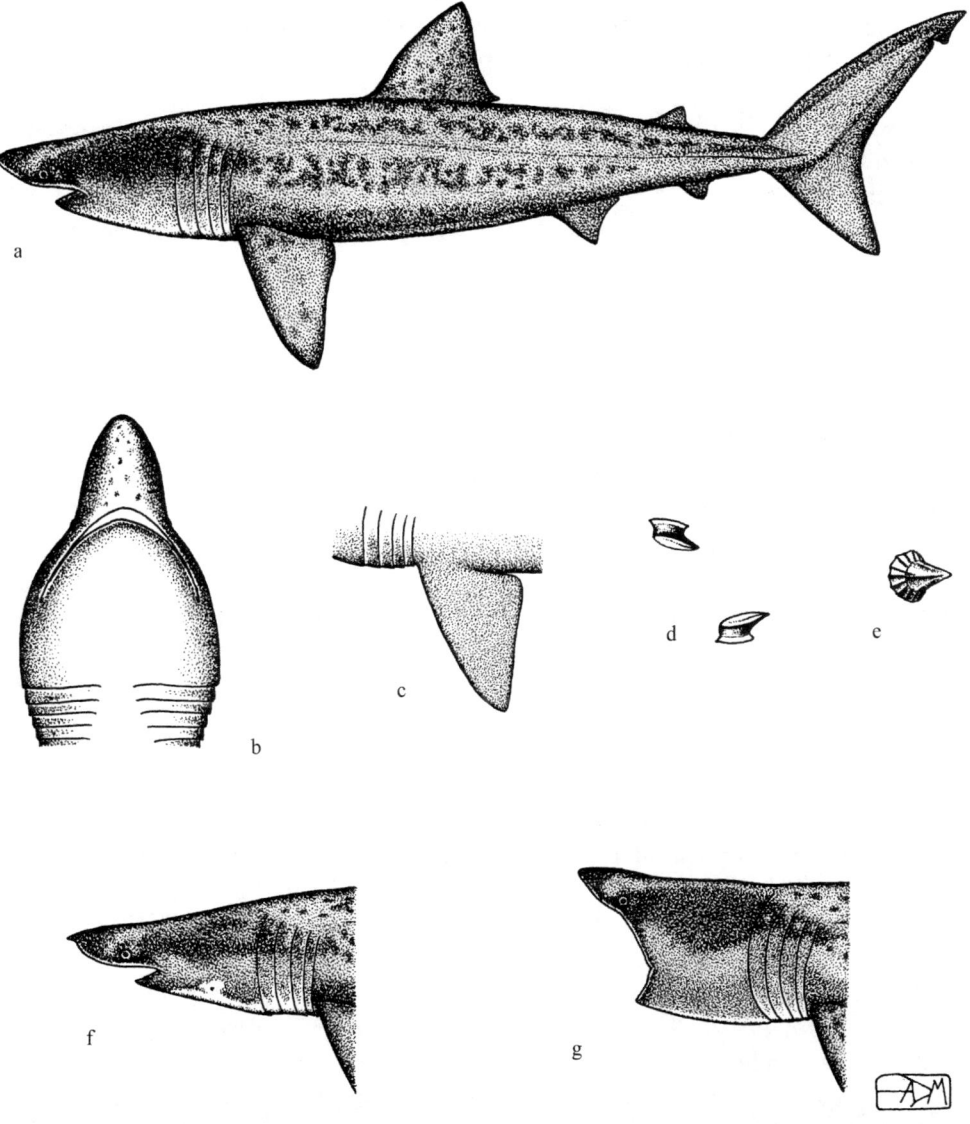

Basking shark (*Cetorhinus maximus*): (a) lateral view, (b) ventral view of the head, (c) ventral view of the pectoral fin, (d) upper and lower teeth, (e) placoid scale, (f) head of a young specimen; (g) head of a feeding adult.

Common names in other languages: French: pélerin; Spanish: peregrino; Italian: cetorino, squalo elefante, squalo gigante; German: riesenhai.

Distinctive characteristics for immediate identification: very long gill slits extending up to the ventral and dorsal surfaces of the head, mouth very wide with very small teeth, wide caudal keels, huge size, from 160 cm up to 1200 cm.

Morphology: Mouth very wide. 5 pairs of very long gill slits, extending up to the ventral and dorsal surfaces of the head, all located anterior to the pectoral fin origin; gill-rakers present on its internal gill slits. Pectoral fins wide but moderately long. First dorsal fin very large, its origin posterior to pectoral fin free rear tip. Second dorsal small. Anal fin about as large as the second dorsal. Caudal fin lunate, with the upper lobe long and the lower lobe relatively short. Wide caudal keels. Snout long and conical, in juveniles the tip is narrow and curved. Eyes small. Spiracles very small.

Coloration: dorsal surfaces brown-grey with irregular dark patches; ventral surfaces similar to the dorsal surfaces or sometimes lighter. The pectoral fin ventral surface is dark like the dorsal surface. Juveniles have the ventral surfaces partially white, with the boundary separating dark from white coloration sharp and indented. Rare cases of albino specimens exist.

Teeth shape: upper teeth with one cusp, curved, very small and very numerous; lower teeth similar.

Dental formula: about 100–about 100 / about 100–about 100.

Maximum size: 980 cm and probably up to 1200 cm.

Size at birth: about 150 cm.

Size at maturity: 460–601 cm (male) and 800 cm (female).

Embryonic development: aplacental viviparous (embryos may be nourished by oophagy).

Gestation: unknown, probably 1–3 years.

Litter size: up to at least 6 young.

Reproduction in the Mediterranean: possibly reproduces in the Mediterranean.

Maximum age: at least 16 years.

Diet: planktonic organisms including crustaceans, bony fish eggs, siphonophores and jellyfishes.

Habitat: pelagic, on continental and insular shelves at depths ranging from the surface to at least 200 m. Lack of pregnant females and new-borns suggest that they are spatially and bathymetrically separated from the rest of their populations.

Geographical distribution in the Mediterranean Sea: Western and Central Mediterranean.

Geographical distribution in the rest of the world: Atlantic, Pacific and Indian Oceans.

Behavior: active and slow, diurnal, solitary or in small to enormous groups (over 100 sharks), migratory, can leap out of the water, can approach divers closely (without showing any aggressive behavior), possibly can segregate by sex (possibly even bathymetrically), usually swims at the surface with its mouth wide open in order to filter the water and capture the planktonic organisms on which they feed thanks to their gillrakers. During mating, the male places its pectoral fin over the female's first dorsal fin and swims very close to her while inserting the clasper.

Dangerousness for man: not dangerous.

Importance for fishery in the Mediterranean: scarce importance.
Status in the Mediterranean: common.
Kind of presence in the Mediterranean: stable.
Specimens of particular interest recorded in the Mediterranean: one of the largest specimens, estimated to be 800–900 cm long, was trapped in a trammel net off Gallipoli, Italy, Ionian Sea, on 5 February 2001, and released alive. The smallest free-swimming specimens caught in these waters were a 150 cm specimen caught off Camogli, Italy, Ligurian Sea in 1888, and a 150 cm specimen caught off Porto Paglia, Sardinia, Italy, in May 1913.
Species with which can be confused: none.
Main references for the Mediterranean: Carruccio (1906), Ariola (1913), Vinciguerra (1923), Monterosso (1931), La Cascia (1935), Tortonese (1956), Cadenat & Blache (1981), Bauchot (1987), Vanni (1992), Moreno (1995), Barrull & Mate (1999), Barrull *et al.* (1999), Soldo *et al.* (1999), Lipej *et al.* (2000), Serena *et al.* (2000), Stephan *et al.* (2000), Zuffa *et al.* (2001), Barrull & Mate (2002), Soldo & Jardas (2002a), Soldo & Jardas (2002b), Capapé *et al.* (2003), Cugini & De Maddalena (2003), Lipej *et al.* (2004), G. Cataldini (pers. comm.).
Other selected non–Mediterranean related references: Sund (1943), Bigelow & Schroeder (1948), Van Deinse & Adriani (1953), Parker & Boeseman (1954), Matthews (1962), Lineaweaver & Backus (1970), Siccardi (1971), Castro (1983), Compagno (1984), Last & Stevens (1994), Fairfax (1998), Sims & Quayle (1998), Sims *et al.* (2000).

Great white shark
Carcharodon carcharias (Linnaeus, 1758)

Classification: Order Lamniformes, family Lamnidae, genus *Carcharodon*.
Common names in other languages: French: grand requin blanc; Spanish: tiburón blanco; Italian: squalo bianco; German: weißer hai.
Distinctive characteristics for immediate identification: caudal fin lunate (caudal fin lower lobe about as along as the upper lobe), gill slits long, body massive, pectoral fins long, wide caudal keels, mouth wide with teeth large, triangular and with serrated margins, protruding from the mouth in lower jaw, large size (from 81 cm up to at least 668 cm).
Morphology: body massive. Snout large and conical. Mouth wide. Eyes moderately large. Caudal fin lunate, with the upper lobe long and the lower slightly shorter than the upper lobe. First dorsal fin large, its origin over the pectoral fin inner margin. Second dorsal fin very small. Anal fin about as large as the second dorsal. Pectoral fins wide and long. Wide caudal keels. Spiracles very small or absent. 5 pairs of long gill slits, all located anterior to the pectoral fin origin, the 4th very close to the 5th.
Coloration: dorsal surfaces grey-brown,, usually with the flanks lighter than the upper surfaces; ventral surfaces white. Boundary separating dorsal from ventral coloration sharp and indented. The pectoral fin ventral surface shows a black patch at the

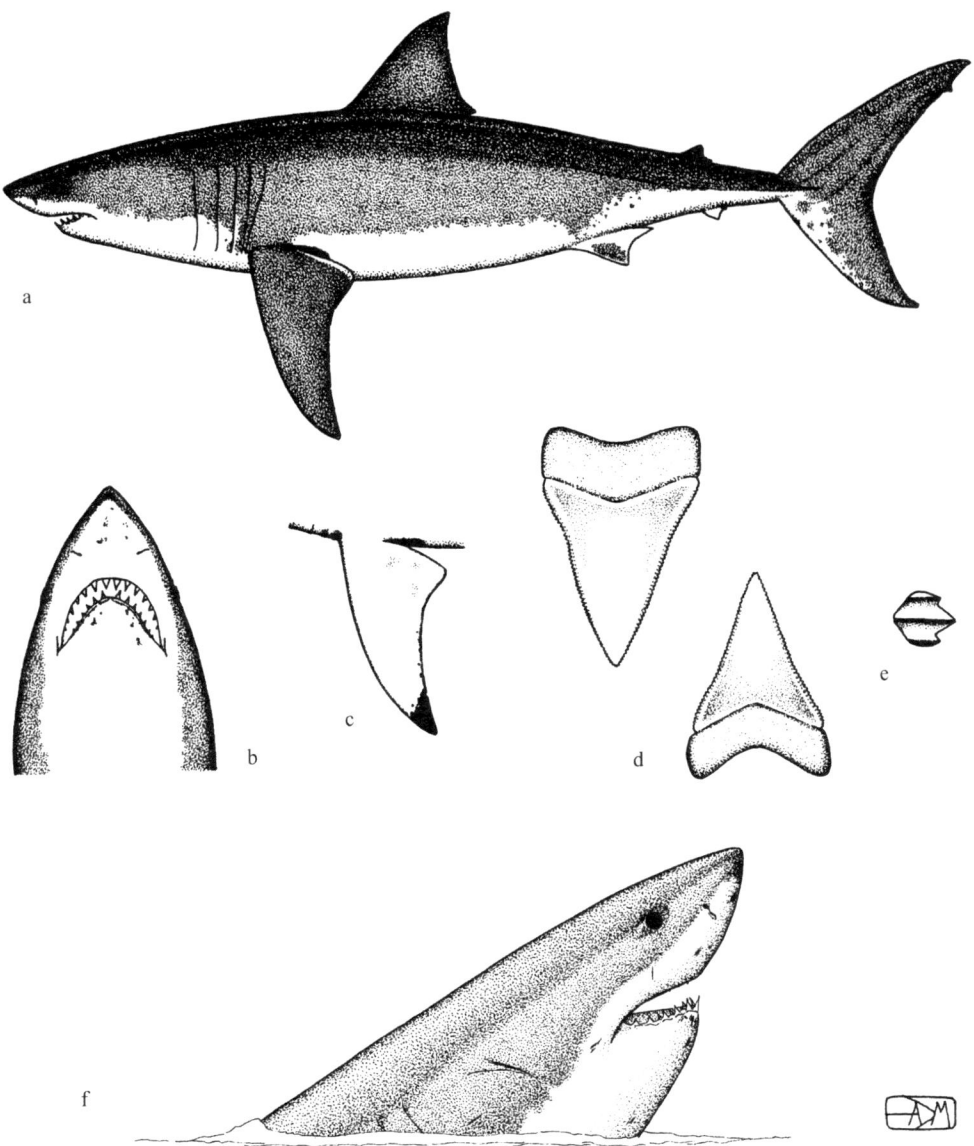

Great white shark (*Carcharodon carcharias*): (a) lateral view, (b) ventral view of the head, (c) ventral view of the pectoral fin, (d) upper and lower teeth, (e) placoid scale, (f) a great white shark lifting its head out of the water looking for prey.

apex and a narrow black band at the posterior margin with some small black spots. At the pectoral fin axil there is a black or grey patch. Eyes dark. Rare cases of albino specimens exist.

Teeth shape: upper teeth with one cusp, large, wide, triangular, with strongly serrated edges; lower teeth similar but narrower. Teeth of the lower jaw protruding from the mouth and visible even when the shark has its mouth closed. New-born sharks have 2 very small cusplets both in upper and lower teeth, and the lower teeth without serrations.

Great white shark

Dental formula: 12 to 14–12 to 14 / 10 to 13–10 to 13.
Maximum size: at least 668 cm and probably over 800 cm.
Size at birth: 81–151 cm.
Size at maturity: about 380 cm (male) and 450–500 cm (female).
Embryonic development: Aplacental viviparous (embryos nourished by oophagy).
Gestation: about 12 months.
Litter size: 2–14 and probably up to 17 young.
Reproduction in the Mediterranean: reproduces in the Mediterranean; data indicates parturition must occur in the Sicilian Channel.
Maximum age: at least 73 years.
Diet: bony fishes, elasmobranchs, marine mammals, molluscs, crustaceans, sea turtles, birds, carcasses.
Habitat: Pelagic, mainly on continental and insular shelves, at depths ranging from the surface to at least 1280 m.
Geographical distribution in the Mediterranean Sea: all Mediterranean.
Geographical distribution in the rest of the world: Atlantic, Pacific and Indian Oceans.
Behavior: particularly active and fast (thanks to their heat-retaining systems), equally diurnal and nocturnal, solitary and in pairs or in small to large groups around a food source, can leap out of the water, migratory, can approach divers closely (often without showing any aggressive behavior), possibly segregate by size and sex (possibly even bathymetrically), can occasionally ingest inedible items, show a social hierarchy when feeding, can perform a threat display with jaws slightly open and pectoral fins depressed, can raise the head out of water in order to observe an object of interest, can perform both horizontal or vertical oriented attacks on a prey by swimming rapidly from deep waters, can use predatory tactics that enable them to eat their prey with minimal risk of injury and minimal energy expenditure (initial attack followed by waiting period while the prey dies from blood loss, then return minutes later to eat the animal), during mating male and female stay belly to belly while inserting the clasper.
Dangerousness for man: highly dangerous.
Importance for fishery in the Mediterranean: scarce importance.
Status in the Mediterranean: uncommon.
Kind of presence in the Mediterranean: stable.
Specimens of particular interest recorded in the Mediterranean: the largest specimens ever recorded have been captured as follows: a 667–687 cm female was caught off L'Estaque, France, on 15 October 1925, a 668–681 cm female was caught off Filfla, Malta, on 17 April 1987, a 666 cm female was caught off Ganzirri, Sicily, Italy, on 19 June 1961, a 597–613 cm female was caught off Enfola, Isola d'Elba, Italy, on 12th August 1938, a 600 cm specimen was caught off Civitanova, Italy, Adriatic Sea, in February 1839 (jaws preserved in the Museo di Anatomia Comparata, Università "La Sapienza" in Rome). A 522 cm female caught in Kvarner, Croatia, on 29 May 1906 is preserved in the Museo civico di Storia Naturale di Trieste and is the largest skin-mounted specimen of Europe. A mold from a 589 cm female captured off Sète, France on 13th October 1956 and preserved in the

Musée Cantonal de Zoologie in Lausanne is the world's largest model prepared from a whole specimen.

Species with which can be confused: the shortfin mako (*Isurus oxyrinchus*), the longfin mako (*Isurus paucus*) and the porbeagle (*Lamna nasus*), but these species have narrower teeth lacking serrations, larger eyes, and a smaller snout, moreover the makos have a narrower body and the porbeagle has a white patch at the dorsal fin free rear tip.

Main references for the Mediterranean: Bonaparte (1839), Doderlein (1881), Brusina (1888), Ninni (1912), Barrull (1993–1994), Fergusson (1996), De Maddalena (1999), De Maddalena (2000a), De Maddalena (2000b), Barrull & Mate (2001), Celona *et al.* (2001), De Maddalena *et al.* (2001), Barrull & Mate (2002), De Maddalena (2002a), Soldo & Jardas (2002a), Soldo & Jardas (2002b), De Maddalena & Reckel (2003), De Maddalena *et al.* (2003), Kabasakal (2003), Galaz & De Maddalena (2004), Lipej *et al.* (2004), De Maddalena & Heim (2012).

Other selected non–Mediterranean related references: Bigelow & Schroeder (1948), Bass *et al.* (1973–1976), Randall (1973), Castro (1983), Ellis (1983), Compagno (1984), Tricas & McCosker (1984), McCosker (1987), Randall (1987), Cliff *et al.* (1989), Ellis & McCosker (1991), Last & Stevens (1994), Collier *et al.* (1996), Francis (1996), Goldman *et al.* (1996), Klimley *et al.* (1996), Mollet *et al.* (1996), Mollet & Cailliet (1996), Pratt (1996), Strong (1996), Uchida *et al.* (1996), Smale & Heemstra (1997), Cliff *et al.* (2000), Klimley *et al.* (2001), Collier (2002), Martin (2003), Le Boeuf (2004), De Maddalena & Heim (2009, 2012), De Maddalena (2014).

Shortfin mako
Isurus oxyrinchus Rafinesque, 1809

Classification: Order Lamniformes, family Lamnidae, genus *Isurus*.
Common names in other languages: French: taupe bleu; Spanish: marrajo; Italian: squalo mako dalle pinne corte; German: kurzflossenmako.
Distinctive characteristics for immediate identification: caudal fin lunate (caudal fin lower lobe about as long as the upper lobe), gill slits long, snout long, narrow, strongly conical and pointed, body strongly spindle-shaped, pectoral fins relatively short (70 percent of the head length), wide caudal keels, teeth long and narrow with cutting edges, protruding from the mouth in lower jaw, iridescent blue coloration, undersurface of head white.
Morphology: body strongly spindle-shaped (quite slender in young but more massive in adults). Snout conical, narrow, long and strongly pointed. Caudal fin lunate, with the upper lobe long and the lower lobe slightly shorter than the upper lobe. First dorsal fin tall, its origin posterior to pectoral fin free rear tip. Second dorsal very small. Anal fin about as large as the second dorsal. Pectoral fins relatively short (70 percent of the head length). Wide caudal keels. Mouth long but narrow in ventral view. Eyes relatively large. Spiracles very small. 5 pairs of long gill slits, all located anterior to the pectoral fin origin, the 4th very close to the 5th.
Coloration: dorsal surfaces brilliant blue to black with pronounced iridescence on the

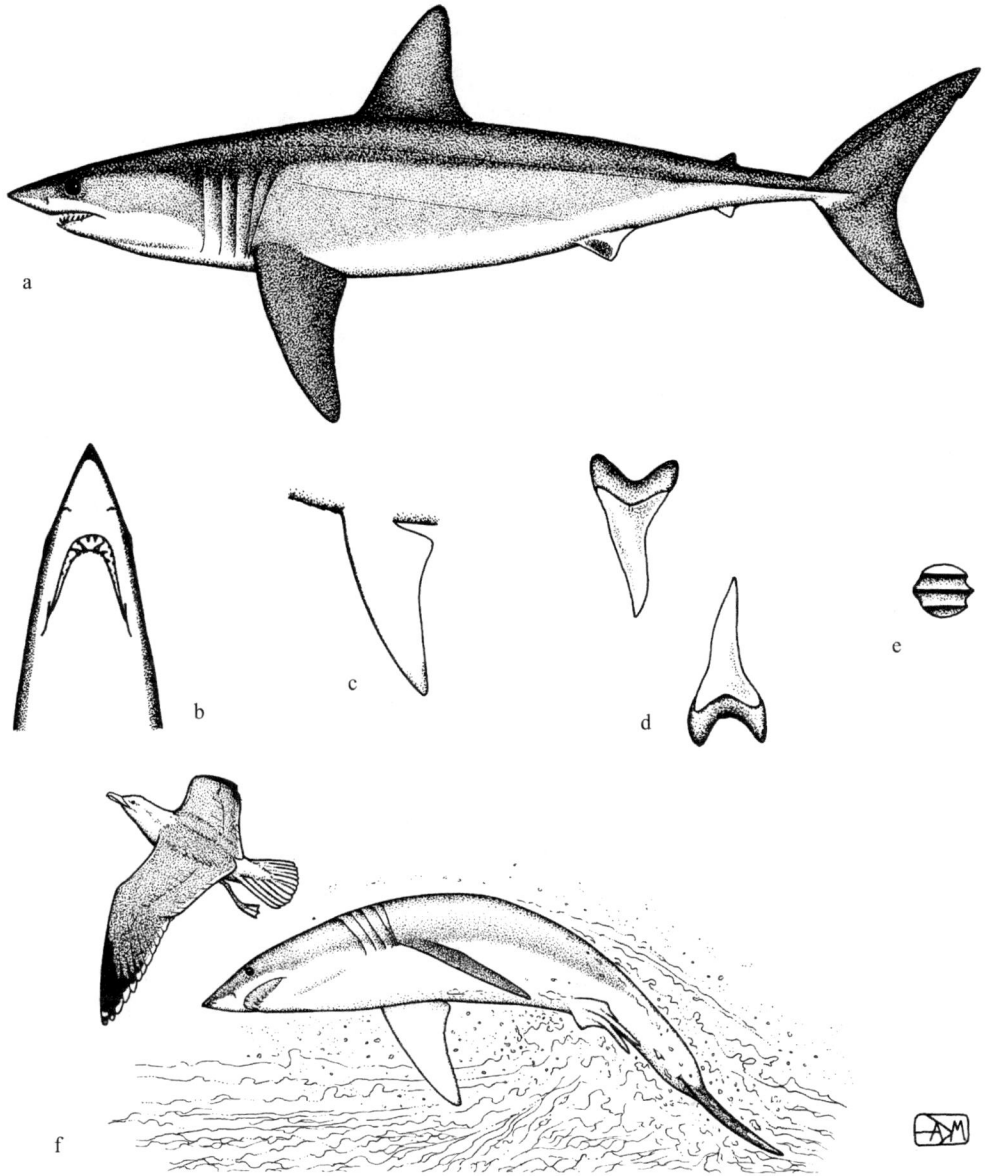

Shortfin mako (*Isurus oxyrinchus*): (a) lateral view, (b) ventral view of the head, (c) ventral view of the pectoral fin, (d) upper and lower teeth, (e) placoid scale, (f) a mako tries to capture a herring gull (*Larus argentatus*) at the sea surface.

sides; ventral surfaces white. Boundary separating dorsal from ventral coloration sharp. The pectoral fin ventral surface is white, sometimes with a small light grayish area at the apex and posterior margin. Eyes black.

Teeth shape: upper teeth with one cusp, large, narrow, long and curved, with cutting edges; lower teeth similar. Teeth of the lower jaw protruding from the mouth and visible when the shark has its mouth closed.

Dental formula: 12 to 14–12 to 14 / 11 to 15–11 to 15.

Maximum size: 585 cm.
Size at birth: 60–70 cm.
Size at maturity: about 195 cm (male) and 273–298 cm (female).
Embryonic development: aplacental viviparous (embryos nourished by oophagy).
Gestation: 15–18 months.
Litter size: 4–25 young.
Reproduction in the Mediterranean: reproduces in the Mediterranean.
Maximum age: at least 25 years.
Diet: bony fishes, elasmobranchs, marine turtles, squids, crustaceans, marine mammals, birds, salps, porifera, carcasses.
Habitat: pelagic, on continental and insular shelves, upper slopes and oceanic basins, at depths ranging from the surface to at least 417 m. Juveniles occur in shallower waters then adults.
Geographical distribution in the Mediterranean Sea: all Mediterranean.
Geographical distribution in the rest of the world: Atlantic, Pacific and Indian Oceans.
Behavior: nervous, particularly active and fast (thanks to their heat-retaining systems), solitary or in large groups, migratory, can leap out of the water, can be timid or aggressive, rarely can approach divers closely (sometimes without showing any aggressive behavior), can segregate by size, can occasionally ingest inedible items.
Dangerousness for man: dangerous.
Importance for fishery in the Mediterranean: notable importance.
Status in the Mediterranean: uncommon.
Kind of presence in the Mediterranean: stable.
Specimens of particular interest recorded in the Mediterranean: the largest specimen ever recorded was an approximately 585 cm female caught off Marmaris, Turkey. Otherwise, the largest specimens recorded in the area were a 445 cm female caught off Six-Fours-Les-Plages, France in September 1973, a 425 specimen caught near Galita Island, Tunisia, on 24 September 1876, a 400 cm shortfin mako caught in the Piombino Channel, Italy, Tyrrhenian Sea, a 400 cm specimen caught off Caska, Croatia, on 13th May 1882, a 390 cm female caught off Bagnara Calabra on 30 November 1991 and a 390 cm specimen caught on 20 September 2000 off Punta Alice, Italy.
Species with which can be confused: the longfin mako (*Isurus paucus*), the great white shark (*Carcharodon carcharias*) and the porbeagle (*Lamna nasus*), but the longfin mako has larger eyes, undersurface of head dark and longer pectoral fins (at least as long as the head), the great white shark has a more massive body, a larger snout and triangular serrated teeth, and the porbeagle has a white patch at the dorsal fin free rear tip and 2 cusplets in each tooth.
Main references for the Mediterranean: Bonaparte (1839), Doria & Gestro (1877), Lawley (1881), Brusina (1888), Capapé (1975a), Capapé (1977), Cadenat & Blache (1981), Bauchot (1987), Vanni (1992), Buencuerpo *et al.* (1998), Celona *et al.* (2001), De Maddalena & Piscitelli (2001), Storai *et al.* (2001), Barrull & Mate (2002), de la Serna *et al.* (2002), Soldo & Jardas (2002a), Celona *et al.* (2004), Lipej *et al.* (2004), Kabasakal & De Maddalena (2011).
Other selected non–Mediterranean related references: Bigelow & Schroeder (1948),

Garrick (1967), Lineaweaver & Backus (1970), Bass et al. (1973–1976), Johnson (1978), Castro (1983), Ellis (1983), Compagno (1984), Randall (1986), Cliff et al. (1990), Stillwell (1991), Moreno & Mòron (1992b), Last & Stevens (1994), Mollet et al. (2000), Ribot Carballal et al. (2003), De Maddalena et al. (2005), Jeff Shindle (pers. comm.).

Longfin mako
Isurus paucus Guitart Manday, 1966

Classification: Order Lamniformes, family Lamnidae, genus *Isurus*.
Common names in other languages: French: petit taupe; Spanish: marrajo negro; Italian: squalo mako dalle pinne lunghe; German: langflossenmako.
Distinctive characteristics for immediate identification: caudal fin lunate (caudal fin lower lobe about as along as the upper lobe), gill slits long, snout short, strongly conical and pointed, body strongly spindle-shaped, pectoral fins long (at least as long as the head), two pairs of caudal keels, teeth long and narrow with cutting edges, protruding from the mouth in lower jaw, eyes large, undersurface of head dark.
Morphology: body strongly spindle-shaped (quite slender in young but more massive in adults). Snout conical, narrow, short and strongly pointed. Caudal fin lunate, with the upper lobe long and the lower slightly shorter than the upper lobe. First dorsal fin tall, its origin posterior to pectoral fin free rear tip. Second dorsal very small. Anal fin about as large as the second dorsal. Pectoral fins long to very long (at least as long as the head). Two pairs of caudal keels: one wide on the caudal peduncle and another small on the sides of the caudal fin, immediately below the caudal peduncle. Mouth long but narrow in ventral view. Eyes large. Spiracles very small. 5 pairs of long gill slits, all located anterior to the pectoral fin origin, the 4th very close to the 5th.
Coloration: dorsal surfaces blue-grey to black; ventral surfaces white, except the underside of the snout and the area around the mouth show the same dark coloration as the upper surfaces. Boundary separating dorsal from ventral coloration sharp and indented. The pectoral fin ventral surface is white with a dark patch having faded margin at the apex, and small extensions of the dorsal coloration can be present at the anterior margin. Eyes black.
Teeth shape: upper teeth with one cusp, large, narrow, long and curved, with cutting edges; lower teeth similar. Teeth of the lower jaw protruding from the mouth and visible when the shark has its mouth closed.
Dental formula: 12 to 13–12 to 13 / 11 to 13–11 to 13
Maximum size: 417 cm.
Size at birth: 84–97 cm.
Size at maturity: about 240 cm (male) and about 240 cm (female).
Embryonic development: aplacental viviparous.
Gestation: unknown.
Litter size: 2 young.
Reproduction in the Mediterranean: does not reproduce in the Mediterranean.

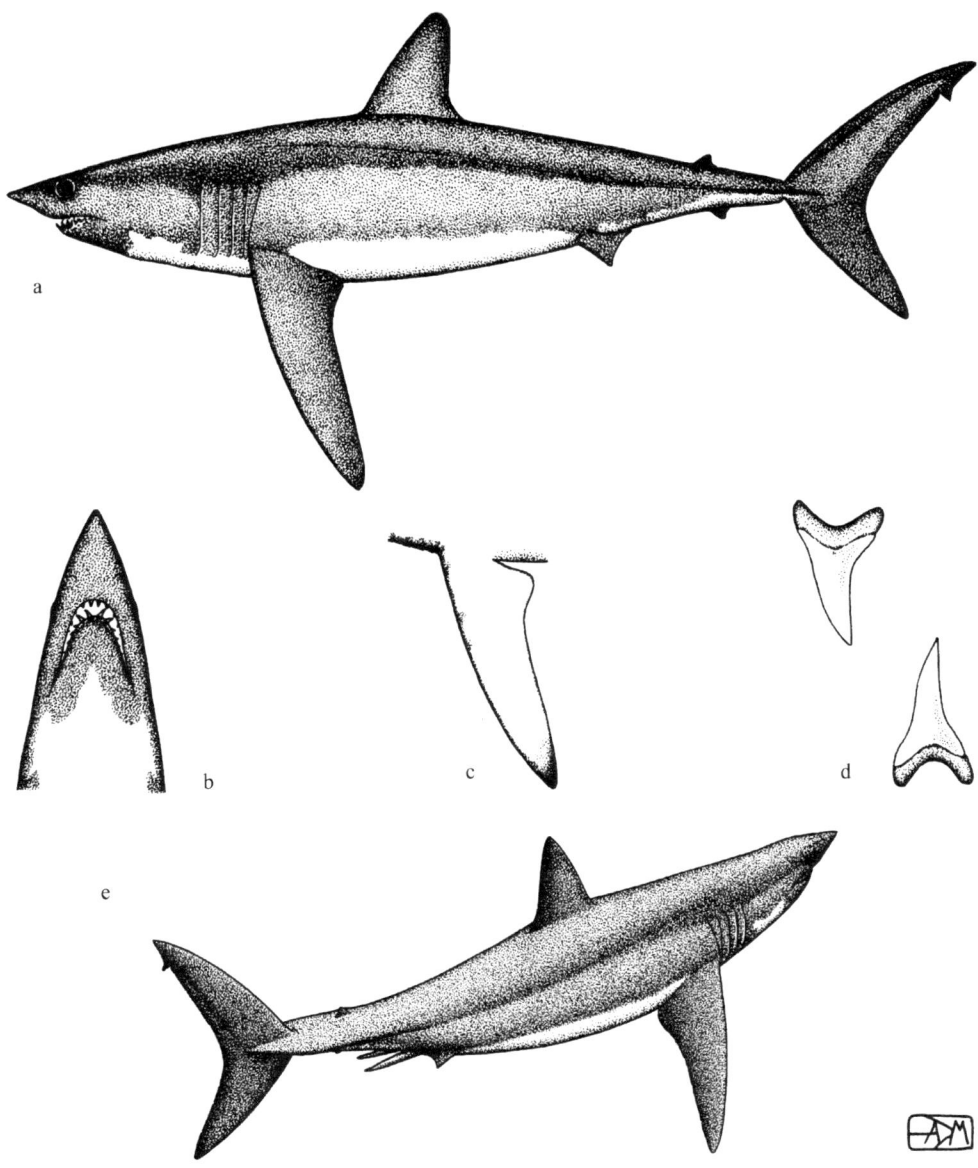

Longfin mako (*Isurus paucus*): (a) lateral view, (b) ventral view of the head, (c) ventral view of the pectoral fin, (d) upper and lower teeth, (e) a swimming longfin mako.

Maximum age: unknown.
Diet: bony fishes and cephalopods.
Habitat: pelagic, outer continental shelves, slopes and oceanic basins, at depths ranging from the surface to at least 748 m.
Geographical distribution in the Mediterranean Sea: Western Mediterranean.
Geographical distribution in the rest of the world: Atlantic, Pacific and Indian Oceans.
Behavior: active, solitary, timid.
Dangerousness for man: potentially dangerous.

Importance for fishery in the Mediterranean: no importance.

Status in the Mediterranean: very rare.

Kind of presence in the Mediterranean: occasional (the specimens recorded must have entered the Mediterranean Sea from the Eastern Atlantic Ocean through the Gibraltar Strait).

Specimens of particular interest recorded in the Mediterranean: only 6 specimens have been recorded from the area including a 207.4 cm specimen caught in the Gibraltar Strait, a 181 cm male, a 162.7 cm male, a 183.7 cm female caught off Morocco, a 280 cm male and a 180 cm female caught off Béni-Saf (Algeria).

Species with which can be confused: the shortfin mako (*Isurus oxyrinchus*), the great white shark (*Carcharodon carcharias*) and the porbeagle (*Lamna nasus*), but the shortfin mako has smaller eyes, undersurface of head white and shorter pectoral fins (70 percent of the head length), the great white shark has a more massive body, a larger snout and triangular serrated teeth, and the porbeagle has a white patch at the dorsal fin free rear tip and 2 cusplets in each tooth.

Main references for the Mediterranean: Bauchot (1987), Moreno (1995), Barrull & Mate (2002).

Other selected non–Mediterranean related references: Garrick (1967), Bass *et al.* (1973–1976), Dodrill & Gilmore (1979), Castro (1983), Compagno (1984), Clark & Kristof (1991).

Porbeagle
Lamna nasus (Bonnaterre, 1788)

Classification: Order Lamniformes, family Lamnidae, genus *Lamna*.

Common names in other languages: French: requin-taupe commun; Spanish: cailón; Italian: smeriglio; German: heringshai.

Distinctive characteristics for immediate identification: caudal fin lunate (caudal fin lower lobe about as along as the upper lobe), gill slits long, snout conical, body stout and strongly spindle-shaped, first dorsal fin very large and with a white patch at the free rear tip, two pairs of caudal keels, teeth relatively small, with 2 cusplets and protruding from the mouth in lower jaw.

Morphology: body spindle-shaped, stout and massive. Snout conical and pointed. Caudal fin lunate, with the upper lobe long and the lower slightly shorter than the upper lobe. First dorsal fin large to very large, its origin over pectoral fin inner margin. Second dorsal fin very small. Anal fin about as large as the second dorsal. Pectoral fins relatively short. Two pairs of caudal keels: one wide on the caudal peduncle and another small on the sides of the caudal fin, immediately below the caudal peduncle. Mouth relatively small. Eyes large. Spiracles very small or absent. 5 pairs of long gill slits, all located anterior to the pectoral fin origin, the 4th very close to the 5th.

Coloration: dorsal surfaces grey-bluish light to black; ventral surfaces white, except the gill slits region, that sometimes shows irregular dark spotted coloration similar to those of the dorsal surfaces. The first dorsal fin free rear tip has a conspicuous white patch. Ventral surface of pectoral fins shows a dark area that extends from the apex towards the base having indented margins and with small spots. Boundary separating dorsal from ventral coloration sharp and indented. Eyes black.

Teeth shape: upper teeth relatively small, with one cusp with cutting edges and two small cusplets; lower teeth similar. Teeth of the lower jaw protruding from the mouth and visible when the shark has its mouth closed. Teeth of juveniles can lack cusplets.

Dental formula: 12 to 16–12 to 16 / 7 to 13–7 to 13.

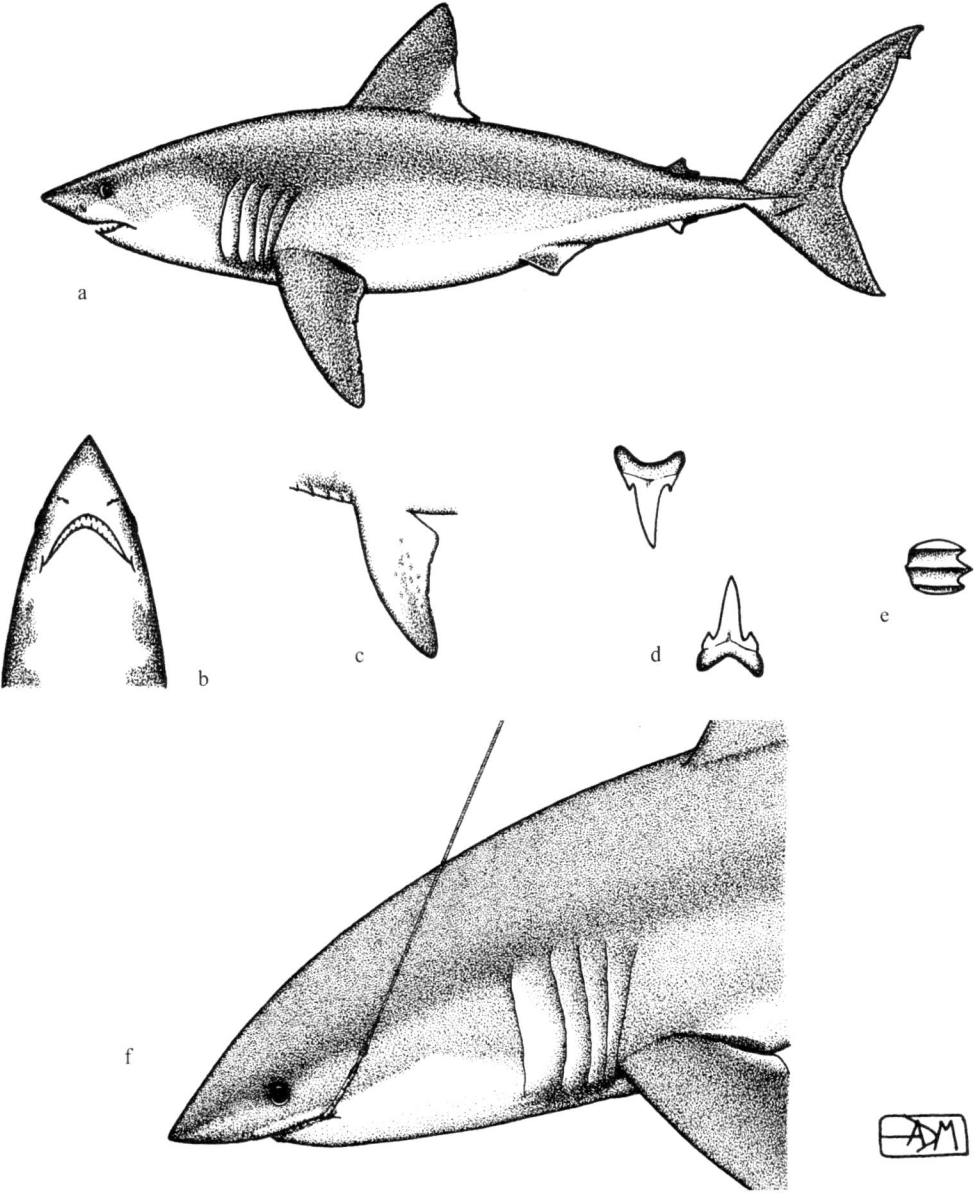

Porbeagle (*Lamna nasus*): (a) lateral view, (b) ventral view of the head, (c) ventral view of the pectoral fin, (d) upper and lower teeth, (e) placoid scale, (f) a porbeagle that has been hooked.

Maximum size: 360 cm.
Size at birth: 68–89 cm.
Size at maturity: 190–217 cm (male) and 200–270 cm (female).
Embryonic development: aplacental viviparous (embryos nourished by oophagy).
Gestation: 8–9 months.
Litter size: 2–6 young.
Reproduction in the Mediterranean: reproduces in the Mediterranean; data indicates parturition must occur in the Western Mediterranean.
Maximum age: 29–46 years.
Diet: bony fishes, sharks, squids, birds.
Habitat: pelagic, on continental shelves and oceanic basins, at depths ranging from the surface to at least 370 m.
Geographical distribution in the Mediterranean Sea: all Mediterranean.
Geographical distribution in the rest of the world: Atlantic, Indian and Pacific Oceans.
Behavior: particularly active and fast (thanks to their heat-retaining systems), solitary or in large groups, migratory, can leap out of the water, timid, can segregate by sex and size.
Dangerousness for man: potentially dangerous.
Importance for fishery in the Mediterranean: some importance.
Status in the Mediterranean: uncommon.
Kind of presence in the Mediterranean: stable.
Specimens of particular interest recorded in the Mediterranean: the smallest pregnant female ever recorded, was almost 200 cm long and carried 3 embryos 58–59 cm long, and was caught in 1984 in the Bay of Málaga, Spain; another 200 cm long pregnant female carrying 4 embryos measuring 58–59 cm was caught in the same waters on 11 May 1989.
Species with which can be confused: the shortfin mako (*Isurus oxyrinchus*), the longfin mako (*Isurus paucus*) and the great white shark (*Carcharodon carcharias*), but these species have a less stout body and lack the white patch at the dorsal fin free rear tip and the 2 cusplets in their teeth (except for newborn white sharks).
Main references for the Mediterranean: Tortonese (1956), Capapé (1975a, 1975b), Cadenat & Blache (1981), Bauchot (1987), Vanni (1992), Marconi & De Maddalena (2001), Barrull & Mate (2002), Cugini & De Maddalena (2003), Lipej *et al.* (2004).
Other selected non–Mediterranean related references: Bigelow & Schroeder (1948), Aasen (1963), Castro (1983), Compagno (1984), Last & Stevens (1994), Francis & Stevens (2000), Jensen *et al.* (2002), Joyce *et al.* (2002), Natanson *et al.* (2002), Campana *et al.* (2003).

Blackmouth catshark
Galeus melastomus Rafinesque, 1810

Classification: Order Carcharhiniformes, family Scyliorhinidae, genus *Galeus*.
Common names in other languages: French: chien espagnol; Spanish: olayo; Italian: boccanera; German: fleckhai.

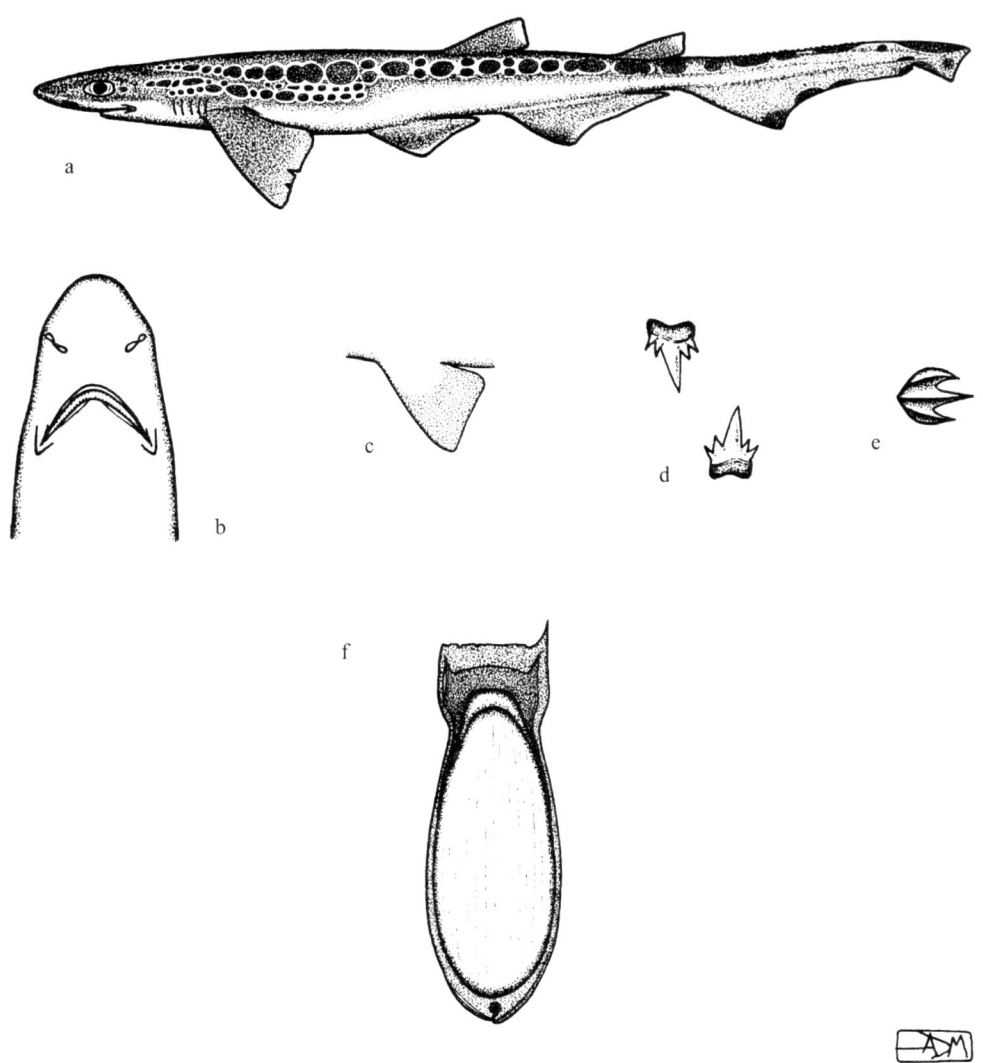

Blackmouth catshark (*Galeus melastomus*): (a) lateral view, (b) ventral view of the head, (c) ventral view of the pectoral fin, (d) upper and lower teeth, (e) placoid scale, (f) egg-case.

Distinctive characteristics for immediate identification: anal fin present and very long, dorsal fins located way back on shark (the first dorsal having its origin posterior to the pelvic fin origin), snout long, dorsal surface with characteristic pattern of regular small and large light spots.

Morphology: body elongated and very slender. Dorsal fins small and of similar size, located far back on shark, the origin of the first dorsal fin over the pelvic fins. Caudal fin with short lower lobe and long upper lobe, elongated on the axis of the body and with wide terminal lobe. Anal fin very long. Pectoral fins short and wide. Snout long and dorso-ventrally flattened. Eyes large. Nostrils wide. Spiracles relatively small. 5 pairs of short gill slits, the 5th over the pectoral fin base.

Coloration: dorsal surfaces light grey-brown with pattern of regular spots slightly darker; ventral surfaces white. Inner mouth surfaces black. The pectoral fin ventral surface is light grey becoming white at the base.

Teeth shape: upper teeth very small, with one cusp and 2 to 6 cusplets; lower teeth similar.

Dental formula: 37 to 42–37 to 42 / 36 to 42–36 to 42.

Maximum size: 90 cm.

Size at birth: about 8 cm.

Size at maturity: 34–45 cm (male) and 38.5–49 cm (female).

Embryonic development: oviparous. Their eggs are 4.1–4.7 cm long, 1.2–1.7 cm wide and 0.8–1.1 cm thick, and have short points at one extremity while the other extremity is rounded.

Gestation: hatching time is unknown.

Litter size: 1–14 young.

Reproduction in the Mediterranean: reproduce in the Mediterranean (possibly the entire Mediterranean).

Maximum age: unknown.

Diet: crustaceans, cephalopods, bony fishes, elasmobranchs, siphonophores, polychaetes, peanut worms, salps, carcasses.

Habitat: benthic, mainly in deep waters, on outer continental shelves and upper slopes, at depths ranging from 50 to at least 1440 m.

Geographical distribution in the Mediterranean Sea: all Mediterranean.

Geographical distribution in the rest of the world: Eastern Atlantic Ocean.

Behavior: torpid and slow, solitary and in large groups, timid, can segregate by size (even bathymetrically), possibly can cooperatively catch their prey, occasionally ingest inedible items.

Dangerousness for man: not dangerous.

Importance for fishery in the Mediterranean: certain importance.

Status in the Mediterranean: very common.

Kind of presence in the Mediterranean: stable.

Specimens of particular interest recorded in the Mediterranean: the largest specimen recorded in this area is a 61.7 cm female caught off Barcelona, Catalan Sea, Spain in 2000.

Species with which can be confused: none.

Main references for the Mediterranean: Tortonese (1956), Ben-Tuvia (1971), Capapé & Zaouali (1976), Macpherson (1980), Cadenat & Blache (1981), Golani (1986–1987), Bauchot (1987), Carrassón et al. (1992), Vanni (1992), Bello (1995), Moreno (1995), Barrull et al. (1999), Sacco et al. (2000), De Maddalena & Piscitelli (2001), Barrull & Mate (2002), Kabasakal (2002a), Rey et al. (2003), Lipej et al. (2004).

Other selected non–Mediterranean related references: Compagno (1984).

Small-spotted catshark

Scyliorhinus canicula (Linnaeus, 1758)

Classification: Order Carcharhiniformes, family Scyliorhinidae, genus *Scyliorhinus*.

Common names in other languages: French: petite roussette; Spanish: pintarroja; Italian: gattuccio minore; German: kleingefleckter katzenhai.

Distinctive characteristics for immediate identification: anal fin present and relatively long, body very slender, dorsal fins small and located way back on shark (the first dorsal having its origin posterior to the pelvic fin origin), snout short, dorsal surface light brown with numerous small simple white and dark spots and bands.

Morphology: body elongated and very slender. Dorsal fins located way back on shark, the origin of the first dorsal fin over the pelvic fins; first dorsal fin small, the second dorsal about as large as the first dorsal. Anal fin relatively long. Pectoral fins short. Caudal fin with short lower lobe and long upper lobe, without posterior notch, with wide terminal lobe and elongated on the axis of the body. Snout short and dorso-ventrally flattened. Eyes large. Nostrils wide. Spiracles medium-sized. 5 pairs of short gill slits, the 5th over the pectoral fin base.

Coloration: dorsal surfaces light brown with numerous small dark and white spots and some darker bands on horseback; ventral surfaces white. The pectoral fin ventral surface is light grey brown with small greyish spots becoming white at the base.

Teeth shape: upper teeth very small, with one pointed cusp and 2 to 4 cusplets; lower teeth similar.

Dental formula: 20 to 25–20 to 25 / 20 to 25–1 to 4–20 to 25.

Maximum size: about 100 cm.

Size at birth: 7–10 cm.

Size at maturity: 34–47.5 cm (male) and 34–47.5 cm (female).

Embryonic development: oviparous. Their eggs are 4.0 cm long, 2.0 cm wide and 1.0 cm thick, and have long filaments so that the egg can attach to algae and gorgonians on the sea bottom.

Gestation: the eggs hatches in 5–11 months.

Litter size: 2 young.

Reproduction in the Mediterranean: reproduce in the Mediterranean (possibly the entire Mediterranean).

Maximum age: at least 8 years.

Diet: bony fishes, sharks, molluscs, crustaceans, polychaetes, siphonophores, echinoderms, salps, carcasses.

Habitat: benthic, on outer continental shelves and upper slopes, at depths ranging from the surface to at least 750 m. Juveniles usually stay in deeper waters than adults.

Geographical distribution in the Mediterranean Sea: all Mediterranean.

Geographical distribution in the rest of the world: Eastern Atlantic Ocean.

Behavior: torpid and slow, nocturnal, solitary or in large groups, timid, can segregate by sex and size (even bathymetrically), during mating the male wraps its body around the female while inserting the clasper.

Dangerousness for man: not dangerous.

Importance for fishery in the Mediterranean: notable importance.

Status in the Mediterranean: very common.

Kind of presence in the Mediterranean: stable.

Specimens of particular interest recorded in the Mediterranean: one of the largest specimens ever reported was about 90–100 cm long and was encountered by diver

Small-spotted catshark

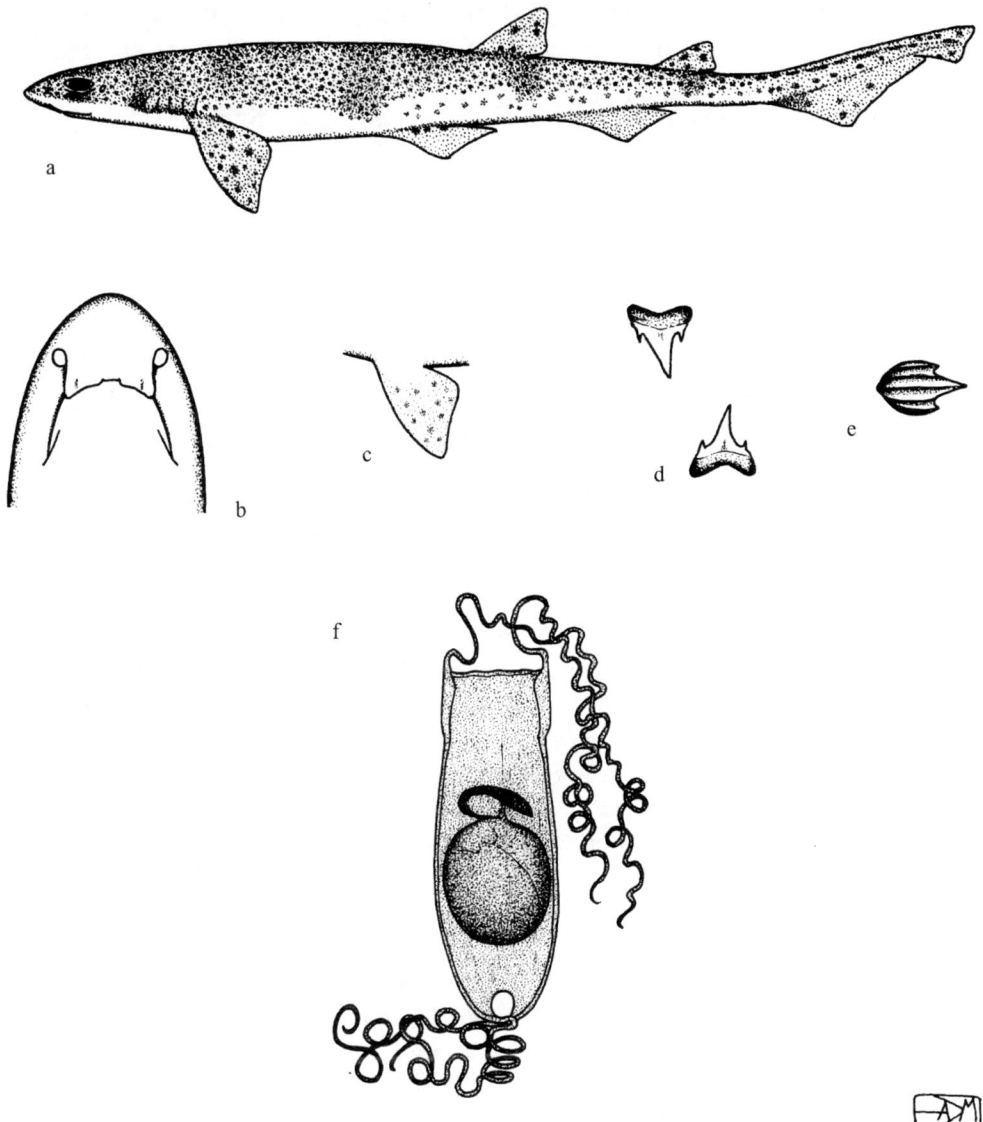

Small-spotted catshark (*Scyliorhinus canicula*): (a) lateral view, (b) ventral view of the head, (c) ventral view of the pectoral fin, (d) upper and lower teeth, (e) placoid scale, (f) egg-case.

Stefano D'Apote off Punta Prita, near Palmi, Italy, South Eastern Tyrrhenian Sea, in summer 2002: the small-spotted catshark was hooked on a lost line and the diver released it alive.

Species with which can be confused: the nursehound (*Scyliorhinus stellaris*), but this species is more massive, with the dorsal part pronounced, and has larger black spots (some uniting to form ring-like patches similar to those of a leopard).

Main references for the Mediterranean: Tortonese (1956), Quignard & Capapé (1971), Jardas (1972), Capapé (1974b), Capapé (1975a), Capapé (1977), Cadenat & Blache (1981), Bauchot (1987), Capapé *et al.* (1991), Vanni (1992), Bello (1997), Barrull *et* al. (1999), Ungaro *et al.* (2000), De Maddalena & Piscitelli (2001), Barrull & Mate (2002), Kabasakal (2001), Kabasakal (2002a), Lipej *et al.* (2004), Stefano D'Apote (pers. comm.).

Other selected non–Mediterranean related references: Lyle (1983), Compagno (1984), Houziaux & Voss (1997).

Nursehound
Scyliorhinus stellaris (Linnaeus, 1758)

Classification: Order Carcharhiniformes, family Scyliorhinidae, genus *Scyliorhinus*.

Common names in other languages: French: grande roussette; Spanish: alitán; Italian: gattuccio maggiore, gattopardo; German: großgefleckter katzenhai.

Distinctive characteristics for immediate identification: anal fin present and relatively long, body very slender but with the dorsal part pronounced, dorsal fins relatively small and located way back on shark (the first dorsal having its origin posterior to the pelvic fin origin), snout short, dorsal surface grey-brown with large black spots (some are united forming ring-like patches similar to those of a leopard).

Morphology: body elongate and slender but with the dorsal part pronounced. Dorsal fins located way back on shark, the origin of the first dorsal fin over the pelvic fins; first dorsal fin relatively small, the second dorsal smaller than the first dorsal. Anal fin relatively long. Pectoral fins short. Caudal fin with short lower lobe and long upper lobe, without posterior notch, with wide terminal lobe and elongated on the axis of the body. Snout short and dorso-ventrally flattened. Eyes large. Nostrils wide. Spiracles medium-sized. 5 pairs of short gill slits, the 5th over the pectoral fin base.

Coloration: dorsal surfaces dark grey-brown with large black spots, some united forming ring-like patches similar to those of a leopard; additional white spots are sometimes present; ventral surfaces white. The pectoral fin ventral surface is grey brown with small and large black spots becoming white in the basal part.

Teeth shape: upper teeth very small, with one pointed cusp and 2 cusplets; lower teeth similar.

Dental formula: 23 to 33–23 to 33 / 30 to 35–0 to 1–30 to 35.

Maximum size: 165 cm.

Size at birth: about 16 cm.

Size at maturity: 63–79 cm (male) and 67–81 cm (female).

Embryonic development: oviparous. The eggs are 10.0–13.0 cm long, 3.0–4.0 cm wide and 3.0 cm thick, and have long filaments at various angles, so that the egg can attach to algae and gorgonians on the sea bottom.

Gestation: the egg-cases hatch in 9 months.

Litter size: 2 young.

Reproduction in the Mediterranean: reproduce in the Mediterranean (possibly in all the Mediterranean).

Maximum age: unknown.

Diet: crustaceans, sharks, molluscs, bony fishes, polychaetes, echinoderms.

Nursehound

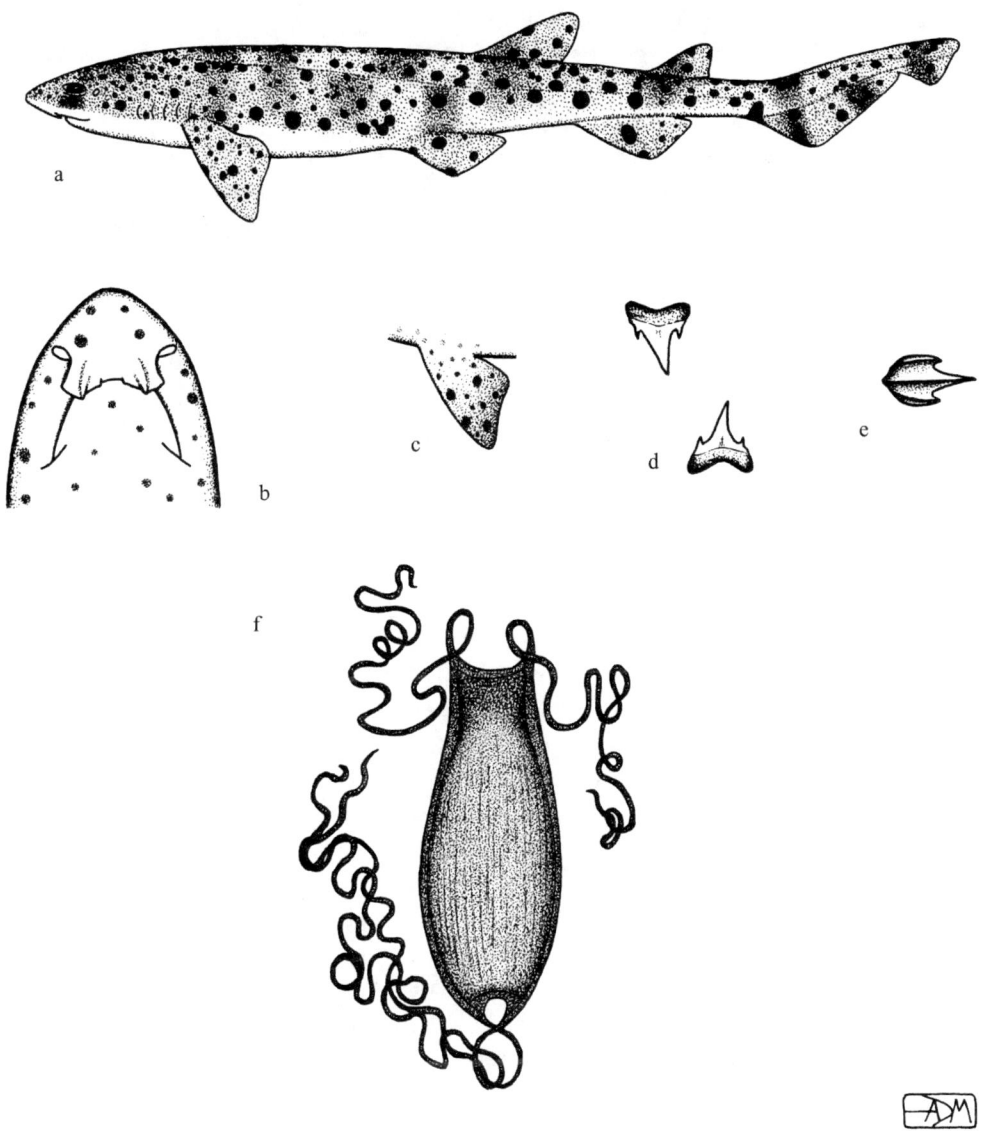

Nursehound (*Scyliorhinus stellaris*): (a) lateral view, (b) ventral view of the head, (c) ventral view of the pectoral fin, (d) upper and lower teeth, (e) placoid scale, (f) egg-case.

Habitat: benthic, on continental shelves, at depths ranging from the surface to at least 200 m.
Geographical distribution in the Mediterranean Sea: all Mediterranean.
Geographical distribution in the rest of the world: Eastern Atlantic Ocean.
Behavior: torpid and slow, nocturnal, solitary or in large groups, timid, can segregate by size, can produce a sound that resembles that of a cat.
Dangerousness for man: not dangerous.
Importance for fishery in the Mediterranean: certain importance.
Status in the Mediterranean: common.

Kind of presence in the Mediterranean: stable.

Specimens of particular interest recorded in the Mediterranean: the largest specimen recorded in this area is a 108 cm male caught off Roses, Catalan Sea, Spain (preserved in the Museo El Cau del Taurò de L'Arboç).

Species with which can be confused: the small-spotted catshark (*Scyliorhinus canicula*), but this species is more slender, with the dorsal part not pronounced, and has smaller dark and white spots that never form ring-like patches similar to those of a leopard.

Main references for the Mediterranean: Tortonese (1956), Capapé (1974c), Capapé (1975a), Capapé (1977), Cadenat & Blache (1981), Bauchot (1987), Vanni (1992), Barrull *et al.* (1999), De Maddalena & Piscitelli (2001), Barrull & Mate (2002), Bruni & Würtz (2002), Lipej *et al.* (2004), Kabasakal & Kabasakal (2004).

Other selected non–Mediterranean related references: Compagno (1984), Patokina & Litvinov (2004).

Tope shark
Galeorhinus galeus (Linnaeus, 1758)

Classification: Order Carcharhiniformes, family Triakidae, genus *Galeorhinus*.

Common names in other languages: French: requin-hâ, milandre; Spanish: cazón; Italian: cagnesca, galeo; German: hundshai.

Distinctive characteristics for immediate identification: caudal fin terminal lobe enormous, first dorsal fin large, second dorsal small, eyes located dorsally on the head, underside of head strongly flattened.

Morphology: First dorsal fin large, its origin over pectoral fin inner margin or posterior to pectoral fin free rear tip. Second dorsal fin small. Anal fin about as large as the second dorsal. Pectoral fins relatively short. Caudal fin with relatively long lower lobe and long upper lobe with enormous terminal lobe. Underside of head strongly flattened. Snout long. Upper labial folds short. Nostrils relatively small. Eyes large and located dorsally on the head. Spiracles small. 5 pairs of short gill slits, the 5th located over the pectoral fin base.

Coloration: dorsal surfaces brown-grey, sometimes with slightly darker spots; ventral surfaces white. The pectoral fin ventral surface is white at the base and partially grey brown, with a darker band parallel to the posterior margin and a narrow whitish band adjacent to the posterior margin. Rare cases of albino specimens exist.

Teeth shape: upper teeth with one cusp, with the medial edge cutting and the lateral edge partially serrated; lower teeth similar.

Dental formula: 17 to 20–17 to 20 / 15 to 18–15 to 18.

Maximum size: 195 cm.

Size at birth: 30–40 cm.

Size at maturity: 120 cm (male) and 130–150 cm (female).

Embryonic development: aplacental viviparous.

Gestation: 10–12 months.

Litter size: 6–52 young.

Tope shark

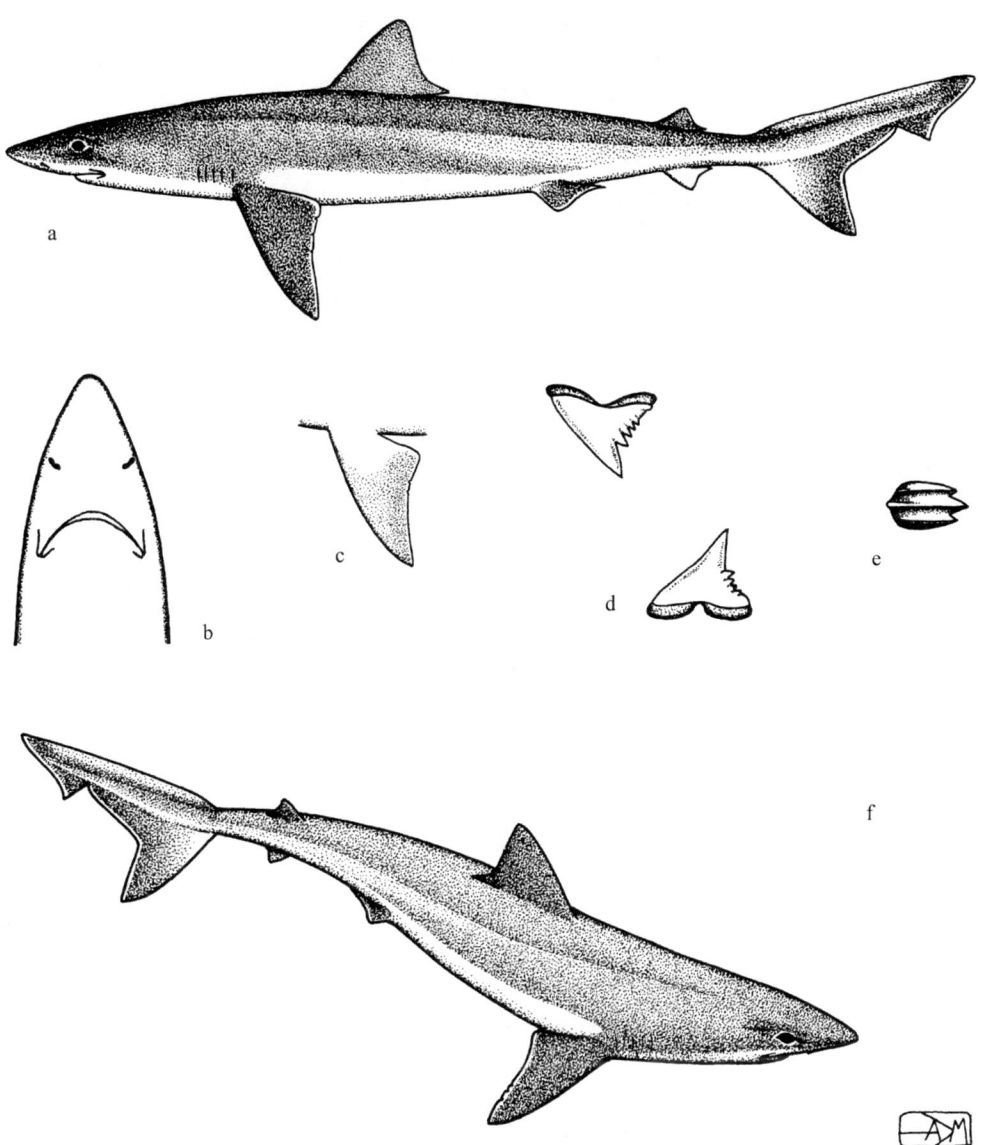

Tope shark (*Galeorhinus galeus*): (a) lateral view, (b) ventral view of the head, (c) ventral view of the pectoral fin, (d) upper and lower teeth, (e) placoid scale, (f) a swimming tope shark.

Reproduction in the Mediterranean: reproduces in the Mediterranean.
Maximum age: at least 25 years.
Diet: bony fishes, cephalopods, crustaceans, annelids, echinoderms, elasmobranchs, carcasses.
Habitat: on continental and insular shelves, at depths ranging from the surface to at least 598 m. Pregnant females give birth close inshore, where juveniles often remain, males stay in deeper waters.
Geographical distribution in the Mediterranean Sea: all Mediterranean.

Geographical distribution in the rest of the world: Atlantic, Pacific and Indian Oceans.

Behavior: active, solitary or in small groups, migratory, sometimes timid but can be curious of divers, can segregate by sex and size.

Dangerousness for man: not dangerous.

Importance for fishery in the Mediterranean: of a certain importance.

Status in the Mediterranean: uncommon.

Kind of presence in the Mediterranean: stable.

Specimens of particular interest recorded in the Mediterranean: one of the largest specimens recorded from the area was a 144 cm male caught off Chioggia, Italy, Adriatic Sea, on 27 November 2002. A specimen was caught off Punta Entinas, Spain, Alboran Sea, between 588 and 598 m depth on 9 May 1999; this is the greater depth ever recorded for this species.

Species with which can be confused: none.

Main references for the Mediterranean: Lo Bianco (1909), Ranzi (1932–1934), Tortonese (1956), Cadenat & Blache (1981), Bauchot (1987), Vanni (1992), Moreno (1995), Francis & Mulligan (1998), Hemida & Labidi (2001), Barrull & Mate (2002), de la Serna *et al.* (2002), Lipej *et al.* (2004).

Other selected non–Mediterranean related references: Roedel & Ripley (1950), Bass *et al.* (1973–1976), Castro (1983), Compagno (1984), Last & Stevens (1994), Lucifora *et al.* (2003).

Starry smooth-hound
Mustelus asterias Cloquet, 1821

Classification: Order Carcharhiniformes, family Triakidae, genus *Mustelus*.

Common names in other languages: French: emissole tachetée; Spanish: musola pinta; Italian: palombo stellato; German: gefleckter glatthai.

Distinctive characteristics for immediate identification: anal fin present, caudal fin terminal lobe large but not enormous, first dorsal fin large, its origin over the pectoral fin base or the inner margin, second dorsal slightly smaller, eyes located dorsally on the head, underside of head strongly flattened, snout long, upper labial folds conspicuously longer than lower folds, nostrils very large and without nasal barbels, internarial space is 1.2 to 1.3 times the nostril width, often with white spotted coloration.

Morphology: first dorsal fin large, its origin over the pectoral fin base or the inner margin. Second dorsal fin slightly smaller. Anal fin much smaller than second dorsal. Pectoral fins relatively short but wide. Caudal fin with short lower lobe and relatively long upper lobe with large terminal lobe. Body relatively slender. Underside of head strongly flattened. Snout long. Upper labial folds conspicuously longer than lower folds. Nostrils very wide. Internarial space is 1.2 to 1.3 times the nostril width. Eyes large and located dorsally on the head. Spiracles medium-sized. 5 pairs of short gill slits, the 4th and 5th located over the pectoral fin base.

Coloration: dorsal surfaces grey-brown, usually with small white spots on the dorsal part and along the lateral line; ventral surfaces white. The pectoral fin ventral surface is partially light grey, white at the base.

Starry smooth-hound

Starry smooth-hound (*Mustelus asterias*): (a) lateral view, (b) ventral view of the head, (c) ventral view of the pectoral fin, (d) upper and lower teeth, (e) placoid scale, (f) female during parturition.

Teeth shape: upper teeth very small, with one low cusp, arranged in a pavement formation; lower teeth similar. In new-born specimens there are minute cusplets.
Dental formula: 40–40 / 40–40.
Maximum size: 153 cm.
Size at birth: 28.5–33 cm.
Size at maturity: 75–87 cm (male) and 85–96 cm (female).
Embryonic development: aplacental viviparous.
Gestation: 12 months.

Litter size: 7–20 young.
Reproduction in the Mediterranean: reproduce in the Mediterranean; data indicates parturition must occur in the Golfe du Lion, France and Adriatic Sea.
Maximum age: at least 4 years.
Diet: crustaceans, bony fishes, cephalopods, sea anemones.
Habitat: benthic, on continental and insular shelves at depths ranging from the surface to at least 1000 m.
Geographical distribution in the Mediterranean Sea: all Mediterranean.
Geographical distribution in the rest of the world: Eastern Atlantic Ocean.
Behavior: active, occur solitary or in groups, timid, can segregate by size.
Dangerousness for man: not dangerous.
Importance for fishery in the Mediterranean: notable importance.
Status in the Mediterranean: common.
Kind of presence in the Mediterranean: stable.
Specimens of particular interest recorded in the Mediterranean: among the largest specimens recorded in the area were a 120 cm pregnant female carrying 20 embryos (the largest litter ever recorded) caught in July 1992 in the Golfe du Lion, France and a 117 cm female caught in an unknown location on 8 May 2000.
Species with which can be confused: the common smooth-hound (*Mustelus mustelus*) and the blackspotted smooth-hound (*Mustelus mediterraneus*); but in both *M. mustelus* and *M. mediterraneus* the first dorsal fin origin is over the pectoral fin free rear tip and the upper labial folds are slightly longer than lower folds, moreover in the common smooth-hound the internarial space is 1.5 to 2.0 times the nostril width, while in the blackspotted smooth-hound the internarial space is 1.1 to 1.3 times the nostril width.
Main references for the Mediterranean: Tortonese (1956), Quignard & Capapé (1972b), Capapé (1974a), Capapé (1977), Cadenat & Blache (1981), Bauchot (1987), Vanni (1992), Moreno (1995), Capapé *et al.* (2000), De Maddalena & Piscitelli (2001), Barrull & Mate (2002), Lipej *et al.* (2004), Kabasakal & Kabasakal (2004).
Other selected non–Mediterranean related references: Poll (1951), Compagno (1984).

Common smooth-hound
Mustelus mustelus (Linnaeus, 1758)

Classification: Order Carcharhiniformes, family Triakidae, genus *Mustelus*.
Common names in other languages: French: emissole lisse; Spanish: musola; Italian: palombo liscio, palombo nocciolo; German: gewöhnlicher glatthai.
Distinctive characteristics for immediate identification: anal fin present, caudal fin terminal lobe large but not enormous, first dorsal fin large, its origin over the pectoral fin free rear tip, second dorsal slightly smaller, eyes located dorsal on the head, underside of head strongly flattened, snout long, upper labial folds slightly longer than lower folds, nostrils very large and without nasal barbels, internarial space is 1.5 to 2.0 times the nostril width, coloration usually without spots.
Morphology: First dorsal fin large, its origin over the pectoral fin free rear tip. Second

Common smooth-hound

Common smooth-hound (*Mustelus mustelus*): (a) lateral view, (b) ventral view of the head, (c) ventral view of the pectoral fin, (d) upper and lower teeth, (e) placoid scale, (f) embryos in the uterus nourished by the placenta.

dorsal slightly smaller. Anal fin much smaller than second dorsal. Pectoral fins relatively short but wide. Caudal fin with short lower lobe and relatively long upper lobe with large terminal lobe. Body relatively slender. Underside of head strongly flattened. Snout long. Upper labial folds slightly longer than lower folds. Nostrils very wide. Internarial space is 1.5 to 2,0 times the nostril width. Eyes large and located dorsal on the head. Spiracles medium-sized. 5 pairs of short gill slits, the 4th and 5th located over the pectoral fin base.

Coloration: dorsal surfaces brown-grey, usually uniform but sometimes with some small dark spots; ventral surfaces white. The pectoral fin ventral surface is partially light grey, white at the base.

Teeth shape: upper teeth very small, with one low cusp, arranged in a pavement formation; lower teeth similar. In new-born specimens there are minute cusplets.

Dental formula: 40–40 / 40–40.

Maximum size: 173 cm.

Size at birth: 39–42 cm.

Size at maturity: 95–130 cm (male) and 125–140 cm (female).

Embryonic development: placental viviparous.

Gestation: 9–11 months.

Litter size: 2–28 young.

Reproduction in the Mediterranean: reproduces in the Mediterranean; data indicates parturition must occur in the Adriatic Sea and the Golfe du Lion, France.

Maximum age: at least 24 years.

Diet: crustaceans, molluscs, bony fishes, sea cucumbers, polychaetes, brittle stars.

Habitat: benthic, on continental shelves and upper slopes, at depths ranging from 5 m to at least 450 m. Adult females and juveniles occur in shallower waters than adult males.

Geographical distribution in the Mediterranean Sea: all Mediterranean.

Geographical distribution in the rest of the world: Eastern Atlantic Ocean.

Behavior: active, nocturnal, solitary or in groups, timid, can segregate by size.

Dangerousness for man: not dangerous.

Importance for fishery in the Mediterranean: notable importance.

Status in the Mediterranean: common.

Kind of presence in the Mediterranean: stable.

Specimens of particular interest recorded in the Mediterranean: one of the three largest common smooth-hounds ever recorded was a 165 cm pregnant female carrying 17 embryos caught in an unknown location of the Adriatic Sea on 15 March 2000.

Species with which can be confused: the starry smooth-hound (*Mustelus asterias*) and the blackspotted smooth-hound (*Mustelus mediterraneus*); but in the starry smooth-hound the internarial space is 1.2 to 1.3 times the nostril width, upper labial folds are conspicuously longer than lower folds, and the first dorsal fin origin is over the pectoral fin base or the inner margin, and in the blackspotted smooth-hound the internarial space is 1.1 to 1.3 times the nostril width and upper labial folds are slightly longer than lower folds and the first dorsal fin origin is over the pectoral fin free rear tip.

Main references for the Mediterranean: Lo Bianco (1909), Tortonese (1956), Capapé (1975a), Capapé & Pantoustier (1975), Cadenat & Blache (1981), Bauchot (1987), Vanni (1992), Moreno (1995), Barrull *et al.* (1999), Capapé *et al.* (2000), Costantini *et al.* (2000), De Maddalena *et al.* (2001), De Maddalena & Piscitelli (2001), Barrull & Mate (2002), Bruni & Würtz (2002), Kabasakal (2002a), Lipej *et al.* (2004), L. Piscitelli (pers. comm.).

Other selected non–Mediterranean related references: Poll (1951), Compagno (1984), Goosen & Smale (1997), Smale & Compagno (1997).

Blackspotted smooth-hound

Mustelus mediterraneus (Quignard & Capapé, 1972)

Classification: Order Carcharhiniformes, family Triakidae, genus *Mustelus*.

Common names in other languages: French: emissole pointillée; Spanish: musola pimienta; Italian: palombo punteggiato; German: schwarzpunkt-glatthai.

Distinctive characteristics for immediate identification: anal fin present, caudal fin terminal lobe large but not enormous, first dorsal fin large, its origin over the pectoral

Blackspotted smooth-hound (*Mustelus mediterraneus*): (a) lateral view, (b) ventral view of the head, (c) ventral view of the pectoral fin, (d) upper and lower teeth, (e) placoid scale, (f) a blackspotted smooth-hound fleeing from a great white shark (*Carcharodon carcharias*).

fin free rear tip, second dorsal slightly smaller, dorsal fin posterior margins prominently fringed, eyes located dorsal on the head, underside of head strongly flattened, snout long, upper labial folds slightly longer than lower folds, nostrils very large and without nasal barbels, internarial space is 1.1 to 1.3 times the nostril width, usually with black spotted coloration.

Morphology: first dorsal fin large, its origin over the pectoral fin free rear tip. Second dorsal slightly smaller. Dorsal fin posterior margins prominently fringed. Anal fin much smaller than second dorsal. Pectoral fins relatively short but wide. Caudal fin with short lower lobe and relatively long upper lobe with large terminal lobe. Body relatively slender. Underside of head strongly flattened. Snout long. Upper labial folds slightly longer than lower folds. Nostrils very wide. Internarial space is 1.1 to 1.3 times the nostril width. Eyes large and located dorsal on the head. Spiracles medium-sized. 5 pairs of short gill slits, the 4th and 5th located over the pectoral fin base.

Coloration: dorsal surfaces brown-grey, usually with small black spots; ventral surfaces white.

Teeth shape: upper teeth very small, with one low cusp, arranged in a pavement formation; lower teeth similar. In new-born sharks there are minute cusplets.

Dental formula: unknown.

Maximum size: 95 cm.

Size at birth: 31 cm.

Size at maturity: 50–55 cm (male) and about 60 cm (female).

Embryonic development: probably placental viviparous.

Gestation: about 12 months.

Litter size: unknown.

Reproduction in the Mediterranean: reproduces in the Mediterranean.

Maximum age: unknown.

Diet: unknown, probably crustaceans.

Habitat: benthic, on continental shelves, probably at depths ranging from the surface to at least 100 m.

Geographical distribution in the Mediterranean Sea: all Mediterranean.

Geographical distribution in the rest of the world: Eastern Atlantic Ocean.

Behavior: unknown.

Dangerousness for man: not dangerous.

Importance for fishery in the Mediterranean: probably of some importance.

Status in the Mediterranean: unknown, probably uncommon.

Kind of presence in the Mediterranean: stable.

Specimens of particular interest recorded in the Mediterranean: there are no detailed records for this species.

Species with which can be confused: the starry smooth-hound (*Mustelus asterias*) and the common smooth-hound (*Mustelus mustelus*); but in the starry smooth-hound the internarial space is 1.2 to 1.3 times the nostril width, the upper labial folds are conspicuously longer than lower folds, and the first dorsal fin origin is over the pectoral fin base or the inner margin, and in the common smooth-hound the internarial space is 1.5 to 2.0 times the nostril width, the upper labial folds are slightly longer than lower folds and the first dorsal fin origin is over the pectoral fin base or the inner margin.

Main references for the Mediterranean: Quignard & Capapé (1972a), Capapé (1977), Cadenat & Blache (1981), Compagno (1984), Bauchot (1987), Tortonese (1987), Hemida *et al.* Lipej *et al.* (2004).

Other selected non–Mediterranean related references: none.

Strait shark
Carcharhinus acarenatus Moreno & Hoyos, 1983

Classification: Order Carcharhiniformes, family Carcharhinidae, genus *Carcharhinus*.

Common names in other languages: French: requin du Détroit; Spanish: jaquetón del Estrecho; Italian: squalo di Gibilterra; German: seestraßenhai.

Distinctive characteristics for immediate identification: snout dorso-ventrally depressed, anal fin, two dorsal fins, the second dorsal much smaller than first dorsal, eyes located laterally on head, no spiracles, characteristic upper labial fold Y-shaped, first dorsal fin relatively large (its origin immediately posterior to the pectoral fin free rear tip), pectoral fins moderately long, no interdorsal ridge.

Morphology: first dorsal fin relatively large, its origin immediately posterior to the pectoral fin free rear tip. Second dorsal small. Anal fin about as large as the second dorsal. Pectoral fins moderately long. Caudal fin with relatively short lower lobe and long upper lobe with medium-sized terminal lobe. No interdorsal ridge. Snout dorso-ventrally depressed and moderately long, rounded in dorso-ventral view. Mouth wide and parabolic in ventral view. Labial folds short, the upper with characteristic Y-shape. Eyes relatively small. Nostrils small. No spiracles. 5 pairs of short gill slits, the 4th and 5th located over the pectoral fin base.

Coloration: dorsal surfaces light grey, with a whitish band on the flanks; ventral surfaces white. Fin apex dark.

Teeth shape: upper teeth with one large cusp with finely serrated edges; lower teeth smaller, with one cusp, narrow and pointed, with very finely serrated edges.

Dental formula: 15–2–15 / 14 to 15–1–14 to 15.

Maximum size: 285 cm.

Size at birth: about 80 cm.

Size at maturity: about 190 cm (male) and 230 cm (female).

Embryonic development: placental viviparous.

Gestation: unknown.

Litter size: at least up to 13 young.

Reproduction in the Mediterranean: unknown.

Maximum age: unknown.

Diet: bony fishes, stingrays, cephalopods, carcasses.

Habitat: pelagic, on continental and insular shelves and upper slopes, at depths ranging from the surface to at least 600 m.

Geographical distribution in the Mediterranean Sea: Western Mediterranean.

Geographical distribution in the rest of the world: Eastern Atlantic Ocean.

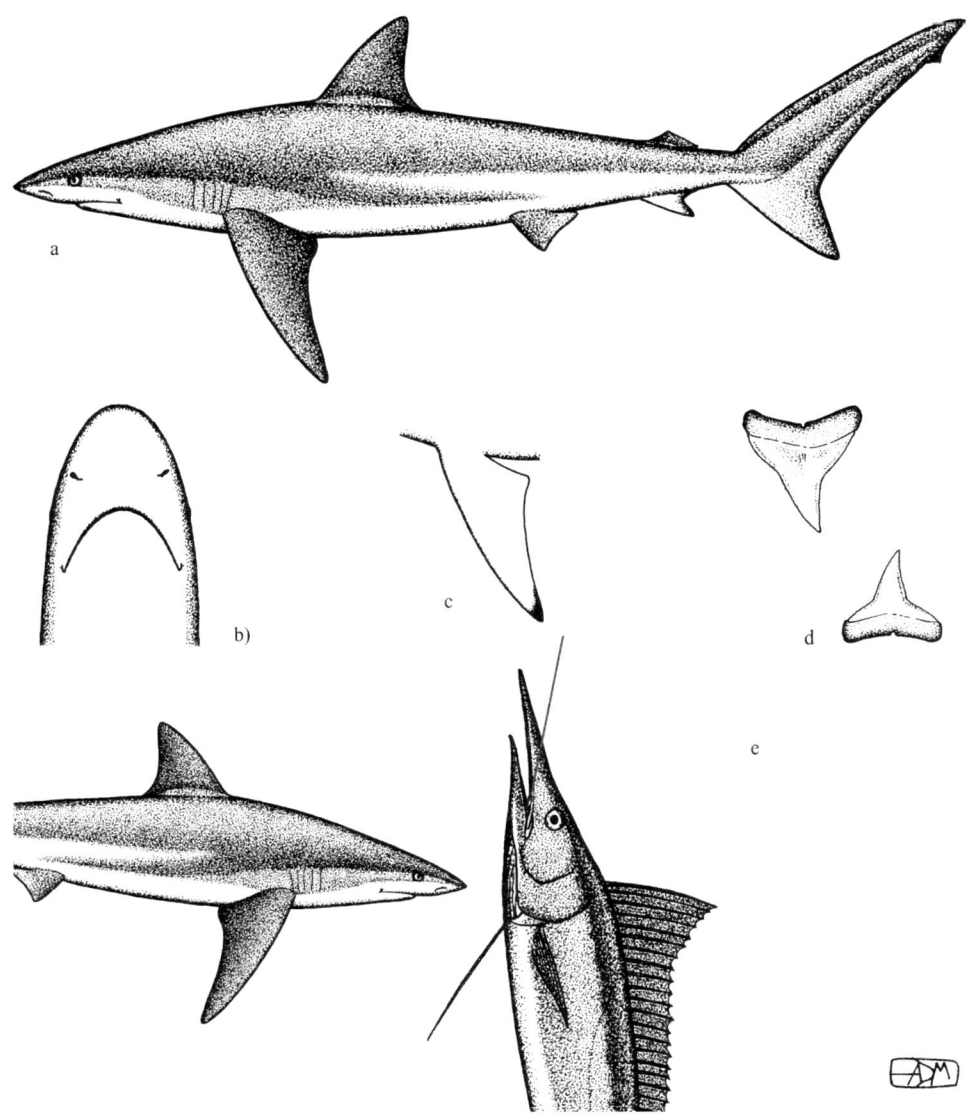

Strait shark (*Carcharhinus acarenatus*): (a) lateral view, (b) ventral view of the head, (c) ventral view of the pectoral fin, (d) upper and lower teeth, (e) a strait shark approaching a hooked Mediterranean spearfish (*Tetrapturus belone*, drawings by Alessandro De Maddalena).

Behavior: active, nocturnal, possibly migratory.
Dangerousness for man: unknown, potentially dangerous.
Importance for fishery in the Mediterranean: of some importance.
Status in the Mediterranean: unknown due to relatively recent description in 1983, probably relatively common.
Kind of presence in the Mediterranean: stable.
Specimens of particular interest recorded in the Mediterranean: one of the largest specimen recorded in the area was a 234.8 cm female caught off the mouth of river Mouluya, between Morocco and Algeria (Sea of Alboran) in early August 1979.

Species with which can be confused: the copper shark (*Carcharhinus brachyurus*), but this species has simple upper labial folds, and usually has an interdorsal ridge and a different dental formula.

Main references for the Mediterranean: Moreno & Hoyos (1983a), Moreno (1995), Barrull & Mate (2002).

Other selected non–Mediterranean related references: none.

Bignose shark
Carcharhinus altimus (Springer, 1950)

Classification: Order Carcharhiniformes, family Carcharhinidae, genus *Carcharhinus*.

Common names in other languages: French: requin babosse; Spanish: jaquetón picoto; Italian: squalo dal muso lungo; German: großnasenhai.

Distinctive characteristics for immediate identification: snout dorso-ventrally depressed, anal fin posterior margin deeply concave, two dorsal fins, the second dorsal much smaller than first dorsal, eyes located laterally on head, no spiracles, first dorsal fin relatively large and usually tall (its origin over the pectoral fin inner margin), usually with the anterior margin describing an angle, pectoral fins long and wide, high interdorsal ridge.

Morphology: first dorsal fin relatively large and usually tall, usually with the anterior margin describing an angle, its origin over the pectoral fin inner margin. Second dorsal small. Anal fin about as large as the second dorsal, its posterior margin deeply concave. Pectoral fins long and wide. Caudal fin with relatively short lower lobe and long upper lobe with medium-sized terminal lobe. High interdorsal ridge. Snout dorso-ventrally depressed and long, rounded in dorso-ventral view. Mouth wide and parabolic in ventral view. Labial folds short. Eyes relatively small. Nostrils small. No spiracles. 5 pairs of short gill slits, the 4th and 5th located over the pectoral fin base.

Coloration: dorsal surfaces light or dark grey with purple iridescence, with an inconspicuous whitish band on the flanks; ventral surfaces white. Fin apex dark. Juveniles can have black fin apex.

Teeth shape: upper teeth with one cusp, relatively large, triangular and serrated, erect to oblique; lower teeth smaller, with one cusp, narrow, pointed and finely serrated.

Dental formula: 15–1 to 2–15 / 14–1–14.

Maximum size: 288 cm.

Size at birth: about 44 cm.

Size at maturity: 216 cm (male) and 220 cm (female).

Embryonic development: placental viviparous.

Gestation: unknown.

Litter size: 15 young.

Reproduction in the Mediterranean: reproduces in the Mediterranean (Eastern Mediterranean).

Maximum age: unknown.

Diet: bony fishes, elasmobranchs, cephalopods, carcasses.

Bignose shark (*Carcharhinus altimus*): (a) lateral view, (b) ventral view of the head, (c) ventral view of the pectoral fin, (d) upper and lower teeth, (e) a male giving a love bite to a female.

Habitat: pelagic, on continental and insular shelves and upper slopes, at depths ranging from the surface to at least 430 m. Juveniles occur in shallower waters than adults.
Geographical distribution in the Mediterranean Sea: Eastern and Western Mediterranean.
Geographical distribution in the rest of the world: Atlantic, Pacific and Indian Oceans.
Behavior: active, nocturnal.
Dangerousness for man: unknown, potentially dangerous.

Importance for fishery in the Mediterranean: no importance.
Status in the Mediterranean: uncommon.
Kind of presence in the Mediterranean: unknown.
Specimens of particular interest recorded in the Mediterranean: the largest specimen reported from the area was a 282 cm male caught off Algeria between 1996 and 2002. A 44 cm new-born female was caught off Israel on 2 September 1990, and is the smallest free-swimming specimen ever recorded (preserved at the Hebrew University in Jerusalem).
Species with which can be confused: the sandbar shark (*Carcharhinus plumbeus*) and the dusky shark (*Carcharhinus obscurus*); but usually both these species have a shorter snout, moreover the sandbar shark has a larger first dorsal fin with its origin over the pectoral fin base or its axil and a more straight pectoral fin anterior margin, and the dusky shark has narrower pectoral fins.
Main references for the Mediterranean: Cadenat & Blache (1981), Compagno (1984), Bauchot (1987), Moreno & Hoyos (1983b), Moreno (1987), Moreno (1995), Golani (1996), Barrull & Mate (2002), Hemida *et al.* (2002).
Other selected non–Mediterranean related references: Bass *et al.* (1973–1976), Garrick (1982), Castro (1983), Randall (1986), Last & Stevens (1994).

Pigeye shark or Java shark
Carcharhinus amboinensis (Müller & Henle, 1839)

Classification: Order Carcharhiniformes, family Carcharhinidae, genus *Carcharhinus*.
Nomi comuni in altre lingue: French: requin balestrine; Spanish: jaquetón chato; Italian: squalo dall'occhio di porco, squalo di Giava; German: Javahai.
Distinctive characteristics for immediate identification: snout dorso-ventrally depressed and short, anal fin, two dorsal fins, the second dorsal much smaller than first dorsal, body massive and relatively stout, eyes located laterally on head, no spiracles, anal fin posterior margin deeply concave, first dorsal fin relatively large, pointed and erect (its origin over the axil or the pectoral fin inner margin), no interdorsal ridge.
Morphology: first dorsal fin relatively large, pointed and erect, its origin over the axil or the pectoral fin inner margin. Second dorsal small and much smaller than first dorsal. Anal fin about as large as the second dorsal, its posterior margin deeply concave. Pectoral fins from relatively short to long and wide. Caudal fin with relatively short lower lobe and long upper lobe with medium-sized terminal lobe. No interdorsal ridge. Body massive and relatively stout, with the dorsal part pronounced. Snout dorso-ventrally depressed and short, rounded in dorso-ventral view. Mouth wide and parabolic in ventral view. Labial folds short. Eyes relatively small. Nostrils small. No spiracles. 5 pairs of short gill slits, the 4th and 5th located over the pectoral fin base.
Coloration: dorsal surfaces light grey, with an inconspicuous whitish band on the flanks; ventral surfaces white. In juveniles, the fin apex and posterior margins have a narrow and inconspicuous darker band.
Teeth shape: upper teeth with one cusp, large, triangular, strongly serrated, from erect

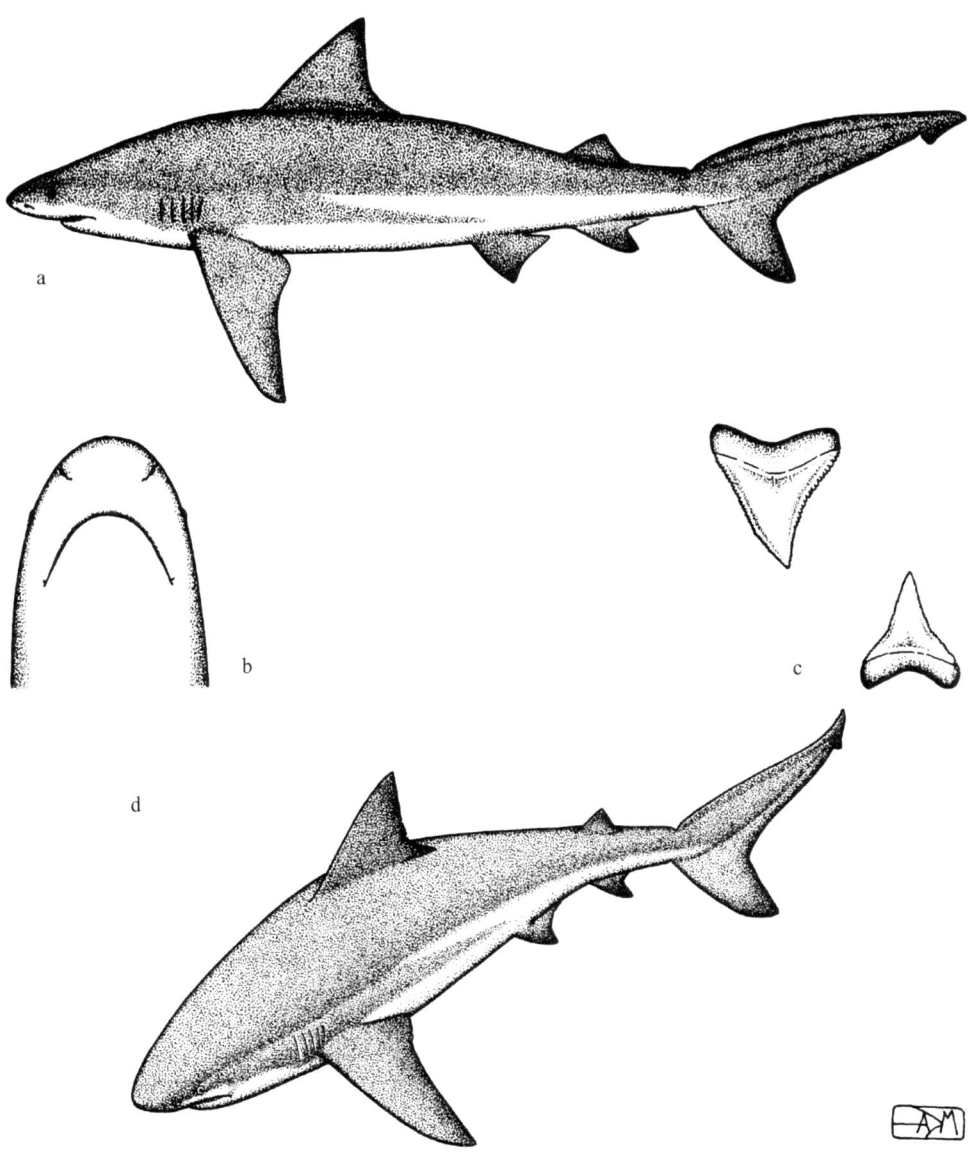

Pigeye shark (*Carcharhinus amboinensis*): (a) lateral view, (b) ventral view of the head, (c) upper and lower teeth, (d) swimming pigeye shark.

to oblique; lower teeth of similar size, with one cusp, wide, triangular, with finely serrated edges, erect to oblique.

Dental formula: 11 to 13–1–11 to 13 / 10 to 12–1–10 to 12.
Maximum size: 280 cm.
Size at birth: 60–72 cm.
Size at maturity: 195–210 cm (male) and 198–223 cm (female).
Embryonic development: placental viviparous.
Gestation: 12 months.
Litter size: 3–13 young.

Reproduction in the Mediterranean: does not reproduce in the Mediterranean.
Maximum age: unknown.
Diet: bony fishes, elasmobranchs, crustaceans, molluscs, cetaceans, carcasses.
Habitat: pelagic, on continental and insular shelves, at depths ranging from the surface to at least 100 m.
Geographical distribution in the Mediterranean Sea: Central Mediterranean.
Geographical distribution in the rest of the world: Eastern Atlantic, Western Pacific and Indian Oceans.
Behavior: solitary, in pairs, or in small groups.
Dangerousness for man: potentially dangerous.
Importance for fishery in the Mediterranean: no importance.
Status in the Mediterranean: very rare.
Kind of presence in the Mediterranean: occasional (the specimen recorded must have entered the Mediterranean Sea from the Eastern Atlantic Ocean through the Gibraltar Strait or possibly from the Red Sea from the Suez Channel).
Specimens of particular interest recorded in the Mediterranean: only one specimen was recorded in the Mediterranean, an approximately 300 cm specimen caught off Crotone, Italy, in summer 2003.
Species with which can be confused: none.
Main references for the Mediterranean: De Maddalena & Della Rovere (2005).
Other selected non–Mediterranean related references: Bass *et al.* (1973–1976), Garrick (1982), Compagno (1984), Randall (1986), Cliff & Dudley (1991), Last & Stevens (1994).

Copper shark or bronze whaler
Carcharhinus brachyurus (Günther, 1870)

Classification: Order Carcharhiniformes, family Carcharhinidae, genus *Carcharhinus*.
Common names in other languages: French: requin cuivre; Spanish: jaquetón cobre; Italian: squalo ramato, squalo bronzeo; German: kupferhai.
Distinctive characteristics for immediate identification: snout dorso-ventrally depressed, anal fin, two dorsal fins, the second dorsal much smaller than first dorsal, eyes located laterally on head, no spiracles, anal fin posterior margin deeply concave, first dorsal fin relatively large, its origin immediately posterior to the pectoral fin free rear tip, pectoral fins long.
Morphology: first dorsal fin relatively large, its origin immediately posterior to the pectoral fin free rear tip. Second dorsal small. Anal fin about as large as the second dorsal, its posterior margin deeply concave. Pectoral fins long. Caudal fin with relatively short lower lobe and long upper lobe with medium-sized to large terminal lobe. Interdorsal ridge present or absent. Snout dorso-ventrally depressed and long, rounded in dorso-ventral view. Mouth wide and parabolic in ventral view. Labial folds short. Eyes relatively small. Nostrils small. No spiracles. 5 pairs of short gill slits, the 4th and 5th located over the pectoral fin base.
Coloration: dorsal surfaces bronze-grey-brown, with a conspicuous whitish band on

the flanks; ventral surfaces white. Boundary separating dorsal from ventral coloration sharp. Sometimes fin apex and posterior margins dark. The pectoral fin ventral surface is white with a small grey patch at the apex.

Teeth shape: upper teeth with one cusp, relatively large, triangular and with serrated edges, oblique; lower teeth smaller, with one cusp, narrow, pointed, with finely serrated edges, erect to oblique.

Dental formula: 14 to 16–1 to 3–14 to 16 / 14 to 15–1 to 3–14 to 15.

Maximum size: 303 cm.

Size at birth: 46–54 cm.

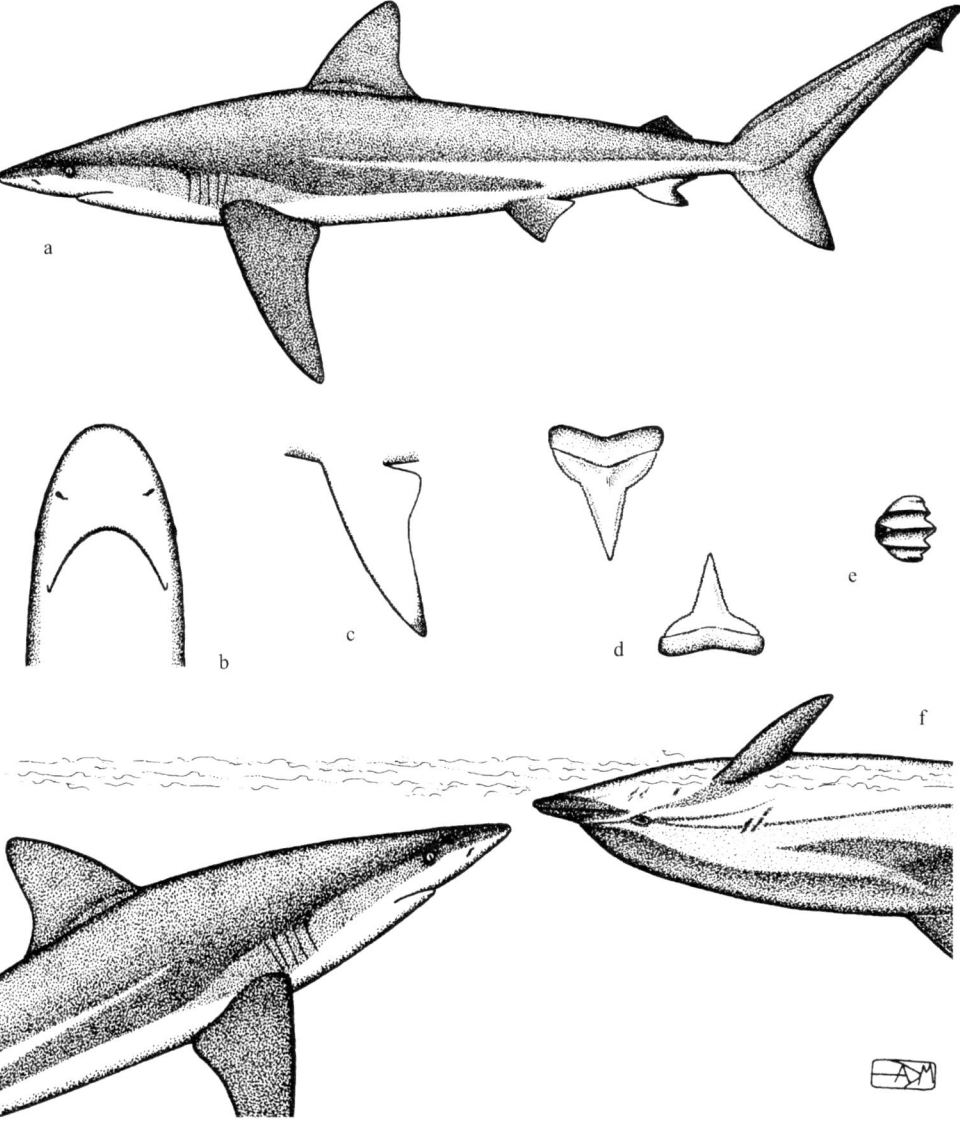

Copper shark (*Carcharhinus brachyurus*): (a) lateral view, (b) ventral view of the head, (c) ventral view of the pectoral fin, (d) upper and lower teeth, (e) placoid scale, (f) a copper shark approaches a striped dolphin (*Stenella coeruleoalba*) carcass to feed on it.

Size at maturity: 200–229 cm (male) and about 244 cm (female).
Embryonic development: placental viviparous.
Gestation: about 12 months.
Litter size: 8–20 young.
Reproduction in the Mediterranean: reproduces in the Mediterranean, possibly in the Tyrrhenian or Ligurian Sea.
Maximum age: at least 12 years.
Diet: bony fishes, elasmobranchs, cephalopods, gastropods, crustaceans, jellyfishes, cetaceans, carcasses.
Habitat: pelagic, on continental shelves, at depths ranging from the surface to at least 100 m. Juveniles favor inshore waters, while adults stay offshore.
Geographical distribution in the Mediterranean Sea: Western and Central Mediterranean.
Geographical distribution in the rest of the world: Atlantic, Pacific and Indian Oceans.
Behavior: active, migratory, solitary or in groups, can segregate by sex and size, feed on schooling fishes simply taking bites from the tightly massed prey.
Dangerousness for man: dangerous.
Importance for fishery in the Mediterranean: scarce importance.
Status in the Mediterranean: uncommon.
Kind of presence in the Mediterranean: stable.
Specimens of particular interest recorded in the Mediterranean: the largest specimen recorded, a 303 cm male, was caught off the Algerian coast between 1996 and 2002. Other large specimens were caught in the waters off Mazara del Vallo, Sicily, Italy, including a 276 cm male caught on 7 July 1983, a 272 cm male caught on 22 July 1983 and a 269 cm male caught on 1 July 1983. A 260 cm female carrying 14 near-term embryos was caught off Punta delle Chianacce, Italy, Tyrrhenian Sea in June 1980.
Species with which can be confused: the strait shark (*Carcharhinus acarenatus*), but this species has characteristic Y-shaped upper labial folds, lack interdorsal ridge and has a different dental formula.
Main references for the Mediterranean: Cadenat & Blache (1981), Garrick (1982), Cigala Fulgosi (1983a), Muñoz-Chapuli (1984), Bauchot (1987), Moreno (1995), Vacchi *et al.* (1996), Orsi Relini (1998), Barrull & Mate (2002), Hemida *et al.* (2002), Morey & Massuttí (2003).
Other selected non–Mediterranean related references: Bass *et al.* (1973–1976), Garrick (1982), Castro (1983), Compagno (1984), Smale (1991), Cliff & Dudley (1992), Last & Stevens (1994).

Spinner shark
Carcharhinus brevipinna (Müller & Henle, 1839)

Classification: Order Carcharhiniformes, family Carcharhinidae, genus *Carcharhinus*.
Common names in other languages: French: requin tisserand; Spanish: jaquetón picudo; Italian: squalo dalle pinne corte; German: spinnerhai.

Spinner shark

Distinctive characteristics for immediate identification: snout dorso-ventrally depressed and long, anal fin, two dorsal fins, the second dorsal much smaller than first dorsal, eyes located laterally on head, no spiracles, pectoral fins short, first dorsal fin relatively small (its origin posterior to or over the pectoral fin free rear tip), no interdorsal ridge.

Morphology: first dorsal fin relatively small, its origin posterior to or over the pectoral fin free rear tip. Second dorsal small. Anal fin about as large as the second dorsal, its posterior margin not deeply concave. Pectoral fins short. Caudal fin with rela-

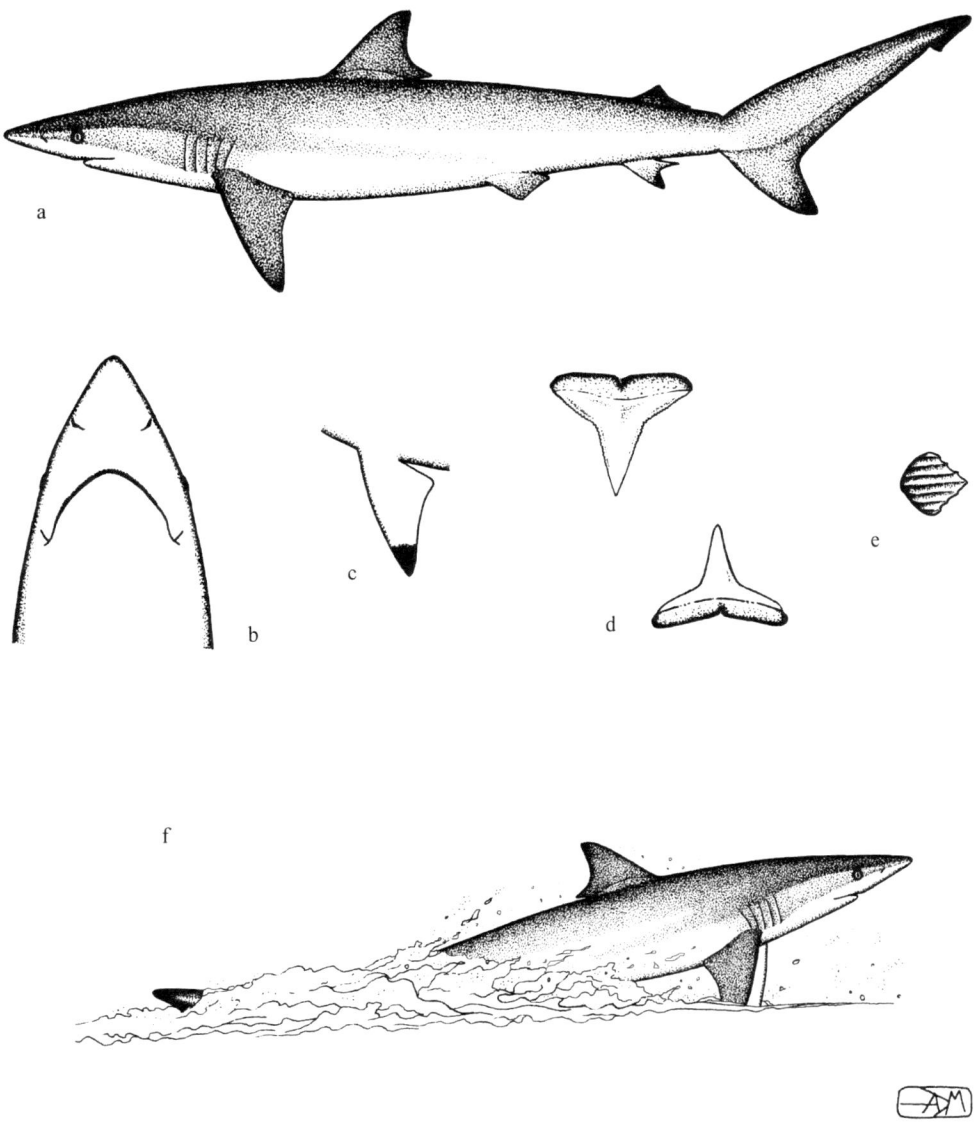

Spinner shark (*Carcharhinus brevipinna*): (a) lateral view, (b) ventral view of the head, (c) ventral view of the pectoral fin, (d) upper and lower teeth, (e) placoid scale, (f) a spinner shark leaps out of the water.

tively short lower lobe and long upper lobe with medium-sized terminal lobe. No interdorsal ridge. Snout dorso-ventrally depressed and long, slightly rounded in dorso-ventral view. Mouth wide and parabolic in ventral view. Labial folds short. Eyes relatively small. Nostrils small. No spiracles. 5 pairs of short gill slits, the 4th and 5th located over the pectoral fin base.

Coloration: dorsal surfaces bronze-grey, with an inconspicuous whitish band on the flanks; ventral surfaces white. Often fin apex black, especially in juveniles.

Teeth shape: upper teeth with one cusp, narrow, pointed and with finely serrated edges, oblique; lower teeth smaller, with one cusp, narrow, pointed, with cutting edges, erect to oblique.

Dental formula: 16–2 to 3–16 / 15 to 16–1 to 3–15 to 16.

Maximum size: 278 cm.

Size at birth: 46–80 cm.

Size at maturity: 170 cm (male) and 180 cm (female).

Embryonic development: placental viviparous.

Gestation: 12–15 months.

Litter size: 2–15 young.

Reproduction in the Mediterranean: possibly reproduces in the Mediterranean.

Maximum age: at least 27 years.

Diet: bony fishes, rays, cephalopods, crustaceans.

Habitat: pelagic, on continental and insular shelves, at depths ranging from the surface to at least 100 m.

Geographical distribution in the Mediterranean Sea: all Mediterranean.

Geographical distribution in the rest of the world: Atlantic, Pacific and Indian Oceans.

Behavior: active and fast, solitary or in large groups, migratory, can leap out of the water (and may rotate up to three times around its axis before dropping back into the water), feeds on small schooling fishes by swimming fast through the school with open mouth spinning along the body axis and leaping out of the water.

Dangerousness for man: potentially dangerous.

Importance for fishery in the Mediterranean: scarce importance.

Status in the Mediterranean: rare.

Kind of presence in the Mediterranean: unknown, possibly stable.

Specimens of particular interest recorded in the Mediterranean: the largest specimen reported from the area was a 220 cm female caught off Mazara del Vallo, Sicily, Italy, on 6 July 1983. A 218 cm female, was caught off Algerian coast between 1996 and 2002.

Species with which can be confused: the silky shark (*Carcharhinus falciformis*), but this species has longer pectoral fins.

Main references for the Mediterranean: Ben-Tuvia (1971), Capapé *et al.* (1979), Cadenat & Blache (1981), Garrick (1982), Cigala Fulgosi (1983a), Bauchot (1987), Moreno (1987), Tortonese (1987), Capapé (1989), Moreno (1995), Barrull & Mate (2002), Hemida *et al.* (2002).

Other selected non–Mediterranean related references: Bigelow & Schroeder (1948), Poll (1951), Bass *et al.* (1973–1976), Garrick (1982), Castro (1983), Compagno (1984), Randall (1986), Branstetter (1987), Last & Stevens (1994).

Silky shark
Carcharhinus falciformis (Bibron, 1839)

Classification: Order Carcharhiniformes, family Carcharhinidae, genus *Carcharhinus*.
Common names in other languages: French: requin soyeux; Spanish: jaquetón sedoso; Italian: squalo sericeo; German: seidenhai.
Distinctive characteristics for immediate identification: snout dorso-ventrally depressed, anal fin posterior margin deeply concave, two dorsal fins, the second

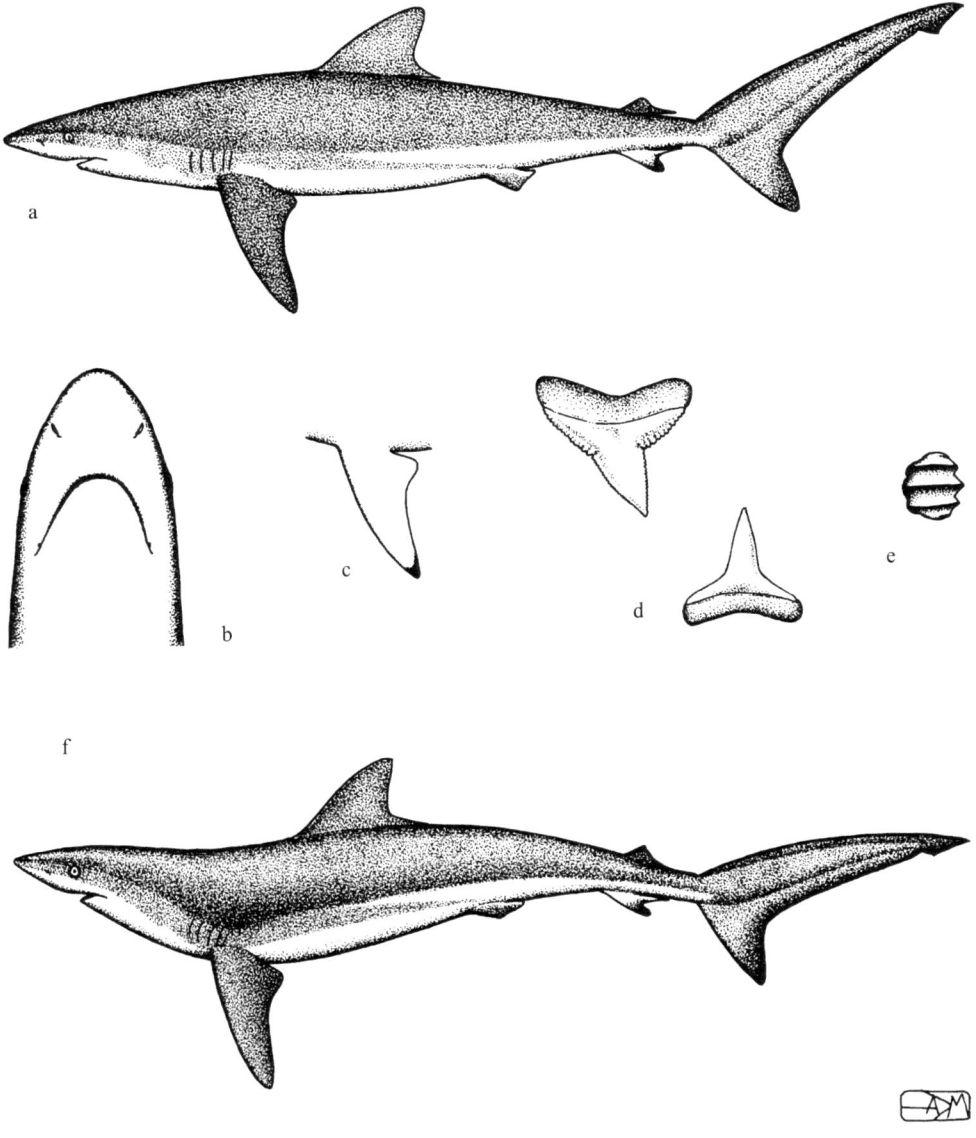

Silky shark (*Carcharhinus falciformis*): (a) lateral view, (b) ventral view of the head, (c) ventral view of the pectoral fin, (d) upper and lower teeth, (e) placoid scale, (f) silky shark performing a threat display.

Silky shark

dorsal much smaller than first dorsal, eyes located laterally on head, no spiracles, pectoral fins relatively short, first dorsal fin usually low (its origin posterior to the pectoral fin free rear tip), second dorsal and anal fin free rear tips long and narrow, pelvic fins very small, body relatively slender, high interdorsal ridge.

Morphology: first dorsal fin moderately large, usually low, its origin posterior to the pectoral fin free rear tip. Second dorsal small and with free rear tip long. Anal fin about as large as the second dorsal, with free rear tip long and posterior margin deeply concave. Pelvic fins very small. Pectoral fins relatively short. Caudal fin with relatively short lower lobe and long upper lobe with medium-sized terminal lobe; lower lobe apex slightly rounded. High interdorsal ridge. Body relatively slender. Snout dorso-ventrally depressed and long, rounded in dorso-ventral view. Mouth wide and parabolic in ventral view. Labial folds short. Eyes relatively small. Nostrils small. No spiracles. 5 pairs of short gill slits, the 4th and 5th located over the pectoral fin base.

Coloration: dorsal surfaces grey to grey-brown or blackish, with an inconspicuous whitish band on the flanks; ventral surfaces white. Fin apex dark, more evident on the anal fin. The pectoral fin ventral surface is white with a small black patch with sharp margin at the apex.

Teeth shape: upper teeth with one cusp, narrow, pointed and with serrated edges, oblique; lower teeth smaller, with one cusp, narrow, pointed, with cutting edges, erect to oblique.

Dental formula: 15 to 16–2–15 to 16 / 15 to 16–1 to 2–15 to 16.

Maximum size: 330 cm.

Size at birth: 63–75 cm.

Size at maturity: 182–217 cm (male) and 180–230 cm (female).

Embryonic development: placental viviparous.

Gestation: about 12 months.

Litter size: 2–15 young.

Reproduction in the Mediterranean: does not reproduce in the Mediterranean.

Maximum age: at least 12 years.

Diet: bony fishes, elasmobranchs, cephalopods, crustaceans, carcasses.

Habitat: pelagic, on continental and insular shelves, slopes and in oceanic basins, at depths ranging from the surface to at least 500 m.

Geographical distribution in the Mediterranean Sea: Western Mediterranean.

Geographical distribution in the rest of the world: Atlantic, Pacific, Indian Oceans.

Behavior: active and fast, nocturnal, solitary or in small to large groups, can approach divers closely (usually without showing any aggressive behavior), can segregate by size, can perform a threat display with back arched, head raised and caudal fin lowered.

Dangerousness for man: potentially dangerous.

Importance for fishery in the Mediterranean: no importance.

Status in the Mediterranean: very rare.

Kind of presence in the Mediterranean: occasional (the specimens recorded must have entered the Mediterranean Sea from the Eastern Atlantic Ocean through the Gibraltar Strait).

Specimens of particular interest recorded in the Mediterranean: a female and a male were caught between Balearic Islands and Algeria.

Species with which can be confused: the spinner shark (*Carcharhinus brevipinna*), but this species has shorter pectoral fins.

Main references for the Mediterranean: Cadenat & Blache (1981), Bauchot (1987), Moreno (1987), Moreno (1995), Barrull & Mate (2002), Hemida *et al.* (2002).

Other selected non–Mediterranean related references: Bigelow & Schroeder (1948), Bass *et al.* (1973–1976), Johnson (1978), Garrick (1982), Castro (1983), Compagno (1984), Randall (1986), Last & Stevens (1994), Ceballos *et al.* (2003), Chen *et al.* (2003).

Blacktip shark
Carcharhinus limbatus (Valenciennes, 1839)

Classification: Order Carcharhiniformes, family Carcharhinidae, genus *Carcharhinus*.

Common names in other languages: French: requin bordé; Spanish: jaquetón manchado; Italian: squalo dalle pinne orlate di nero; German: schwarzspitzenhai.

Distinctive characteristics for immediate identification: snout dorso-ventrally depressed and long, anal fin, two dorsal fins, the second dorsal much smaller than first dorsal, eyes located laterally on head, no spiracles, pectoral fins moderately long, perfectly falcate and pointed, first dorsal fin pointed, erect, tall (its origin over the pectoral fin inner margin), fin apex and posterior margins with a well evident small black area (sometimes with the exception of the anal fin).

Morphology: first dorsal fin pointed, erect, with the upper part narrow, moderately large to large and usually tall, its origin over the pectoral fin inner margin. Second dorsal small. Anal fin about as large as the second dorsal, its posterior margin not deeply concave. Pectoral fins perfectly falcate, pointed and moderately long. Caudal fin with relatively short lower lobe and long upper lobe with medium-sized terminal lobe. Dorsal part of the body pronounced. No interdorsal ridge. Snout dorso-ventrally depressed and long, slightly rounded in dorso-ventral view. Mouth wide and parabolic in ventral view. Labial folds short. Eyes relatively small. Nostrils small. No spiracles. 5 pairs of short gill slits, the 4th and 5th located over the pectoral fin base.

Coloration: dorsal surfaces grey or bronze-grey, with a conspicuous whitish band on the flanks; ventral surfaces white. Fin apex and posterior margins black (usually with the exception of the anal fin): the extension of these black areas is small. The pectoral fin ventral surface is white with a small black patch with sharp margin at the apex.

Teeth shape: upper teeth with one cusp, quite narrow, pointed and with finely serrated edges, slightly oblique; lower teeth smaller, with one cusp, narrow, pointed, with very finely serrated edges, erect.

Dental formula: 14 to 15–1 to 3–14 to 15 / 13 to 15–1 to 2–13 to 15.

Maximum size: 255 cm.

Size at birth: 38–72 cm.

Blacktip shark

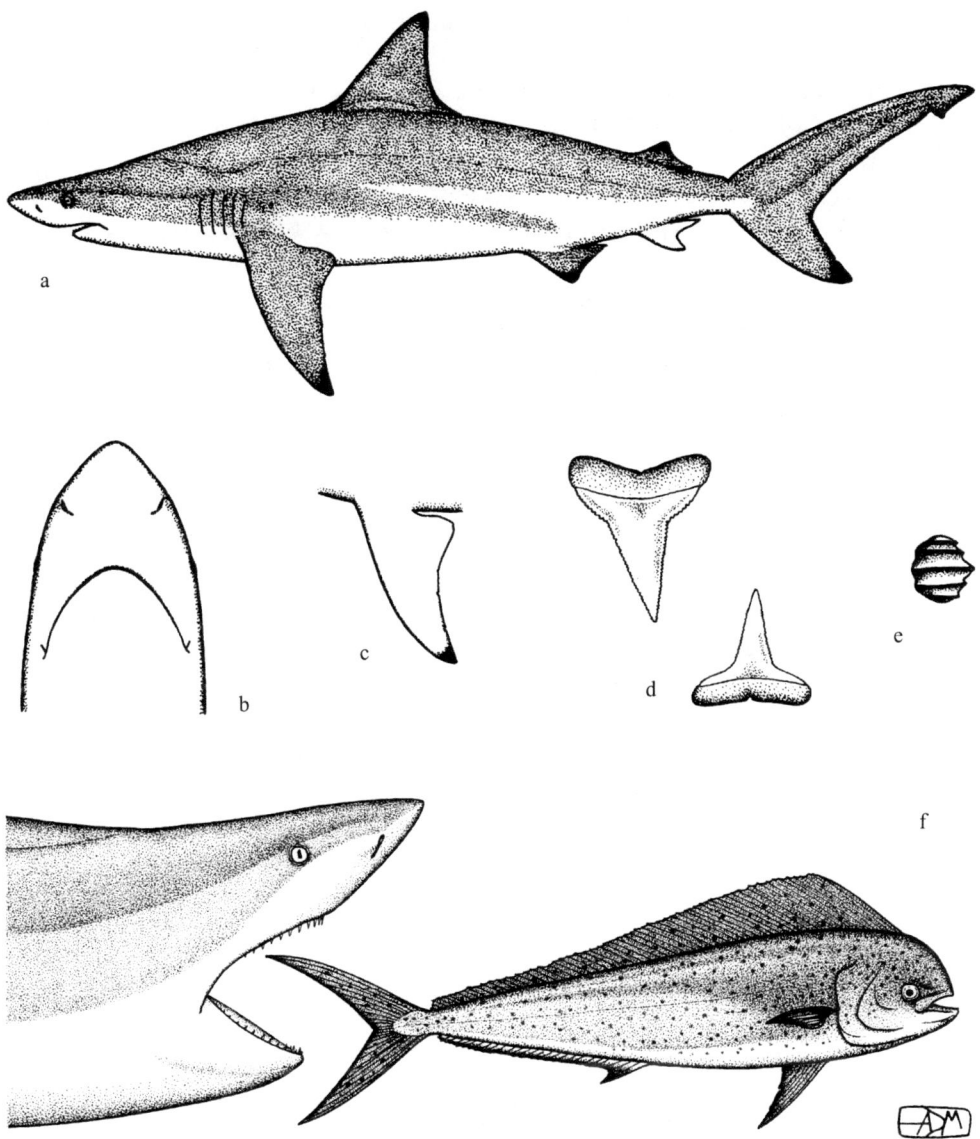

Blacktip shark (*Carcharhinus limbatus*): (a) lateral view, (b) ventral view of the head, (c) ventral view of the pectoral fin, (d) upper and lower teeth, (e) placoid scale, (f) a blacktip shark pursuing a common dolphinfish (*Coryphaena hippurus*).

Size at maturity: 160–200 cm (male) and 145–170 cm (female).
Embryonic development: placental viviparous.
Gestation: 12 months.
Litter size: 1–10 young.
Reproduction in the Mediterranean: unknown.
Maximum age: at least 10 years.
Diet: bony fishes, elasmobranchs, cephalopods, crustaceans, carcasses.
Habitat: pelagic, on continental and insular shelves, at depths ranging from the surface

to at least 100 m. Pregnant females give birth close inshore where juveniles often remain.

Geographical distribution in the Mediterranean Sea: all Mediterranean.

Geographical distribution in the rest of the world: Atlantic, Pacific and Indian Oceans.

Behavior: active and fast, solitary or in groups, migratory, can leap out of the water (and may rotate up to three times around its axis before dropping back into the water), can approach divers closely (often without showing any aggressive behavior), can segregate by size, pregnant females give birth close inshore where juveniles often remain, possibly feed on small schooling fishes by swimming fast through the school with open mouth spinning along their axis and leaping out of the water (like the spinner shark).

Dangerousness for man: dangerous.

Importance for fishery in the Mediterranean: scarce importance.

Status in the Mediterranean: rare.

Kind of presence in the Mediterranean: unknown, likely occasional (the specimens recorded could have entered the Mediterranean Sea from the Red Sea through the Suez Channel).

Specimens of particular interest recorded in the Mediterranean: the largest specimen caught in this area was 210 cm long and was caught off Israel.

Species with which can be confused: none.

Main references for the Mediterranean: Ben-Tuvia (1953), Mouneimne (1977), Capapé et al. (1979), Cadenat & Blache (1981), Garrick (1982), Bauchot (1987), Moreno (1987), Capapé (1989), Moreno (1995), Barrull & Mate (2002).

Other selected non–Mediterranean related references: Bigelow & Schroeder (1948), Bass et al. (1973–1976), Johnson (1978), Garrick (1982), Castro (1983), Compagno (1984), Randall (1986), Last & Stevens (1994), Castillo-Géniz et al. (1998), White & Potter (2004).

Oceanic whitetip shark
Carcharhinus longimanus (Poey, 1861)

Classification: Order Carcharhiniformes, family Carcharhinidae, genus *Carcharhinus*.

Common names in other languages: French: requin océanique; Spanish: jaquetón de ley; Italian: longimano; German: weißspitzen-hochseehai.

Distinctive characteristics for immediate identification: snout dorso-ventrally depressed, anal fin, two dorsal fins, the second dorsal much smaller than first dorsal, eyes located laterally on head, no spiracles, first dorsal fin very large and tall, with wide apex and tall, pectoral fins very long and with wide apex, first dorsal, pectoral, pelvic and caudal fin apex with a conspicuous irregular white patch.

Morphology: first dorsal fin very large and tall, its origin over the pectoral fin inner margin. Second dorsal small. Anal fin larger than the second dorsal and with a long apex, its posterior margin deeply concave. Pectoral fins very long and wide, their apex slightly rounded. Caudal fin with relatively long lower lobe and very

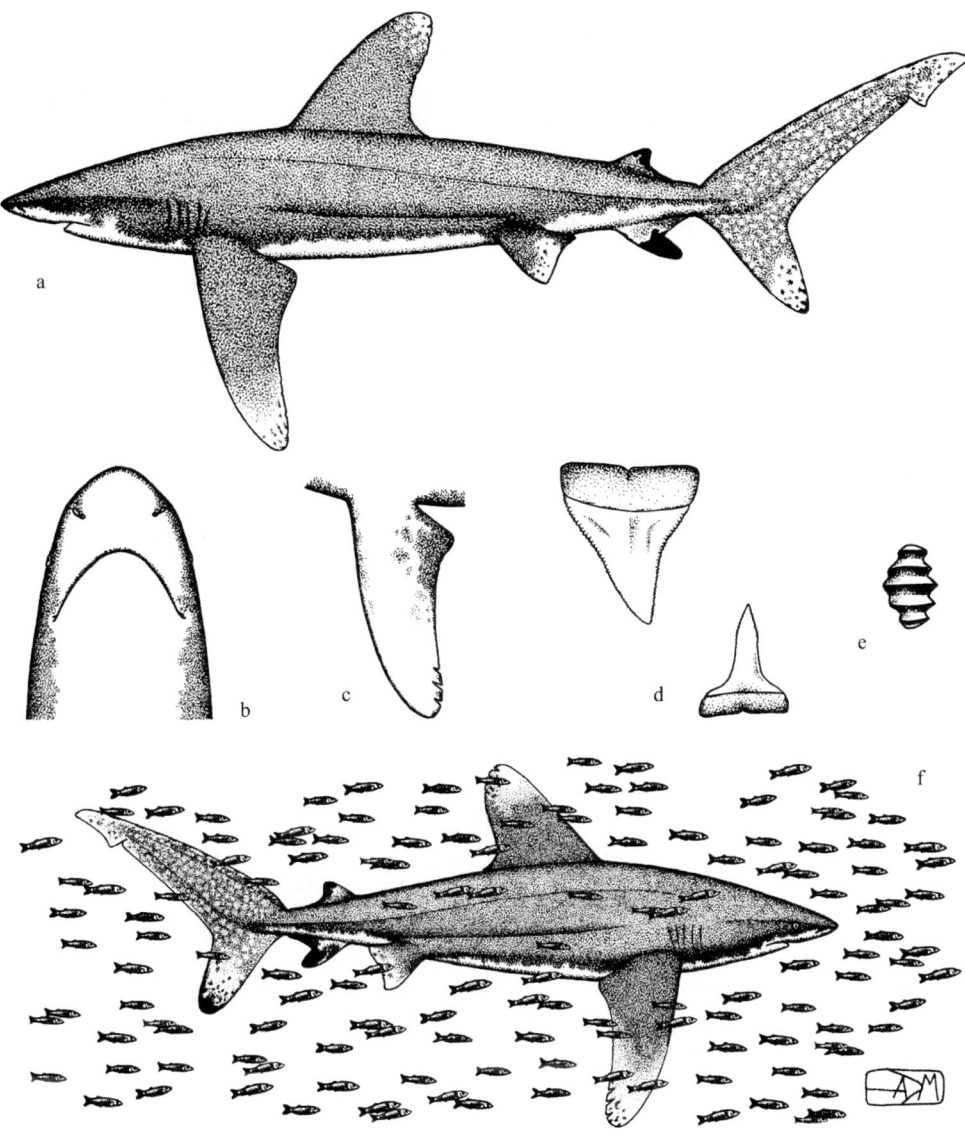

Oceanic whitetip shark (*Carcharhinus longimanus*): (a) lateral view, (b) ventral view of the head, (c) ventral view of the pectoral fin, (d) upper and lower teeth, (e) placoid scale, (f) an oceanic whitetip swims hidden behind a school of small fish.

long upper lobe with medium-sized terminal lobe. Low interdorsal ridge present or absent. Snout dorso-ventrally depressed and relatively long, rounded in dorso-ventral view. Mouth wide and parabolic in ventral view. Labial folds short. Eyes relatively small. Nostrils small. No spiracles. 5 pairs of short gill slits, the 4th and 5th located over the pectoral fin base.

Coloration: dorsal surfaces bronze-grey; ventral surfaces white. First dorsal, pectoral, pelvic and caudal fin upper and lower apex with a conspicuous irregular white patch; second dorsal and anal fins with conspicuous irregular black patch at the apex, more extended on the anal fin; additional small dark spots scattered on all fins' apex. Boundary separating dorsal from ventral coloration sharp and indented. The pectoral fin ventral surface is partially white and partially covered by the same dark indented coloration of the dorsal surface, particularly at the inner margin, free rear tip and posterior margin.

Teeth shape: upper teeth with one cusp, large, triangular, with strongly serrated edges; lower teeth smaller, with one cusp, narrow, pointed, with very finely serrated edges in the upper part, erect to oblique.

Dental formula: 14 to 15–1 to 2–14 to 15 / 13 to 15–1–13 to 15.

Maximum size: 395 cm.

Size at birth: 60–70 cm.

Size at maturity: 175–198 cm (male) and 180–200 cm (female).

Embryonic development: placental viviparous.

Gestation: about 12 months.

Litter size: 1–15 young.

Reproduction in the Mediterranean: does not reproduce in the Mediterranean.

Maximum age: at least 16 years.

Diet: bony fishes, stingrays, cephalopods, sea turtles, cetaceans, gastropods, crustaceans, carcasses.

Habitat: pelagic, on continental and insular shelves, slopes and oceanic basins, at depths ranging from the surface to at least 152 m.

Geographical distribution in the Mediterranean Sea: Western and Central Mediterranean.

Geographical distribution in the rest of the world: Atlantic, Pacific and Indian Oceans.

Behavior: active and usually slow (but able to swim at high speed), equally nocturnal and diurnal, solitary or in large to enormous groups around a food source, can approach divers closely (sometimes without showing any aggressive behavior), can segregate by sex and size, can occasionally ingest inedible items, feed on schooling fishes by simply taking bites from the tightly massed prey and possibly swimming through the school with their mouths wide open and ingesting prey that inadvertently swim into their jaws, possibly their white fin apex serves to bait prey into the strike zone (seen from a distance its white patches may appear like a school of small fishes and when the prey approaches, the shark quickly accelerates and attacks).

Dangerousness for man: highly dangerous.

Importance for fishery in the Mediterranean: no importance.

Status in the Mediterranean: very rare.

Kind of presence in the Mediterranean: occasional (the specimens recorded must have entered the Mediterranean Sea from the Eastern Atlantic Ocean through the Gibraltar Strait and from the Red Sea through the Suez Channel).

Specimens of particular interest recorded in the Mediterranean: an approximately 250 cm specimen was caught in one of the channels of Venice, Italy, Adriatic Sea, in the spring of 1978. A possible oceanic whitetip shark, estimated 300 cm long, was encountered off Martigues, France, Golfe du Lion, by a scuba diver in 1998.

Species with which can be confused: none.
Main references for the Mediterranean: Bigelow & Schroeder (1948), Cadenat & Blache (1981), Bauchot (1987), Barrull & Mate (2002), Lipej et al. (2004), R. Ilgrande (pers. comm.), M. Motti (pers. comm.).
Other selected non–Mediterranean related references: Cousteau & Cousteau (1970), Lineaweaver & Backus (1970), Bass et al. (1973–1976), Johnson (1978), Garrick (1982), Castro (1983), Compagno (1984), Randall (1986), Myrberg (1987), Last & Stevens (1994).

Blacktip reef shark
Carcharhinus melanopterus (Quoy & Gaimard, 1824)

Classification: Order Carcharhiniformes, family Carcharhinidae, genus *Carcharhinus*.
Common names in other languages: French: requin pointes noires; Spanish: jaquetón de puntas negras; Italian: squalo dalle pinne nere di scogliera; German: schwarzspitzen-riffhai.
Distinctive characteristics for immediate identification: snout dorso-ventrally depressed, anal fin, two dorsal fins, the second dorsal much smaller than first dorsal, eyes located laterally on head, no spiracles, first dorsal fin moderately large (its origin over the pectoral fin inner margin), pectoral fins relatively short, no interdorsal ridge, all fins have an irregular black patch at their apex, that is very wide on the first dorsal fin and caudal fin lower lobe.
Morphology: first dorsal fin moderately large, its origin over the pectoral fin inner margin. Second dorsal small. Anal fin about as large as the second dorsal, its posterior margin not deeply concave. Pectoral fins relatively short. Caudal fin with relatively short lower lobe and long upper lobe with medium-sized terminal lobe. No interdorsal ridge. Snout dorso-ventrally depressed and relatively short, very rounded in dorso-ventral view. Mouth wide and parabolic in ventral view. Labial folds short. Eyes relatively small. Nostrils small. No spiracles. 5 pairs of short gill slits, the 4th and 5th located over the pectoral fin base.
Coloration: dorsal surfaces light grey-brown or bronze-grey, with a conspicuous whitish band on the flanks; ventral surfaces white. All fin apexes and the caudal fin posterior margin are conspicuously black, and the black patch is particularly wide on the first dorsal fin and the caudal fin lower lobe, moreover the first dorsal fin shows a whitish area below the black patch. The pectoral fin ventral surface is white with a black patch having a sharp margin at the apex and posterior margin.
Teeth shape: upper teeth with one cusp, relatively large and moderately wide, with edges finely serrated in its upper part becoming more strongly serrated at the base, erect to oblique; lower teeth with one cusp, narrow, pointed, with very finely serrated edges, erect to oblique.
Dental formula: 12–2–12 / 11–1 to 3–11.
Maximum size: 267 cm.
Size at birth: 33–52 cm.
Size at maturity: 91–100 cm (male) and 96–112 cm (female).

Blacktip reef shark

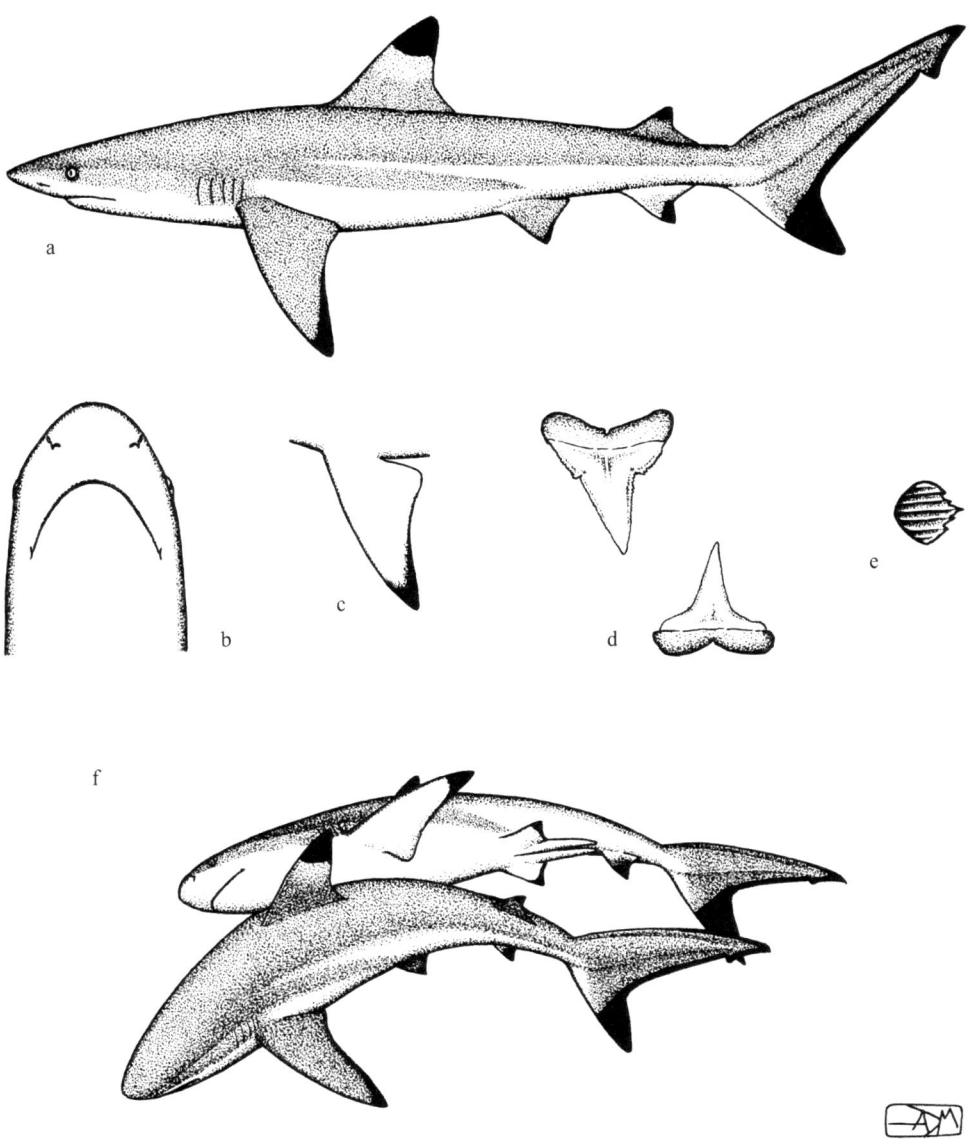

Blacktip reef shark (*Carcharhinus melanopterus*): (a) lateral view, (b) ventral view of the head, (c) ventral view of the pectoral fin, (d) upper and lower teeth, (e) placoid scale, (f) a male and a female during courtship.

Embryonic development: placental viviparous.
Gestation: 10 months.
Litter size: 2–14 young.
Reproduction in the Mediterranean: unknown.
Maximum age: unknown.
Diet: bony fishes, sharks, cephalopods, crustaceans.
Habitat: on continental and insular shelves, at depths ranging from the surface to at least 100 m. Can occur close to shore in very shallow waters, especially the juveniles.

Geographical distribution in the Mediterranean Sea: Southern Central and Eastern Mediterranean.
Geographical distribution in the rest of the world: Western and Central Pacific, Indian Oceans.
Behavior: active and fast, nocturnal, solitary or in small groups, usually timid but can approach divers closely (often without showing any aggressive behavior), can segregate by size.
Dangerousness for man: dangerous.
Importance for fishery in the Mediterranean: scarce importance.
Status in the Mediterranean: uncommon.
Kind of presence in the Mediterranean: possibly stable or maybe occasional (the specimens recorded could have entered the Mediterranean Sea from the Red Sea through the Suez Channel).
Specimens of particular interest recorded in the Mediterranean: a 267 cm pregnant female carrying 14 embryos caught in the Gulf of Gabès, Tunisia, on 7 September 1973 is the largest specimen ever reported.
Species with which can be confused: none.
Main references for the Mediterranean: Tortonese (1956), George et al. (1964), Capapé (1974a), Capapé et al. (1979), Cadenat & Blache (1981), Garrick (1982), Compagno (1984), Bauchot (1987), Capapé (1989), Moreno (1995), Golani (1996), Barrull & Mate (2002).
Other selected non–Mediterranean related references: Bass et al. (1973–1976), Johnson (1978), Garrick (1982), Randall (1986), Last & Stevens (1994), I. France Porcher (pers. comm.).

Dusky shark
Carcharhinus obscurus (Le Sueur, 1818)

Classification: Order Carcharhiniformes, family Carcharhinidae, genus *Carcharhinus*.
Common names in other languages: French: requin sombre; Spanish: jaquetón lobo; Italian: squalo bruno; German: düsterer hai.
Distinctive characteristics for immediate identification: snout dorso-ventrally depressed, anal fin, two dorsal fins, the second dorsal much smaller than first dorsal, eyes located laterally on head, no spiracles, anal fin posterior margin deeply concave, first dorsal fin relatively large (its origin over the pectoral fin inner margin), pectoral fins moderately long, interdorsal ridge.
Morphology: first dorsal fin relatively large, its origin over the pectoral fin inner margin. Second dorsal much smaller than first dorsal but still large. Anal fin about as large as the second dorsal, its posterior margin deeply concave. Pectoral fins moderately long. Caudal fin with relatively short lower lobe and long upper lobe with medium-sized terminal lobe. Low interdorsal ridge. Snout dorso-ventrally depressed and long, rounded in dorso-ventral view. Mouth wide and parabolic in ventral view. Labial folds short. Eyes relatively small. Nostrils small. No spiracles. 5 pairs of short gill slits, the 4th and 5th located over the pectoral fin base.

Dusky shark

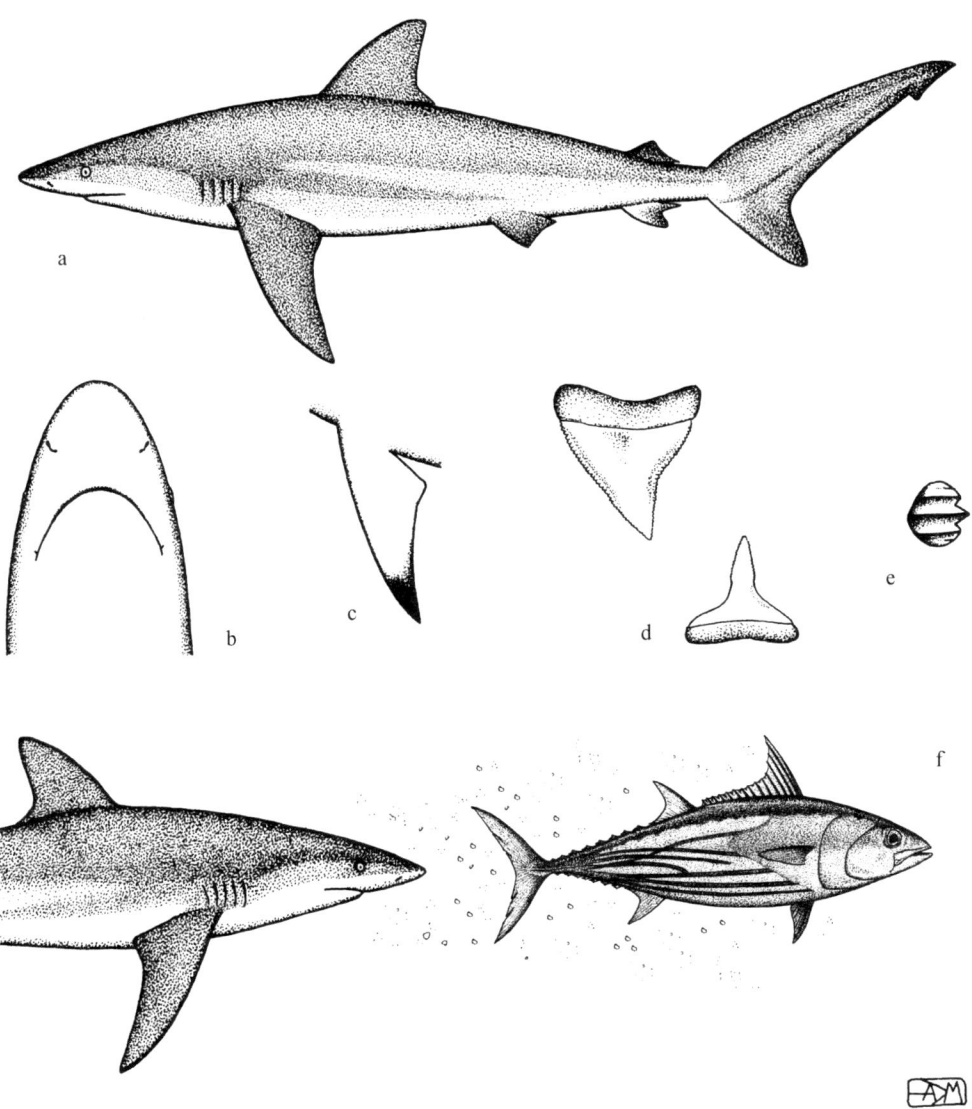

Dusky shark (*Carcharhinus obscurus*): (a) lateral view, (b) ventral view of the head, (c) ventral view of the pectoral fin, (d) upper and lower teeth, (e) placoid scale, (f) a dusky shark pursues a skipjack tuna (*Katsuwonus pelamis*).

Coloration: dorsal surfaces dark grey-brown, slightly bluish, with an inconspicuous whitish band on the flanks; ventral surfaces white. Sometimes fin apex dark, more evident on the anal fin. The pectoral fin ventral surface is white with a black patch with faded margin at the apex and posterior margin.

Teeth shape: upper teeth with one cusp, large, triangular and with serrated edges, erect to oblique; lower teeth smaller, with one cusp, narrow, pointed, with finely serrated edges, erect to oblique.

Dental formula: 14 to 15–1 to 3–14 to 15 / 14 to 15–1 to 3–14 to 15.

Maximum size: 400 cm.

Size at birth: 75–100 cm.
Size at maturity: about 280 cm (male) and 257–300 cm (female).
Embryonic development: placental viviparous.
Gestation: possibly 8–9 or 16 months.
Litter size: 3–14 young.
Reproduction in the Mediterranean: unknown.
Maximum age: at least 45 years.
Diet: bony fishes, elasmobranchs, crustaceans, cephalopods, cetaceans, bryozoans, barnacles, carcasses.
Habitat: pelagic, on continental and insular shelves and oceanic basins, at depths ranging from the surface to at least 400 m. Pregnant females can give birth in shallow waters that are preferred by juveniles.
Geographical distribution in the Mediterranean Sea: all Mediterranean.
Geographical distribution in the rest of the world: Atlantic, Pacific and Indian Oceans.
Behavior: active and fast, solitary or in large groups, migratory, can approach divers closely (usually without showing any aggressive behavior), can segregate by size, can occasionally ingest inedible items.
Dangerousness for man: dangerous.
Importance for fishery in the Mediterranean: scarce importance.
Status in the Mediterranean: uncommon.
Kind of presence in the Mediterranean: possibly occasional (the specimens recorded must have entered the Mediterranean Sea from the Eastern Atlantic Ocean through the Gibraltar Strait and possibly from the Red Sea from the Suez Channel).
Specimens of particular interest recorded in the Mediterranean: the largest specimen ever reported was a 400 cm pregnant female carrying 7 term embryos caught off Sidi Daoud, Tunisia. Another large specimen was a 349 cm female caught off Mazara del Vallo, Sicily, Italy, on 6 August 1983.
Species with which can be confused: the sandbar shark (*Carcharhinus plumbeus*) and the bignose shark (*Carcharhinus altimus*); but both these species have wider pectoral fins, moreover the sandbar shark has a larger first dorsal fin (usually much larger and taller) with its origin over the pectoral fin base or its axil and a shorter snout, and the bignose shark usually has a longer snout.
Main references for the Mediterranean: Capapé *et al.* (1979), Cadenat & Blache (1981), Bauchot (1987), Moreno (1987), Tortonese (1987), Moreno (1995), Fergusson & Compagno (2000), Barrull & Mate (2002), Hemida *et al.* (2002), Zogaris & De Maddalena (2014).
Other selected non–Mediterranean related references: Bigelow & Schroeder (1948), Bass *et al.* (1973–1976), Garrick (1982), Castro (1983), Compagno (1984), Randall (1986), Smale (1991), Last & Stevens (1994), Natanson *et al.* (1995).

Sandbar shark
Carcharhinus plumbeus (Nardo, 1827)

Classification: Order Carcharhiniformes, family Carcharhinidae, genus *Carcharhinus*.

Sandbar shark

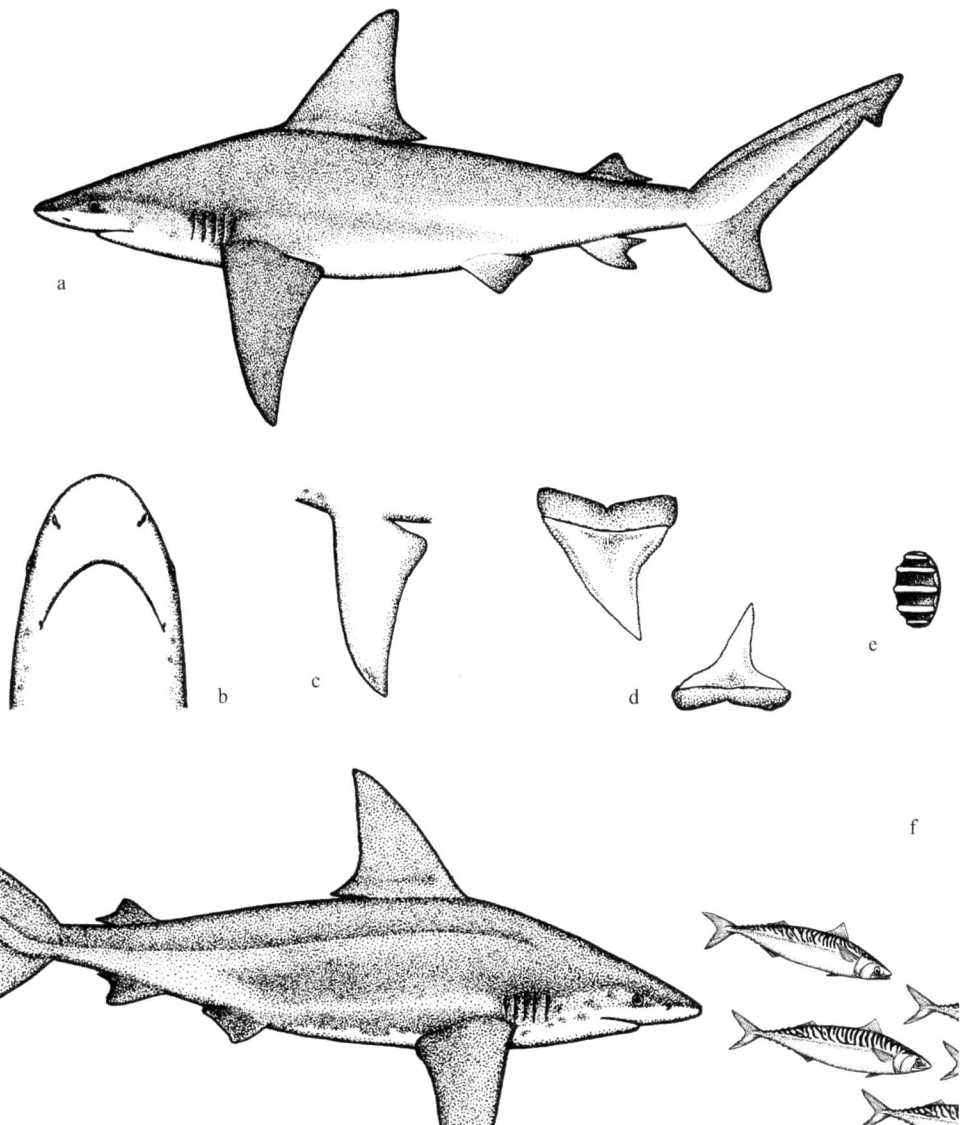

Sandbar shark (*Carcharhinus plumbeus*): (a) lateral view, (b) ventral view of the head, (c) ventral view of the pectoral fin, (d) upper and lower teeth, (e) placoid scale, (f) a sandbar shark catches a school of Atlantic mackerels (*Scomber scombrus*).

Common names in other languages: French: requin gris; Spanish: jaquetón de Milberto; Italian: squalo grigio; German: sandbankhai.

Distinctive characteristics for immediate identification: snout dorso-ventrally depressed, anal fin, two dorsal fins, the second dorsal much smaller than first dorsal, eyes located laterally on head, no spiracles, anal fin posterior margin deeply concave, first dorsal fin large to enormous and very tall (its origin over the pectoral fin base or its axil), pectoral fins long and wide, interdorsal ridge.

Morphology: first dorsal fin large to enormous, usually very tall, its origin over the pectoral fin base or its axil. Second dorsal relatively small. Anal fin about as large as the second dorsal, its posterior margin deeply concave. Pectoral fins long and wide. Caudal fin with relatively short lower lobe and long upper lobe with medium-sized terminal lobe. Body relatively stout, its dorsal part pronounced. Narrow inter-dorsal ridge. Snout dorso-ventrally depressed and short, rounded in dorso-ventral view. Mouth wide and parabolic in ventral view. Labial folds short. Eyes relatively small. Nostrils small. No spiracles. 5 pairs of short gill slits, the 4th and 5th located over the pectoral fin base.

Coloration: dorsal surfaces grey-brown, with an inconspicuous whitish band on the flanks; ventral surfaces white. The pectoral fin ventral surface is whitish but darker at the apex, posterior margin and anterior margin.

Teeth shape: upper teeth with one cusp, large, triangular and with serrated edges, erect to oblique; lower teeth smaller, with one cusp, narrow, pointed, with edges very finely serrated in its upper part and cutting in the lower part, erect to oblique.

Dental formula: 14 to 16–2–14 to 16 / 12 to 15–1–12 to 15.

Maximum size: 249 cm.

Size at birth: 56–75 cm.

Size at maturity: 130 cm (male) and 147 cm (female).

Embryonic development: placental viviparous.

Gestation: 9–12 months.

Litter size: 1 to at least 14 and perhaps to 18 young.

Reproduction in the Mediterranean: reproduces in the area; data indicates in particular parturition must occur in the Adriatic Sea and the Ionian Sea.

Maximum age: at least 30 years and possibly up to 50.

Diet: bony fishes, elasmobranchs, molluscs, crustaceans.

Habitat: pelagic, on continental and insular shelves and upper slopes, at depths ranging from the surface to at least 315 m. Pregnant females give birth in shallow waters where newborns remain.

Geographical distribution in the Mediterranean Sea: all Mediterranean.

Geographical distribution in the rest of the world: Atlantic, Pacific and Indian Oceans.

Behavior: active and fast, primarily nocturnal, solitary or in large groups, migratory, timid, can segregate by sex and size, pregnant females can give birth close inshore, where juveniles often remain.

Dangerousness for man: potentially dangerous.

Importance for fishery in the Mediterranean: scarce importance.

Status in the Mediterranean: uncommon.

Kind of presence in the Mediterranean: stable.

Specimens of particular interest recorded in the Mediterranean: among the largest specimens recorded in the area were a 203 cm female caught off Algerian coast between 1996 and 2002, and a 185 cm female caught off Trieste, Italy, Adriatic Sea, in 1869.

Species with which can be confused: the dusky shark (*Carcharhinus obscurus*) and the bignose shark (*Carcharhinus altimus*); but usually both these species have a longer snout, a smaller first dorsal fin with its origin over the pectoral fin inner margin and a more rounded pectoral fin anterior margin, moreover the dusky shark has narrower pectoral fins.

Main references for the Mediterranean: Lo Bianco (1909), Tortonese (1938), Tortonese (1956), Capapé (1974a), Capapé et al. (1979), Cadenat & Blache (1981), Bauchot (1987), Moreno (1987), Capapé (1989), Vanni (1992), Moreno (1995), Mizzan (1996), Kovacic (1998), Lipej et al. (2000), Barrull & Mate (2002), Hemida et al. (2002), Costantini & Affronte (2003), Lipej et al. (2004), Zogaris & De Maddalena (2014).

Other selected non–Mediterranean related references: Bigelow & Schroeder (1948), Springer (1960), Bass et al. (1973–1976), Garrick (1982), Castro (1983), Compagno (1984), Casey et al. (1985), Randall (1986), Casey & Natanson (1992), Last & Stevens (1994), Sminkey & Music (1995), Kohler et al. (1996).

Tiger shark
Galeocerdo cuvier (Peron & LeSueur, 1822)

Classification: Order Carcharhiniformes, family Carcharhinidae, genus *Galeocerdo*.
Common names in other languages: French: requin tigre; Spanish: tiburón tigre; Italian: squalo tigre; German: tigerhai.
Distinctive characteristics for immediate identification: snout dorso-ventrally depressed, anal fin, two dorsal fins, second dorsal much smaller than first dorsal, eyes located laterally on head, short snout with an almost straight anterior margin, spiracle small, upper labial folds very long, caudal fin upper lobe long and narrow, anal and pelvic fins falcate, small caudal keels, large size (from 76 to 740 cm), coloration usually dark striped.
Morphology: first dorsal fin relatively large, its origin over the pectoral fin inner margin or the free rear tip or posterior to it. Second dorsal small. Anal fin larger then the second dorsal, falcate, its posterior margin deeply concave. Pelvic fins falcate. Pectoral fins relatively short. Caudal fin with relatively short lower lobe and long and narrow upper lobe with small terminal lobe. Small caudal keels. Anterior part of the body massive, posterior relatively slender. Interdorsal ridge. Snout dorso-ventrally depressed and short, its anterior margin almost straight in dorso-ventral view. Mouth very wide and parabolic in ventral view. Upper labial folds very long. Eyes relatively small. Nostrils moderately large. Spiracles small. 5 pairs of short gill slits, the 4th and 5th located over the pectoral fin base.
Coloration: dorsal surfaces dark grey-brown, with dark vertical stripes and patches very evident in young and fading or absent in adults; ventral surfaces white. Boundary separating dorsal from ventral coloration sharp and indented. The pectoral fin ventral surface is partially white, with an extended grayish area at the apex, posterior margin and anterior margin.
Teeth shape: upper teeth with one cusp, large, cockscomb-shaped, with a large notch on the lateral margin and strongly serrated edges (the large serrae are themselves secondarily serrated); lower teeth similar.
Dental formula: 9 to 13–1–8 to 13 / 9 to 13–1—9 to 13.

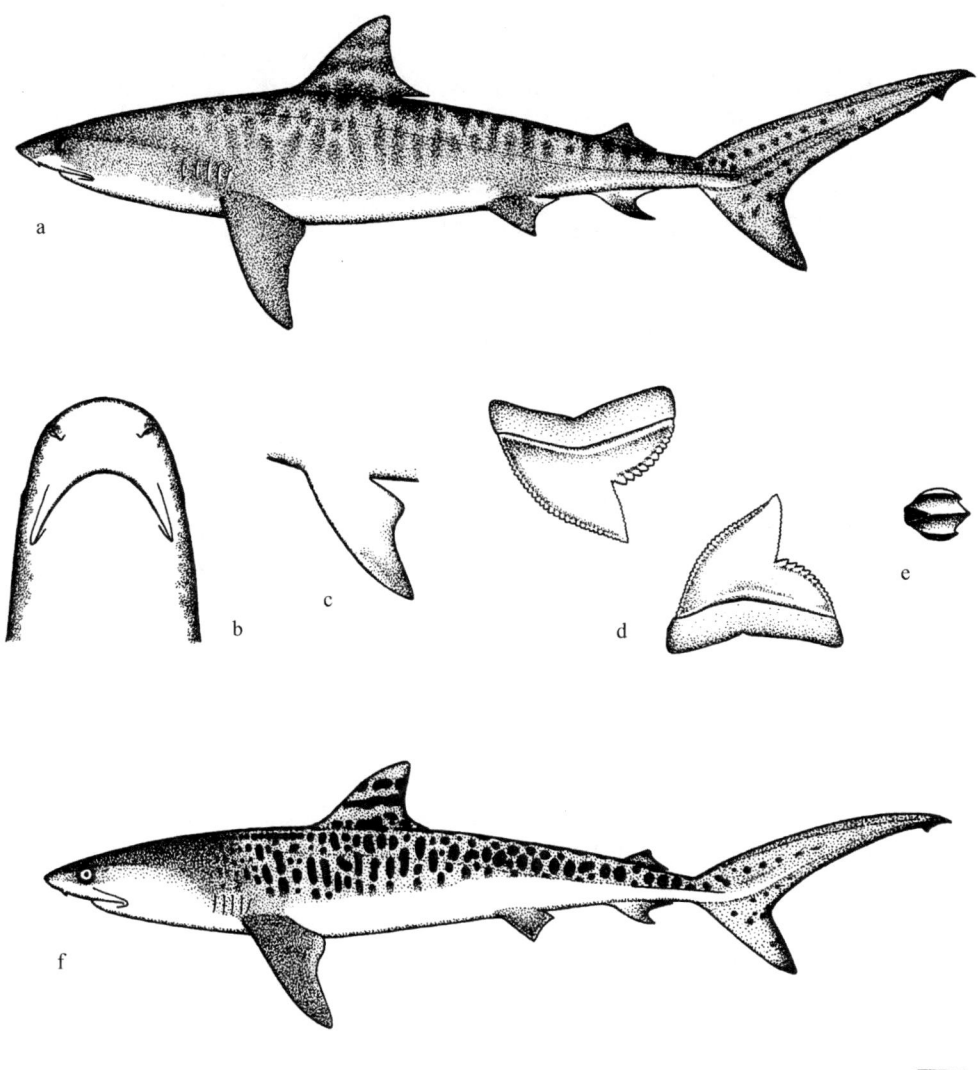

Tiger shark (*Galeocerdo cuvier*): (a) lateral view, (b) ventral view of the head, (c) ventral view of the pectoral fin, (d) upper and lower teeth, (e) placoid scale, (f) newborn tiger shark.

Maximum size: at least 740 cm, possibly up to 910 cm.
Size at birth: 51–76 cm.
Size at maturity: 226–290 cm (male) and 250–350 cm (female).
Embryonic development: aplacental viviparous.
Gestation: possibly over 12 months.
Litter size: 10–82 young.
Reproduction in the Mediterranean: does not reproduce in the Mediterranean.
Maximum age: at least 27 years.
Diet: bony fishes, elasmobranchs, marine mammals, marine reptiles, cephalopods, gastropods, crustaceans, birds, marine mammals, tunicates, jellyfishes, carcasses.

Habitat: pelagic, on continental and insular shelves, at depths ranging from the surface to at least 305 m., live offshore during the day and move close inshore at night.
Geographical distribution in the Mediterranean Sea: Western and Central Mediterranean.
Geographical distribution in the rest of the world: Atlantic, Pacific and Indian Oceans.
Behavior: active and slow (but able to swim at high speed), primarily nocturnal, solitary or in small groups around a source of food, migratory, can approach divers closely (sometimes without showing any aggressive behavior), often ingests inedible items.
Dangerousness for man: highly dangerous.
Importance for fishery in the Mediterranean: no importance.
Status in the Mediterranean: very rare.
Kind of presence in the Mediterranean: occasional (the specimens recorded must have entered the Mediterranean Sea from the Eastern Atlantic Ocean through the Gibraltar Strait and possibly from the Red Sea through the Suez Channel).
Specimens of particular interest recorded in the Mediterranean: only four specimens have been recorded from the Mediterranean: a 200 cm male caught off Algeciras, Spain in 1981 (preserved in the Laboratorio de Vertebrados, Faculdad de Biologìa, Universidad Complutense de Madrid), an approximately 300 cm specimen caught off rìo Moulouya between Morocco and Algeria, Sea of Alboran, a 400 cm specimen caught in June 1991 off Manilva, Spain (jaws preserved in the Museo-Acuario Aula del Mar in Málaga) and an approximately 300 cm female caught in July 1998 off Maregrosso, Sicily, Italy. A tooth of this species was found on a beach in San Benedetto del Tronto, Italy, Adriatic Sea, in September 2002.
Species with which can be confused: none.
Main references for the Mediterranean: Cadenat & Blache (1981), Bauchot (1987), De La Rosa (1994), Celona (2001), Barrull & Mate (2002), J.A. Moreno (pers. comm.).
Other selected non–Mediterranean related references: Bigelow & Schroeder (1948), Fourmanoir (1961), Bass *et al.* (1973–1976), Johnson (1978), Castro (1983), Compagno (1984), Randall (1986), Clark & Kristof (1991), Last & Stevens (1994), Natanson *et al.* (1999).

Blue shark
Prionace glauca (Linnaeus, 1758)

Classification: Order Carcharhiniformes, family Carcharhinidae, genus *Prionace*.
Common names in other languages: French: peau bleue; Spanish: tintorera; Italian: verdesca, squalo azzurro; German: blauhai.
Distinctive characteristics for immediate identification: snout dorso-ventrally depressed, anal fin, two dorsal fins, the second dorsal much smaller than first dorsal, eyes located laterally on head, no spiracles, snout very long and narrow, pectoral fins very long and narrow, small caudal keels, eyes large, coloration bright blue.
Morphology: first dorsal fin relatively large, its origin well posterior to the pectoral fin free rear tip. Second dorsal small. Anal fin about large as the second dorsal. Pectoral

Blue shark

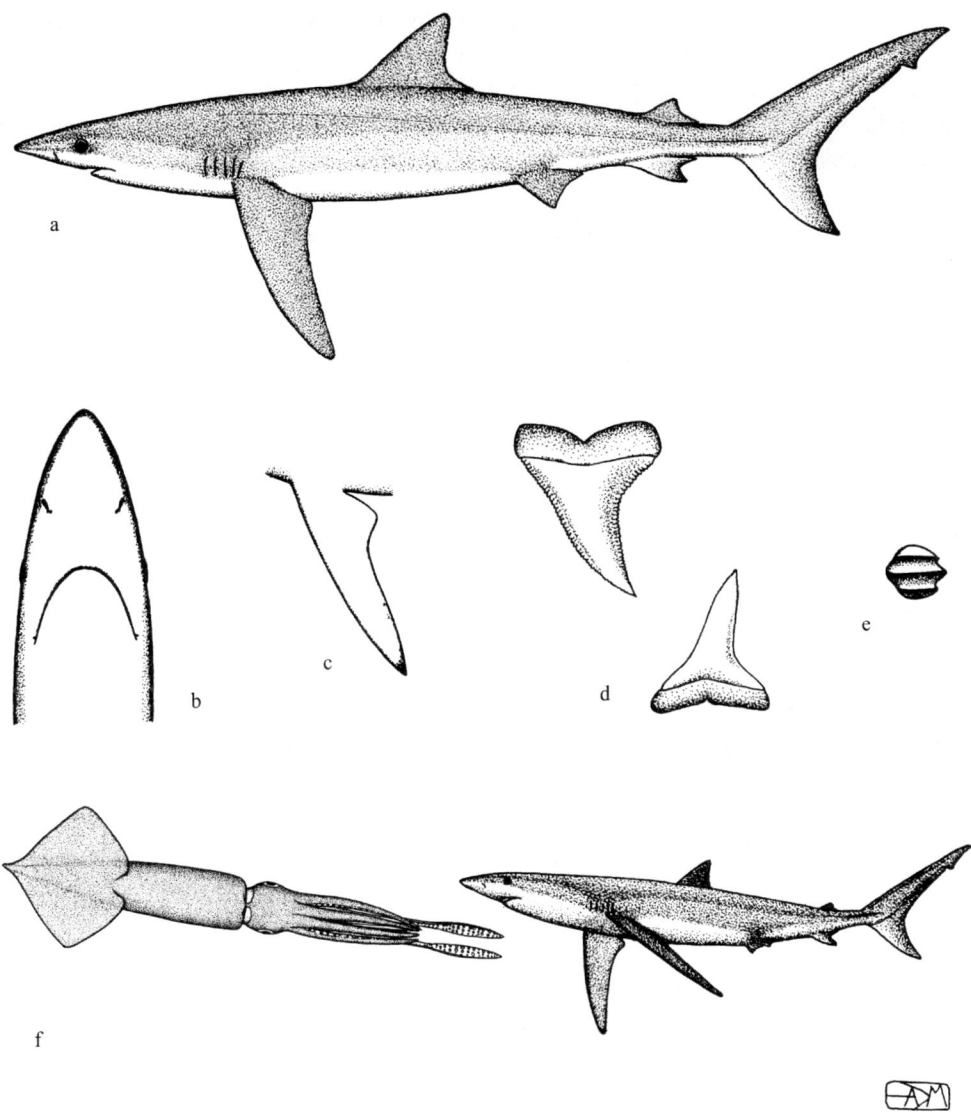

Blue shark (*Prionace glauca*): (a) lateral view, (b) ventral view of the head, (c) ventral view of the pectoral fin, (d) upper and lower teeth, (e) placoid scale, (f) a blue shark pursues a large flying squid (*Todarodes sagittatus*).

fins very long and narrow. Caudal fin with moderately long lower lobe and much longer and narrow upper lobe with large terminal lobe. Small caudal keels. Body slender. No interdorsal ridge. Snout very long and narrow. Mouth wide and parabolic in ventral view. Labial folds short. Eyes large. Nostrils small. No spiracles. 5 pairs of short gill slits, the 4th and 5th located over the pectoral fin base.

Coloration: dorsal surfaces bright blue, sometimes iridescent; ventral surfaces white. The fin apex and posterior margins have a narrow and inconspicuous black band. The pectoral fin ventral surface is white with a small black patch at the apex and a narrow black band on the posterior margin.

Teeth shape: upper teeth with one cusp, large, long, relatively narrow, curved, oblique, with strongly serrated edges; lower teeth with one cusp, narrower, oblique, with edges finely serrated in the upper part and smooth at the base.
Dental formula: 14 to 16–1 to 2–14 to 16 / 13 to 16–1 to 4–13 to 16.
Maximum size: 383 cm.
Size at birth: 35–52 cm.
Size at maturity: 175–281 cm (male) and 145–221 cm (female).
Embryonic development: placental viviparous.
Gestation: 9–12 months.
Litter size: 3–135 young.
Reproduction in the Mediterranean: reproduces in the Mediterranean; data indicates parturition must occur in the Adriatic Sea.
Maximum age: at least 20 years.
Diet: molluscs, bony fishes and their eggs, sharks, crustaceans, cetaceans, nematodes, birds, carcasses.
Habitat: pelagic, on continental and insular shelves and oceanic basins, at depths ranging from the surface to at least 610 m. Offshore during the day but can move close inshore at night. Pregnant females give birth in shallower waters.
Geographical distribution in the Mediterranean Sea: all Mediterranean.
Geographical distribution in the rest of the world: Atlantic, Pacific and Indian Oceans.
Behavior: active and fast, primarily nocturnal, solitary or in large to enormous groups around a source of food, migratory, can approach divers closely (usually without showing any aggressive behavior), can segregate by sex and size, feed on schooling fishes and squids by simply taking bites from the tightly massed prey by swimming through the school with their mouths wide open and ingesting prey that inadvertently swim into their jaws, females can preserve the sperm for long periods.
Dangerousness for man: dangerous.
Importance for fishery in the Mediterranean: notable importance.
Status in the Mediterranean: relatively common.
Kind of presence in the Mediterranean: stable.
Specimens of particular interest recorded in the Mediterranean: chondrocranium and jaws of an estimated 380 cm specimen caught off Nice, France, Ligurian Sea, in 1899 and preserved in the Národní muzeum in Prague may represent the largest specimen preserved worldwide and the largest reported from the Mediterranean. Another of the largest specimens ever reported was about 350 cm long and was caught off Pescara, Italy, Western Adriatic Sea, on 11 July 2002.
Species with which can be confused: none.
Main references for the Mediterranean: Tortonese (1956), Capapé (1977), Cadenat & Blache (1981), Bauchot (1987), Vanni (1992), Moreno (1995), Bianchi *et al.* (1997), Clò & Bianchi (1997), Politi (1997), Pomi (1997), Buencuerpo *et al.* (1998), Barrull *et al.* (1999), De Maddalena & Piscitelli (2001), Barrull & Mate (2002), de la Serna *et al.* (2002), Cugini & De Maddalena (2003), Lipej *et al.* (2004), Patokina & Litvinov (2004), Šanda & De Maddalena (2004).
Other selected non–Mediterranean related references: Bigelow & Schroeder (1948),

Bass *et al.* (1973–1976), Sciarrotta & Nelson (1977), Castro (1983), Compagno (1984), Last & Stevens (1994), Skomal & Natanson (2002), Acuña & Villaroel (2003).

Milk shark
Rhizoprionodon acutus (Rüppell, 1837)

Classification: Order Carcharhiniformes, family Carcharhinidae, genus *Rhizoprionodon*.

Common names in other languages: French: requin à museau pointu; Spanish: tiburón lechoso; Italian: squalo latteo; German: milchhai.

Distinctive characteristics for immediate identification: snout dorso-ventrally depressed, anal fin, two dorsal fins, the second dorsal much smaller than first dorsal, eyes located laterally on head, no spiracles, anal fin with elongated pre-anal ridges, large eyes, long snout, short pectoral fins.

Morphology: first dorsal fin relatively large, its origin over the pectoral fin free rear tip. Second dorsal small. Anal fin larger than the second dorsal, with a long free rear tip, elongated pre-anal ridges and its posterior margin slightly concave. Pectoral fins short. Caudal fin with relatively short lower lobe and long upper lobe with medium-sized terminal lobe. Interdorsal ridge absent or low. Snout long. Mouth wide and parabolic in ventral view. Labial folds relatively short. Eyes large. Nostrils relatively small. No spiracles. 5 pairs of short gill slits, the 4th and 5th located over the pectoral fin base.

Coloration: dorsal surfaces grey, grey-brown or purplish brown; ventral surfaces white. Pectoral, pelvic, anal posterior margins and caudal fin upper lobe posterior margin light. In juveniles, the dorsal fin apex and caudal fin upper lobe are dark.

Teeth shape: upper teeth with one cusp, oblique, with edges finely serrated or cutting; lower teeth similar.

Dental formula: 12-1-12 / 12-12.

Maximum size: 178 cm.

Size at birth: 24–41 cm.

Size at maturity: 68–72 cm (male) and 70–81 cm (female).

Embryonic development: placental viviparous.

Gestation: 12 months.

Litter size: 1–8 young.

Reproduction in the Mediterranean: does not reproduce in the Mediterranean.

Maximum age: at least 8 years.

Diet: bony fishes, cephalopods, crustaceans, gastropods.

Habitat: pelagic, on continental shelves, at depths ranging from the surface to at least 490 m.

Geographical distribution in the Mediterranean Sea: Central Mediterranean.

Geographical distribution in the rest of the world: Eastern Atlantic, Pacific and Western Indian Oceans.

Behavior: active and fast, pregnant females can give birth close inshore, where juveniles often remain.

Milk shark

Milk shark (*Rhizoprionodon acutus*): (a) lateral view, (b) ventral view of the head, (c) ventral view of the pectoral fin, (d) upper and lower teeth, (e) a milk shark being attacked by a shortfin mako (*Isurus oxyrinchus*).

Dangerousness for man: not dangerous.
Importance for fishery in the Mediterranean: no importance.
Status in the Mediterranean: very rare.
Kind of presence in the Mediterranean: occasional (the specimens recorded must have entered the Mediterranean Sea from the Eastern Atlantic Ocean through the Gibraltar Strait or from the Red Sea through the Suez Channel).
Specimens of particular interest recorded in the Mediterranean: only one specimen

was reported from the Mediterranean, a 72.5 cm female caught off Taranto, Italy, Ionian Sea, around 1984 (preserved in the Museo civico di Storia Naturale di Verona).

Species with which can be confused: none.

Main references for the Mediterranean: Pastore & Tortonese (1984).

Other selected non–Mediterranean related references: Springer (1964), Bass *et al.* (1973–1976), Castro (1983), Compagno (1984), Randall (1986), Last & Stevens (1994), Patokina & Litvinov (2004), White & Potter (2004).

Scalloped hammerhead

Sphyrna lewini (Griffith & Smith, 1834)

Classification: Order Carcharhiniformes, family Sphyrnidae, genus *Sphyrna*.

Common names in other languages: French: requin-marteau halicorne; Spanish: cornuda negra; Italian: pesce martello smerlato; German: bogenstirn-hammerhai.

Distinctive characteristics for immediate identification: very wide hammer-shaped head, its anterior margin curved with a median notch and its posterior margin concave, second dorsal fin small, anal fin larger.

Morphology: very wide hammer-shaped head (also called "cephalofoil"), dorsoventrally depressed and expanded laterally, its anterior margin curved with a median notch and its posterior margin concave. First dorsal large and tall, its origin over the pectoral fin free rear tip. Second dorsal small with a long free rear tip. Anal fin larger than the second dorsal and falcate. Pectoral fins relatively short. Caudal fin with relatively short lower lobe and long upper lobe with medium-sized terminal lobe. Dorsal part pronounced. Mouth wide and parabolic in ventral view. Labial folds short. Eyes small. Nostrils long. No spiracles. 5 pairs of gill slits, the 4th and 5th located over the pectoral fin base.

Coloration: dorsal surfaces grey-brown or olive or bronzy; ventral surfaces white. Pectoral fin ventral surface with a small black patch with faded margin at the apex. Rare cases of albino specimens exist.

Teeth shape: upper teeth with one cusp, with finely serrated edges; lower teeth similar. In juveniles, the teeth lack serration.

Dental formula: 15 to 16–1 to 2–15 to 16 / 15 to 16–1–15 to 16.

Maximum size: 370–420 cm and possibly over.

Size at birth: 38–50 cm.

Size at maturity: 140–210 (male) and 200–230 cm (female).

Embryonic development: placental viviparous.

Gestation: 9–10 months.

Litter size: 13–38 young.

Reproduction in the Mediterranean: does not reproduce in the Mediterranean.

Maximum age: at least 15 years.

Diet: bony fishes, elasmobranchs, molluscs, crustaceans, sea snakes.

Habitat: pelagic, on continental and insular shelves, at depths ranging from the surface to at least 275 m. Pregnant females give birth close inshore where newborns remain.

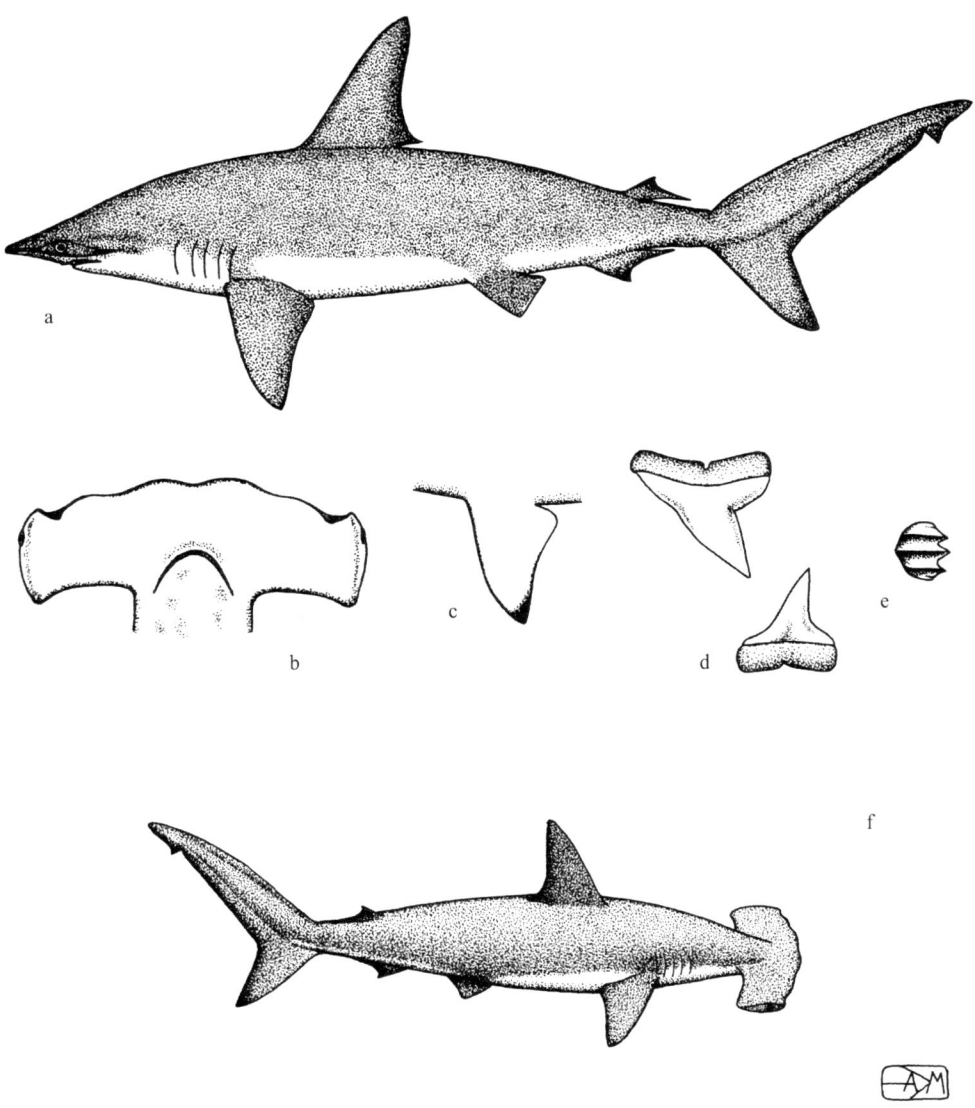

Scalloped hammerhead (*Sphyrna lewini*): (a) lateral view, (b) ventral view of the head, (c) ventral view of the pectoral fin, (d) upper and lower teeth, (e) placoid scale; (f) a scalloped hammerhead swimming.

Geographical distribution in the Mediterranean Sea: unknown.
Geographical distribution in the rest of the world: Atlantic, Pacific and Indian Oceans.
Behavior: active and fast, primarily nocturnal, solitary or in enormous groups, migratory, usually timid but can approach divers closely (usually without showing aggressive behavior), can segregate by sex and size, show a social hierarchy and a complex social behavior, use their hammer-shaped head (that has a wide electroreceptive area) to detect and scoop up rays buried under sand and probably pin them to the sea floor while taking bites from their body (other functions of the cephalofoil are

an increase of swimming maneuverability, maybe increasing sensitivity to vibrations, visual stereoscopy and increased olfactory sensibility).
Dangerousness for man: potentially dangerous.
Importance for fishery in the Mediterranean: scarce importance.
Status in the Mediterranean: very rare.
Kind of presence in the Mediterranean: occasional (the specimens recorded must have entered the Mediterranean Sea from the Eastern Atlantic Ocean through the Gibraltar Strait or from the Red Sea through the Suez Channel).
Specimens of particular interest recorded in the Mediterranean: a scalloped hammerhead from the Mediterranean is preserved in the British Museum of Natural History in London (United Kingdom).
Species with which can be confused: the great hammerhead (*Sphyrna mokarran*), the golden hammerhead (*Sphyrna tudes*) and the smooth hammerhead (*Sphyrna zygaena*), but their hammers have a different shape: the great hammerhead has the anterior margin almost straight with a median notch and its posterior margin slightly concave, the smalleye hammerhead has the anterior margin curved with a median notch and its posterior margin about straight, and the smooth hammerhead has the anterior margin curved without a median notch and its posterior margin concave.
Main references for the Mediterranean: Tortonese (1956), Tortonese (1987), Séret (1999), Cadenat & Blache (1981), Bauchot (1987).
Other selected non–Mediterranean related references: Bigelow & Schroeder (1948), Gilbert (1967), Clarke (1971), Bass *et al.* (1973–1976), Castro (1983), Compagno (1984), Randall (1986), McEachran & Séret (1987), Chen *et al.* (1988), Klimley *et al.* (1988), Stevens & Lyle (1989), Holland *et al.* (1993), Last & Stevens (1994), Liu *et al.* (1999), Kajiura (2001), Kajiura & Holland (2002).

Great hammerhead
Sphyrna mokarran (Rüppell, 1837)

Classification: Order Carcharhiniformes, family Sphyrnidae, genus *Sphyrna*.
Common names in other languages: French: grand requin-marteau; Spanish: tiburón martillo; Italian: pesce martello maggiore; German: großer Hammerhai.
Distinctive characteristics for immediate identification: very wide hammer-shaped head, its anterior margin almost straight with a median notch and its posterior margin slightly concave, first dorsal, pectoral, anal and caudal fins strongly falcate, second dorsal fin tall and as large as the anal fin.
Morphology: very wide hammer-shaped head (also called "cephalofoil"), dorso-ventrally depressed and laterally expanded, its anterior margin almost straight with a median notch and its posterior margin slightly concave. First dorsal, pectoral, anal and caudal fins strongly falcate. First dorsal large and very tall, its origin over the pectoral fin inner margin. Second dorsal much smaller than the first dorsal but relatively large and tall. Anal fin about as large as the second dorsal. Pelvic fins long. Pectoral fins relatively short. Caudal fin with long and narrow lower lobe and very long and narrow upper lobe with small terminal lobe. Dorsal part pronounced. Mouth wide

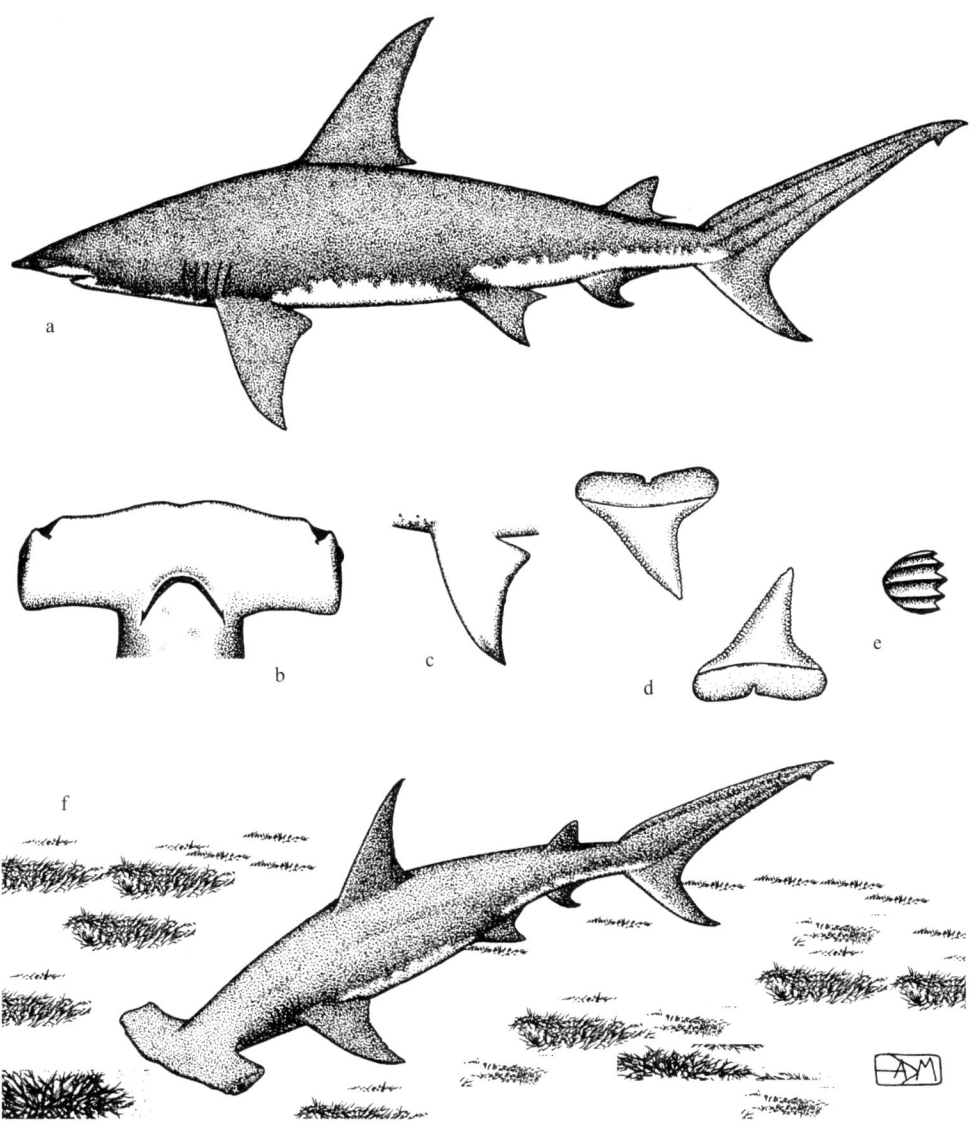

Great hammerhead (*Sphyrna mokarran*): (a) lateral view, (b) ventral view of the head, (c) ventral view of the pectoral fin, (d) upper and lower teeth, (e) placoid scale, (f) a great hammerhead uses the wide electroreceptive area of its head to detect prey buried under sand.

and parabolic in ventral view. Labial folds short. Eyes small. Nostrils long. No spiracles. 5 pairs of gill slits, the 4th and 5th located over the pectoral fin base.

Coloration: dorsal surfaces bronze-olive-grey; ventral surfaces whitish. Boundary separating dorsal from ventral coloration sharp and indented. The pectoral fin ventral surface has a dark band on the apex and posterior margin. Rare cases of albino specimens exist.

Teeth shape: upper teeth with one cusp, triangular, oblique and strongly serrated; lower teeth similar.

Great hammerhead

Dental formula: 17–2 to 3–17 / 17–1–17.
Maximum size: at least 550–610 cm and possibly larger.
Size at birth: 50–70 cm.
Size at maturity: 225–269 cm (male) and 210–300 cm (female).
Embryonic development: placental viviparous.
Gestation: 11 months.
Litter size: 6–45 young.
Reproduction in the Mediterranean: likely does not reproduce in the Mediterranean.
Maximum age: unknown.
Diet: bony fishes, elasmobranchs, crustaceans, molluscs, sea cucumbers, marine turtles, carcasses.
Habitat: pelagic, on continental and insular shelves, slopes and oceanic basins, at depths ranging from the surface to at least 80 m.
Geographical distribution in the Mediterranean Sea: Western Mediterranean.
Geographical distribution in the rest of the world: Atlantic, Pacific and Indian Oceans.
Behavior: active and fast, primarily nocturnal, solitary or in pairs, migratory, can approach divers closely (often without showing aggressive behavior), rarely ingest inedible items, use their hammer-shaped head (that has a wider electroreceptive area) to detect and scoop up rays buried under sand and pin them to the sea floor while taking bites from their body (other functions of the cephalofoil are increasing of swimming maneuverability, possibly increasing sensitivity to vibration detection, visual stereoscopy and increased olfactory sensibility).
Dangerousness for man: dangerous.
Importance for fishery in the Mediterranean: no importance.
Status in the Mediterranean: very rare.
Kind of presence in the Mediterranean: unknown.
Specimens of particular interest recorded in the Mediterranean: only one capture of this species has been recorded from the area: an approximately 300 cm specimen was caught in the tuna-trap off Camogli, Ligurian Sea, Italy, on 21 September 1969; the hammerhead had a harpoon like those used in the Southern Tyrrhenian Sea to catch swordfish, embedded in its body.
Species with which can be confused: the golden hammerhead (*Sphyrna tudes*), the smooth hammerhead (*Sphyrna zygaena*) and the scalloped hammerhead (*Sphyrna lewini*), but they have a smaller second dorsal fin, first dorsal and pelvic fins not falcate and their hammer has a different shape: the smalleye hammerhead has the anterior margin curved with a median notch and its posterior margin nearly straight, the smooth hammerhead has the anterior margin curved without a median notch and its posterior margin concave, and the scalloped hammerhead has the anterior margin curved with a median notch and its posterior margin concave.
Main references for the Mediterranean: Boero & Carli (1977), Cadenat & Blache (1981), Bauchot (1987), Moreno (1995), de la Serna *et al.* (2002).
Other selected non–Mediterranean related references: Bigelow & Schroeder (1948), Gilbert (1967), Bass *et al.* (1973–1976), Castro (1983), Compagno (1984), Randall (1986), Stevens & Lyle (1989), Strong *et al.* (1990), Last & Stevens (1994), Cliff (1995), Martin (1995), Chapman & Gruber (2002), J. Abernethy (pers. comm.).

Golden hammerhead or smalleye hammerhead
Sphyrna tudes (Valenciennes, 1822)

Classification: Order Carcharhiniformes, family Sphyrnidae, genus *Sphyrna*.
Common names in other languages: French: requin-marteau à petits yeux; Spanish: cornuda ojichica; Italian: pesce martello dorato; German: kleinaugen-hammerhai.
Distinctive characteristics for immediate identification: very wide hammer-shaped

Golden hammerhead (*Sphyrna tudes*): (a) lateral view, (b) ventral view of the head, (c) ventral view of the pectoral fin, (d) upper and lower teeth, (e) placoid scale, (f) juvenile smalleye hammerhead.

head, its anterior margin curved with a median notch and its posterior margin nearly straight, anal fin much longer than second dorsal.

Morphology: very wide hammer-shaped head (also called "cephalofoil"), dorso-ventrally depressed and greatly expanded laterally, its anterior margin curved with a median notch and its posterior margin nearly straight. Fins not falcate. First dorsal large and tall, its origin over the pectoral fin inner margin. Second dorsal small. Anal fin larger than the second dorsal, with a long base. Pelvic fins short. Pectoral fins relatively short. Caudal fin with relatively short lower lobe and long upper lobe with medium-sized terminal lobe. Dorsal part of body pronounced. Mouth wide and parabolic in ventral view. Labial folds short. Eyes small. Nostrils long. No spiracles. 5 pairs of gill slits, the 4th and 5th located over the pectoral fin base.

Coloration: dorsal surfaces grey or grey-yellowish and partially yellow or orange with iridescence; ventral surfaces yellow or orange.

Teeth shape: upper teeth with one cusp, oblique, with cutting edges; lower teeth narrower, with one cusp, pointed, with cutting edges.

Dental formula: 15 to 16–15 to 16 / 15 to 16–1—15 to 16.

Maximum size: 152 cm.

Size at birth: about 30 cm.

Size at maturity: about 80 cm (male) and about 98 cm (female).

Embryonic development: placental viviparous.

Gestation: 10 months.

Litter size: 5–12 young.

Reproduction in the Mediterranean: does not reproduce in the Mediterranean.

Maximum age: unknown.

Diet: bony fishes and their eggs, sharks, crustaceans, squids.

Habitat: pelagic, on continental and insular shelves, at depths ranging from the surface to at least 36 m. Pregnant females give birth in shallow waters.

Geographical distribution in the Mediterranean Sea: Eastern and Central Mediterranean.

Geographical distribution in the rest of the world: Atlantic Ocean.

Behavior: active and fast, solitary or in large groups, timid, can segregate by sex and size, probably use their hammer-shaped head (that has a wider electroreceptive area) to detect and scoop up rays buried under sand and pin them to the sea floor while taking bites from their body (other functions of the cephalofoil are increasing swimming maneuverability, maybe even increasing sensitivity to vibration, visual stereoscopy and increased olfactory sensibility).

Dangerousness for man: potentially dangerous.

Importance for fishery in the Mediterranean: no importance.

Status in the Mediterranean: very rare.

Kind of presence in the Mediterranean: occasional (the specimens recorded must have entered the Mediterranean Sea from the Eastern Atlantic Ocean through the Gibraltar Strait).

Specimens of particular interest recorded in the Mediterranean: some young specimens have been recorded from the area, including a 34.2 cm female caught off Nice, France, Ligurian Sea (preserved in the Muséum National d'Histoire Naturelle in Paris), and a 55 cm male caught off Livorno, Italy, Tyrrhenian Sea (preserved in Pisa).

Species with which can be confused: the great hammerhead (*Sphyrna mokarran*), the smooth hammerhead (*Sphyrna zygaena*) and the scalloped hammerhead (*Sphyrna lewini*), but their hammer has a different shape: the great hammerhead has the anterior margin almost straight with a median notch and its posterior margin slightly concave, the smooth hammerhead has the anterior margin curved without a median notch and its posterior margin concave, and the scalloped hammerhead has the anterior margin curved with a median notch and its posterior margin concave.

Main references for the Mediterranean: Canestrini (1874), Brusina (1888), Kolombatović (1894), Tortonese (1956), Cadenat & Blache (1981), Bauchot (1987), McEachran & Séret (1987), Lipej *et al.* (2004).

Other selected non–Mediterranean related references: Bigelow & Schroeder (1948), Gilbert (1967), Castro (1983), Compagno (1984), Castro (1989).

Smooth hammerhead
Sphyrna zygaena (Linnaeus, 1758)

Classification: Order Carcharhiniformes, family Sphyrnidae, genus *Sphyrna*.
Common names in other languages: French: requin-marteau commun; Spanish: cornuda; Italian: pesce martello comune; German: glatter hammerhai.
Distinctive characteristics for immediate identification: very wide hammer-shaped head, its anterior margin curved without a median notch and its posterior margin concave, second dorsal fin small, anal fin about as large as the second dorsal.
Morphology: very wide hammer-shaped head (also called "cephalofoil"), dorsoventrally depressed and expanded laterally, its anterior margin curved without a median notch and its posterior margin concave. Fins not falcate. First dorsal large and tall, its origin over the pectoral fin inner margin. Second dorsal small. Anal fin about as large as the second dorsal. Pelvic fins short. Pectoral fins relatively short. Caudal fin with relatively short lower lobe and long upper lobe with medium-sized terminal lobe. Dorsal part pronounced. Mouth wide and parabolic in ventral view. Labial folds short. Eyes small. Nostrils long. No spiracles. 5 pairs of gill slits, the 4th and 5th located over the pectoral fin base.
Coloration: dorsal surfaces olive dark or grey-brown; ventral surfaces white. Pectoral fin ventral surface have a small black patch at the apex.
Teeth shape: upper teeth with one cusp, oblique, with cutting edges except for a fine serrated part at the base of the lateral edge; lower teeth smaller, with one cusp pointed and oblique.
Dental formula: 14 to 15–1 to 2–14 to 15 / 14–1–14.
Maximum size: 370 or 400 cm.
Size at birth: 46–61 cm.
Size at maturity: 210–250 cm (male) and 210–265 cm (female).
Embryonic development: placental viviparous.
Gestation: unknown.

Smooth hammerhead

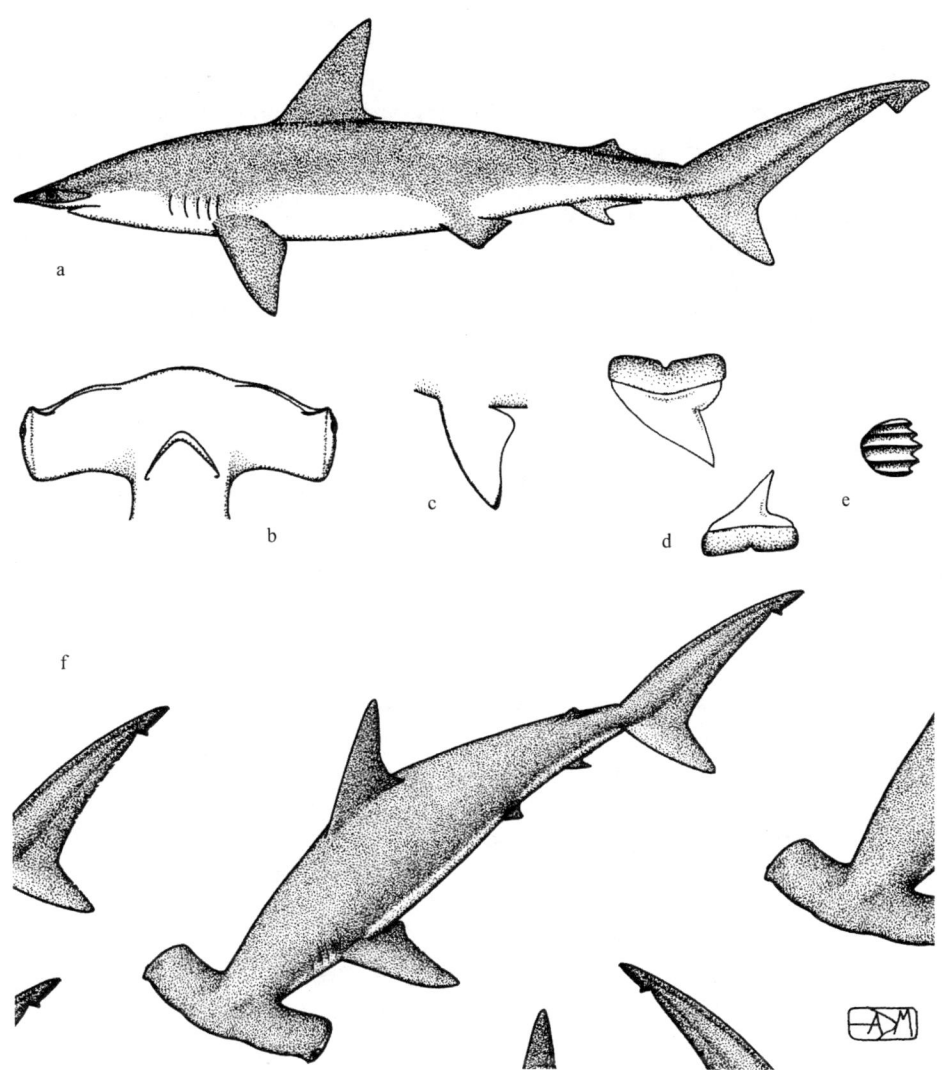

Smooth hammerhead (*Sphyrna zygaena*): (a) lateral view, (b) ventral view of the head, (c) ventral view of the pectoral fin, (d) upper and lower teeth, (e) placoid scale, (f) smooth hammerheads swimming in a group (drawings by Alessandro De Maddalena).

Litter size: 29–37 young.
Reproduction in the Mediterranean: reproduce in the Mediterranean, possibly off the Algerian coast.
Maximum age: unknown.
Diet: bony fishes, elasmobranchs, cetaceans, crustaceans, molluscs, carcasses.
Habitat: pelagic, on continental and insular shelves, slopes and oceanic basins, at depths ranging from the surface to at least 100 m. Pregnant females can give birth close inshore, where juveniles often remain while adults stay offshore.
Geographical distribution in the Mediterranean Sea: all Mediterranean.
Geographical distribution in the rest of the world: Atlantic, Pacific and Indian Oceans.

Behavior: active and fast, solitary or in enormous groups (up to 1200 specimens), migratory, timid, can segregate by size, probably use their hammer-shaped head (that has a wider electroreceptive area) to detect and scoop up rays buried under sand and pin them to the sea floor while taking bites from their body (other functions of the cephalofoil are increasing swimming maneuverability, maybe increasing sensitivity to vibration, visual stereoscopy and increased olfactory sensibility).

Dangerousness for man: potentially dangerous.

Importance for fishery in the Mediterranean: some importance.

Status in the Mediterranean: rare.

Kind of presence in the Mediterranean: stable.

Specimens of particular interest recorded in the Mediterranean: one of the largest specimens recorded, a 360 cm female, was caught in the Gulf of Genoa, Italy. The smallest free-swimming specimen ever recorded, was 46.7 cm long and was caught off the Algerian coast (preserved in the Muséum National d'Histoire Naturelle in Paris). Large schools of these sharks have been repeatedly observed by divers around Lampedusa, Italy, Channel of Sicily.

Species with which can be confused: the great hammerhead (*Sphyrna mokarran*), the golden hammerhead (*Sphyrna tudes*) and the scalloped hammerhead (*Sphyrna lewini*), but their hammer has a different shape: the great hammerhead has the anterior margin almost straight with a median notch and its posterior margin slightly concave, the smalleye hammerhead has the anterior margin curved with a median notch and its posterior margin nearly straight, and the scalloped hammerhead has the anterior margin curved with a median notch and its posterior margin concave.

Main references for the Mediterranean: Tortonese (1956), Gilbert (1967), Capapé (1974a), Cadenat & Blache (1981), Bauchot (1987), Vanni (1992), Moreno (1995), Buencuerpo *et al.* (1998), Barrull *et al.* (1999), Barrull & Mate (2002), Lipej *et al.* (2004), Celona & De Maddalena (2005).

Other selected non–Mediterranean related references: Bigelow & Schroeder (1948), Lineaweaver & Backus (1970), Bass *et al.* (1973–1976), Castro (1983), Compagno (1984), Randall (1986), Smale (1991), Last & Stevens (1994).

Glossary

Annelid—taxonomic classification of segmented worms
Anterior—forward portion of shark or fin
Axil of Fin—Posterior insertion point of the pectoral fin on the shark, the "arm pit" of the fin
Barbel—whisker like projection from the mouth that has a taste function
Bathymetric Segregation—varies with depth. For example, bathymetric segregation by size means that the size of sharks of the same species vary with depth.
Benthic—associated with the sea floor
Bryozoan—taxonomic group of colonial animals known as "moss animal" due to the plant like appearance and adherence to structure.
Caudal Fin—main part of a shark's tail, typically having upper and lower lobes
Caudal Fin Subterminal Notch—Discontinuity on the posterior edge of the caudal fin upper lobe near the tip
Caudal Fin Terminal Lobe—Additional lobe at the end of the caudal fin upper lobe
Caudal Peduncle—the zone that transitions the caudal fin to the body of the shark
Cephalopod— taxonomic group containing squid and octopi
Cetacean—taxonomic group including dolphins and whales
Crustacean—taxonomic group containing crabs, shrimp and lobster
Cusp—the point of a tooth
Cusplet—smaller points on a tooth
Depressed—flattened in the dorsal-to-ventral direction
Dermal Denticle—a tooth like scale found on sharks, also known as a placoid scale
Dorsal—top of the shark
Dorso-Ventral View—view looking down on shark from above and looking up at shark from below
Dorsal View—view looking down on shark from above
Echinoderms—taxonomic classification including starfish, brittle starfish, sea cucumbers, sea urchins and sea pens
Elasmobranches—taxonomic group that contains sharks, ray and skates
Fin Apex—Tip of fin farthest from shark body
Fin Free Rear Tip—tip of the fin formed by the inner margin and the posterior margin, located close to the body of the shark opposite the apex of the fin and the origin of the fin.
Fin Origin—the anterior insertion point of the fin on the shark

Foraminifera—taxonomic group of single cell protists with a hard shell
Gastropod—taxonomic group that includes sea slugs and snails
Gill Rakers—projections from the gill arches that prevent small prey from escaping through the gills. Gill rakers are prevalent in sharks that feed on small prey, like the basking shark.
Inner Margin of Fin—edge of the fin extending from the axil to the free rear tip
Interdorsal Ridge—sharp transition between the right hand and left hand dorsal side of the shark
Internarial Space—distance between the nostrils
Keels—A horizontal projection that serves as stability function, typically on the caudal peduncle or the base of the caudal fin
Labial Fold—fold of skin at the corner of the mouth, on upper and lower jaws
Lateral View—Side view of shark
Lunate—"moon like," shaped like a new moon
Margin of fin—edge of fin
Mollusc—taxonomic group including sea slugs, sea snails, squids and octopi, and bivalves (clams)
Nematodes—taxonomic group of unsegmented worm, round worms
Ocelli—white spots with dark margins
Ophiurids—taxonomic group including brittle starfish
Parturition—giving birth
Pelagic—free swimming in open water
Planktonic—free floating or drifting in open water
Polychaetes—taxonomic group containing marine segmented worms
Porifera—taxonomic group containing sponges
Posterior—rear or aft portion of shark or fin
Pronounced—accentuated. For example, a pronounced dorsal portion of a shark is almost humped
Salps—free swimming tunicate that is planktonic and transparent. Can form long chains.
Segregate by Sex—sharks of the same sex are found together, while those of the opposite sex are absent
Segregate by Size—sharks of the same species of the same size found together. This is typical in nursery areas where small sharks are found in an area devoid of larger sharks of the same species.
Siphonophores—taxonomic group containing certain jellyfish like creatures, notably the manowar
Spiracles—Pores above the eyes on some sharks that serve as a second entrance for water to the gills, typical found in benthic sharks that lay on the bottom
Terminal Mouth—mouth located at the most anterior part of the shark
Tunicates—taxonomic group of invertebrates that have a "notochord." Some attach to structure and have characteristic siphons while others are free swimming
Ventral—bottom of shark
Ventral View—view looking up at shark from below

Bibliography

Aasen, O. (1963). Length and growth of the porbeagle (*Lamna nasus*) in the North West Atlantic. *Rep. Norwegian Fish. Mar. Invest.*, 13: 20–37.

Acuña, E., & Villaroel, J.C. (2003). Distribution, abundance and reproductive biology of the blue shark *Prionace glauca* in the Southeastern Pacific Ocean. *AES Abstracts Manaus, Brazil, June 27–June 30*: 36.

Adams, D.H., & McMichael, R.H. Jr. (1999). Mercury levels in four species of sharks from the Atlantic coast of Florida. *Fishery Bulletin*, 97: 372–379.

Alonso, M.K., Crespo, E.A., Garcia, N.A., Pedraza, S.N., Mariotti, P.A. & Mora, N.J. (2002). Fishery and ontogenetic driven changes in the diet of the spiny dogfish, *Squalus acanthias*, in Patagonian waters, Argentina. *Environmental Biology of Fishes*, 63: 193–202.

Arcidiacono, F. (1931). La pesca del pesce vacca (*Hexanchus griseus* L.) nella marina di Riposto. *Bollettino della Pesca, Piscicultura e Idrobiologia*, 1931: 608–612.

Ariola, V. (1913). Cattura di squali nel Golfo di Genova. *Atti della Società Ligustica di Scienze Naturali e Geografiche*, 24: 3–19.

Barrull, J. (1993–1994). Cita histórica de tiburón blanco *Carcharodon carcharias* (Linnaeus, 1758), en el Mar Catalán (Mar Mediterráneo), documentada con dientes de la mandíbula. *Miscellània Zoològica*, 17: 283–285.

Barrull, J., & Mate, I. (1995). Presencia de tiburón dormilón *Somniosus rostratus* (Risso, 1826) en el Mar Catalán (Mar Mediterráneo). *Miscellània Zoològica*, 18: 200–202.

Barrull, J., & Mate, I. (1998). Pesca comercial de tiburones en aguas catalanas. *Boletín de la Asociación Española de Elasmobranquios*, 1: 40–44.

Barrull, J., & Mate, I. (1999). Registros de tiburón peregrino (*Cetorhinus maximus*) en aguas del Mediterráneo. *Boletín de la Asociación Española de Elasmobranquios*, 2: 37–52.

Barrull, J., & Mate, I. (2000). Biología de la cañabota *Hexanchus griseus* (Bonnaterre, 1788) en el Mar Mediterráneo. *Boletín de la Asociación Española de Elasmobranquios*, 3: 13–20.

Barrull, J., & Mate, I. (2001). Presence of the Great White Shark *Carcharodon carcharias* (Linnaeus, 1758) in the Catalonian Sea (NW Mediterranean): review and discussion of records, and notes about its ecology. *Annales, Series historia naturalis*, 11(1): 3–12.

Barrull, J., & Mate, I. (2001). First confirmed record of Angular Roughshark *Oxynotus centrina* (Linnaeus, 1758) predation on shark egg case of small-spotted catshark *Scyliorhinus canicula* (Linnaeus, 1758) in Mediterranean waters. *Annales, Series historia naturalis*, 11(1): 23–28.

Barrull, J., & Mate, I. (2001). First record of a pregnant female of little sleeper shark *Somniosus rostratus* (Risso, 1826) in Spanish Mediterranean coast. *Boletín Instituto Español de Oceanografía*, 17: 323–325.

Barrull, J., & Mate, I. (2002). *Tiburones del Mediterráneo*. Llibreria El Set-ciències, Arenys de Mar, 292 pp.

Barrull, J., Mate, I. & Bueno, M. (1999). Observaciones de tiburones (Chondrichthyes, Euselachii) en aguas de Cataluña (Mediterráneo NO), con algunos aspectos generales de su ecología. *Scientia gerundensis*, 24: 127–151.

Bass, A.J., D'Aubrey, J.D. & Kistnasamy, N. (1973–1976). Sharks of the east coast of Southern Africa. 1–6, *Investigational Report of the Oceanographic Research Institute, Durban*, 33, 37, 38, 39, 43, 45.

Basusta, N. (2002). Occurrence of a sawback angelshark (*Squatina aculeata* Cuvier, 1829) off the Eastern Mediterranean coast of Turkey. *Turkish Journal of Veterinary & Animal Sciences*, 26: 1177–1179.

Bauchot, M.L. (1987). Requins. In W. Fischer, M. Schneider & M.-L. Bauchot (Eds.), *Fiches FAO d'identification des espèces pour les besoins de la peche. (Révision I). Méditerranée et Mer Noire. Zone de peche 37. Vol. 2. Vertébrés*, pp. 767–843. Rome, CEE, FAO.

Bello, G. (1995). Cephalopods in the stomach contents of *Galeus melastomus* (Selachii, Scyliorhinidae) from the Adriatic Sea. *Atti della Società italiana di Scienze naturali e del Museo Civico di Storia naturale di Milano*, 134: 33–40.

Bello, G. (1997). Cephalopods from the stomach contents of demersal chondrichthyans caught

in the Adriatic Sea. *Vie et milieu*, 47(3): 221–227.
Bello, G. (1998). The feeding ecology of the velvet bellly, *Etmopterus spinax* (Chondrichthyes: Squalidae), of the Adriatic Sea on the basis of its stomach contents. *Atti della Società italiana di Scienze naturali e del Museo Civico di Storia naturale di Milano*, 139: 187–193.
Ben-Tuvia, A. (1953). Mediterranean fishes of Israel. *Bulletin Sea Fisheries Research Station of Israel, Haifa*, 8: 1–40.
Ben-Tuvia, A. (1971). Revised list of the Mediterranean fishes of Israel. *Israel Journal of Zoology*, 20: 1–39.
Bianchi, I., Clò, S., & Costantini, M. (1997). Medtag e baby shark: due progetti per la marcatura degli squali. Primi risultati, riflessioni e prospettive. *Quaderni della Civica Stazione Idrobiologica di Milano*, 22: 51–64.
Bigelow, H.B., & Schroeder, W.C. (1948). Sharks. In *Fishes of the Western North Atlantic. Part one: Lancelets, Ciclostomes, Sharks*, pp. 53–576. Memoir Sears Foundation for Marine Research, Yale University.
Bigelow, H.B., & Schroeder, W.C. (1957). A study of the sharks of the suborder Squaloidea. *Bulletin of the Museum of Comparative Zoology, Harvard University*, 117(1): 1–150.
Boero, F., & Carli, A. (1977). Prima segnalazione mediterranea di *Sphyrna mokarran* (Rüppell) (Selachii, Sphyrnidae). *Bollettino dei Musei e degli Istituti Biologici dell'Università di Genova*, 45: 91–93.
Boero, F., & Carli, A. (1979). Catture di Elasmobranchi nella tonnarella di Camogli (Genova) dal 1950 al 1974. *Bollettino del Museo dell'Istituto di Biologia dell'Università di Genova*, 47: 27–34.
Bonaparte, C. (1839). *Iconografia della fauna italica per le quattro classi degli animali vertebrati. Tomo III. Pesci.* Tipografia Salviucci, Roma.
Borri, C. (1934). Catalogo delle Collezioni dei Vertebrati del R. Museo Zoologico di Pisa. II. Squali. *Atti della Società Toscana di Scienze Naturali*, 44.
Branstetter, S. (1987). Age and growth estimates for blacktip, *Carcharhinus limbatus*, and spinner, *C. brevipinna*, sharks from the Northwestern Gulf of Mexico. *Copeia*, 1987(4): 964–974.
Bruni, M., & Würtz, M. (2002). The Chondrichthyan fish collection of the Oceanographic Museum of Monaco: history and present status. In M. Vacchi, G. La Mesa, F. Serena, & B. Sèret (Eds.), *Proc. 4th European Elasmobranch Association Meeting, Livorno (Italy)*, 2000, 49–63. ICRAM, ARPAT & SFI, 2002.
Brusina, S. (1888). Morski psi Sredozemnoga i Crljenog mora (Sharks of the Adriatic and the Black Sea). Glasnik hrvatskoga naravoslovnoga družtva. III: 167–230, Zagreb.
Buencuerpo, V., Rios, S., & Moron, J. (1998). Pelagic sharks associated with the swordfish, *Xiphias gladius*, fishery in the eastern North Atlantic Ocean and the Strait of Gibraltar. *Fishery Bulletin*, 96(4): 667–685.
Cadenat, J., & Blache, J. (1981). Requins de Méditerranée et d'Atlantique (plus particulièrement de la Côte Occidentale d'Afrique). *Faune Tropicale, ORSTOM, Paris*, 21: 1–330.
Campana, S., Joyce, W., & Marks, L. (2003). Status of the porbeagle shark (*Lamna nasus*) population in the Northwest Atlantic in the context of species at risk. Canadian Science Advisory Secretariat, Research Document 2003/007: 1–31.
Canestrini, G. (1874). *Fauna d'Italia. Parte terza. Pesci.* Milano: Vallardi.
Capapé, C. (1974a). Observation sur la sexualité, la reproduction et la fécondité de 8 Sélaciens pleurotrêmes vivipares placentaires des côtes tunisiennes. *Archives de l'Institut Pasteur de Tunis*, 51(4): 329–344.
Capapé, C. (1974b). Contribution à la biologie des Scyliorhinidae des côtes tunisiennes. II. *Scyliorhinus canicula* (Linné, 1758): Regime alimentaire. *Annales de l'Institut Michel Pacha*, 7: 13–29.
Capapé, C. (1974c). Contribution à la biologie des Scyliorhinidae des côtes tunisiennes. IV. *Scyliorhinus stellaris* (Linné, 1758). Régime alimentaire. *Archives de l'Institut Pasteur de Tunis*, 52: 383–394.
Capapé, C. (1975a). Observations sur le régime alimentaire de 29 Selaciens pleurotêrmes des côtes tunisiennes. *Archives de l'Institut Pasteur de Tunis*, 52(4): 395–414.
Capapé, C. (1975b). Sélaciens nouveaux et rares le long des côtes tunisiennes. Premières observations biologiques. *Archives de l'Institut Pasteur de Tunis*, 52(4): 395–414.
Capapé, C. (1977). Liste commentée des sélaciens de la région de Toulon (de la Ciotat à Saint-Tropez). *Bull. Mus. Hist. Nat. Marseille*, 37: 5–9.
Capapé, C. (1980). Nouvelle description de *Heptranchias perlo* (Bonnaterre, 1788) (Pisces, Pleurotremata, Hexanchidae). Données sur la biologie de la reproduction et le régime alimetaire des spécimens des côtes tunisiennes. *Bull. Offn. Natn. Pêch. Tunisie*, 4 (2): 231–264.
Capapé, C. (1985). Nouvelle description de *Centrophorus granulosus* (Schneider, 1801) (Pisces, Squalidae).Données sur la biologie de la reproduction et le régime alimentaire des spécimens des côtes tunisiennes. *Bull. Inst. Natn. Scient. Tech. Océanogr. Pêche Salambô*, 12: 97–141.
Capapé, C. (1989). Les Sélaciens des côtes méditerranéennes: aspects generaux de leur écologie et exemples de peuplements. *Océanis*, 15 (3): 309–331.
Capapé, C., Guélorget, O., Barrull, J., Mate, I., Hemida, F., Seridji, R. Bensaci, J., & Nejmeddine Bradaï, M. (2003). Records of the bluntnose sixgill shark, *Hexanchus griseus* (Bonnaterre, 1788) (Chondrichthyes: Hexanchidae) in the Mediterranean Sea: a historical survey. *Annales, Series historia naturalis*, 13(2): 157–166.
Capapé, C., Hemida, F., Bensaci, J., Saïdi, B., &

Nejmeddine Bradaï, M. (2003). Records of the basking sharks, *Cetorhinus maximus* (Gunnerus, 1765) (Chondrichthyes: Cetorhinidae) off the Maghrebin shore (southern Mediterranean): a survey. *Annales, Series historia naturalis*, 13(1): 13–18.

Capapé, C., Hemida, F., Guélorget, O., Barrull, J., Mate, I., Ben Souissi, J., & M. Nejmeddine Bradaï (2003). Reproductive biology of the bluntnose sixgill shark *Hexanchus griseus* (Bonnaterre, 1788) (Chondrichthyes: Hexanchidae) from the Mediterranean Sea: a review. *Acta Adriatica*, 45(1): 95–106.

Capapé, C., & Pantoustier, G. (1975). Anomalies chez quelques Sélaciens des côtes tunisiennes. *Archives de l'Institut Pasteur de Tunis*, 52(3): 251–262.

Capapé, C., Quignard, J.P., & Mellinger, J. (1990). Reproduction and development of two angel shaks, *Squatina squatina* and *S. oculata* (Pisces: Squatinidae), off Tunisian coasts: semi-delayed vitellogenesis, lack of egg capsules, and lecithrotrophy. *Journal of Fish Biology*, 37: 347–256.

Capapé, C., Tomasini, J.A., & Bouchereau, J.L. (1991). Observations sur la biologie de la reproduction de la petite roussette *Scyliorhinus canicula* (Linnaeus, 1758) (Pisces, Scyliorhinidae) du Golfe du Lion (France Méridionale). *Ichthyophysiologica Acta*, 13: 87–109.

Capapé, C., Tomasini, J.A., & Quignard, J.P. (2000). Les Elasmobranches Pleurotrêmes de la côte du Languedoc (France Méridionale): observations biologiques et démographiques. *Vie et Milieu*, 50(2): 123–133.

Capapé, C., & Zaouali, J. (1976). Contribution à la biologie des Scyliorhinidae des côtes tunisiennes. V. *Galeus melastomus* (Rafinesque, 1810). Régime alimentaire. *Archives de l'Institut Pasteur de Tunis*, 53: 281–292.

Capapé, C., Zaouali, J., & Desoutter, M. (1979). Note sur la présence en Tunisie de *Carcharhins obscurus* (Lesueur, 1818) (Pisces, Pleurotremata) avec clé de détermination des Carcharhinidae des côtes tunisiennes. *Bulletin de l'Office national des Pêches, Tunisie*, 3(2): 171–182.

Carrasson, M., Stefanescu, C., & Cartes, J.E. (1992). Diets and bathymetric distributions of two bathyal sharks of the Catalan deep sea (Western Mediterranean). *Marine Ecology Progress Series*, 82: 21–30.

Carruccio, A. (1906). Sulla *Selache maxima* Günn. *Bollettino della Società Zoologica Italiana*, 1906: 191–202.

Casey, J. G., & Natanson, L.J. (1992). Revised estimates of age and growth of the sandbar shark (*Carcharhinus plumbeus*) from the western North Atlantic. *Canadian Journal of Fisheries and Aquatic Science*, 49(7): 1474–1477.

Casey, J. G., Pratt, H.L. Jr., & Stillwell, C. E. (1985). Age and growth of the sandbar shark, *Carcharhinus plumbeus*, from the Western North Atlantic. *Canadian Journal of Fisheries and Aquatic Science*, 42: 963–975.

Castillo-Geniz, J.L., Marquez-Farias, J.F., Rodriguez de la Cruz, M.C., Cortes, E., & Cid del Prado, A. (1998). The Mexican artisanal shark fishery in the Gulf of Mexico: towards a regulated fishery. *Marine & Freshwater Research*, 49: 611–620.

Castro, J. (1983). *The Sharks of North American Waters*. College Station: Texas A&M University Press, 180 pp.

Castro, J.I. (1989). The biology of the Golden Hammerhead, *Sphyrna tudes*, off Trinidad. *Environmental Biology of Fishes*, 24(1): 3–11.

Ceballos, P., Galvan, F., & Hoyos, M. (2003). Reproductive biology of silky shark *Carcharhinus falciformis* off the west coast of Baja California Sur. *AES Abstracts Manaus, Brazil, June 27–June 30*: 40.

Celona, A. (2001). First record of a tiger shark *Galeocerdo cuvier* (Peron & LeSueur, 1822) in the Italian waters. *Annales, Series historia naturalis*, 10(2): 207–210.

Celona, A., & De Maddalena, A. (2005). The hammerhead sharks (family Sphyrnidae Gill, 1872) in the Sicilian waters (Italy, Mediterranean Sea). *Annales, Series historia naturalis*, 15(1).

Celona, A., De Maddalena, A., & Romeo, T. (2003). The bluntnose sixgill shark, *Hexanchus griseus* (Bonnaterre, 1788), in the Eastern North Sicilian waters.

Celona, A., Donato N., & De Maddalena, A. (2001). In relation to the captures of a great white shark *Carcharodon carcharias* (Linnaeus, 1758) and a shortfin mako, *Isurus oxyrinchus* Rafinesque, 1809 in the Messina Strait. *Annales, Series historia naturalis*, 11(1): 13–16.

Celona, A., Piscitelli, L., & De Maddalena, A. (2004). Two large shortfin makos, *Isurus oxyrinchus*, Rafinesque, 1809, caught off Sicily, Western Ionian Sea. *Annales, Series historia naturalis*, 14(1): 35–42.

Chapman, D., & Gruber, S. H. (2002). A further observation of the prey-handling behavior of the great hammerhead shark, *Sphyrna mokarran*: predation on the spotted eagle ray, *Aetobatus narinari*. *Bulletin of Marine Science*, 70(3): 947–952.

Chen, C.T., Joung, S.G., & Lee, S.H. (2003). Some aspects of fishery biology of the silky shark, *Carcharhinus falciformis*, in Taiwanese waters. *AES Abstracts Manaus, Brazil, June 27–June 30*: 6.

Chen, C.-T., Leu, T.-C. & Joung, S.-J. (1988). Notes on reproduction in the scalloped hammerhead, *Sphyrna lewini*, in Northeastern Taiwan waters. *Fishery Bulletin*, 86(2): 389–393.

Chen, C. T., Liu, K.M., & Chang, Y. C. (1997). Reproductive biology of the bigeye thresher shark, *Alopias superciliosus* (Lowe, 1839) (Chondrichthyes: Alopiidae) in the northwestern Pacific. *Ichthyological Research*, 43(3): 227–235.

Cigala Fulgosi, F. (1983a). Confirmation of the presence of *Carcharhinus brachyurus* (Gunther, 1870) (Pisces, Selachii, Carcharhinidae) in the

Mediterranean. *Doriana (Suppl. Ann. Mus. Civ. St. nat. "G. Doria")*, 5(249): 1–5.

Cigala Fulgosi, F. (1983b). First record of the "big-eyed thresher" *Alopias superciliosus* (Lowe, 1840) (Selachii, Alopiidae) in the Mediterranean, with notes on some fossil species of the genus *Alopias*. *Annali del Museo Civico di Storia Naturale "G. Doria,"* Genova, 84: 211–229.

Cigala Fulgosi, F., & Gandolfi, G. (1983). Redescription of the external morphology of *Somniosus rostratus* (Risso, 1826), with special reference to its squamation and cutaneous sensory organs, and aspects of both their functional morphology (Pisces, Selachii , Squalidae). *Monitore zoologico Italiano*, N.S.: 17, 27–70.

Cipria, G. (1937). Embrione di *Echinorhinus spinosus* Gmelin. *Memorie R. Comitato Talassografico Italiano*, 245: 3–7.

Clark, E., & Kristof, E. (1991). How deep do sharks go? Reflections on deep sea sharks. In S.H. Gruber (Ed.), Discovering sharks, pp. 77–78. *Underwater Naturalist, Bulletin American Littoral Society*, 19(4)-20(1).

Clarke, T.C. (1971). The ecology of the scalloped hammerhead shark, *Sphyrna lewini*, in Hawaii. *Pacific Science*, 25: 133–144.

Cliff, G. (1995). Sharks caught in the protective gill nets off Kwazulu-Natal, South Africa. 8. The great hammerhead shark *Sphyrna mokarran* (Rüppell). *South African Journal of Marine Sciences*, 15: 105–114.

Cliff, G., Compagno, L.J.V., Smale, M.J., Van Der Elst, R.P., & Wintner, S.P. (2000). First records of white sharks, *Carcharodon carcharias*, from Mauritius, Zanzibar, Madagascar and Kenya. *South African Journal of Science*, 96. 365–367.

Cliff, G., & Dudley, S.F.J. (1991). Sharks caught in the protective gill nets off Natal, South Africa. 5. The Java shark *Carcharhinus amboinensis* (Müller & Henle). *South African Journal of Marine Sciences*, 11: 443–453.

Cliff, G., & Dudley, S.F.J. (1992). Sharks caught in the protective gill nets off Natal, South Africa. 6. The copper shark *Carcharhinus brachyurus* (Günther). *South African Journal of Marine Sciences*, 12: 663–674.

Cliff, G., Dudley, S.F.J., & Davis, B. (1989). Sharks caught in the protective gill nets off Natal, South Africa. 2. The great white shark *Carcharodon carcharias* (Linnaeus). *South African Journal of Marine Sciences*, 8: 131–144.

Cliff, G., Dudley, S.F.J., & Davis, B. (1989). Sharks caught in the protective gill nets off Natal, South Africa. 3. The shortfin mako shark *Isurus oxyrinchus* (Linnaeus). *South African Journal of Marine Sciences*, 9: 115–126.

Clò, S., & Bianchi, I. (1997). Osservazioni sul comportamento alimentare della verdesca, *Prionace glauca* (Linnaeus, 1758) (Chondrichthyes: Carcahrhinidae). *Quaderni della Civica Stazione Idrobiologica di Milano*, 22: 79–93.

Collier, R. (2002). *Shark Attacks of the Twentieth Century from the Pacific Coast of North America*. Chatsworth: Scientia, 296 pp.

Collier, R.S., Marks, M., & R.W. Warner (1996). White shark attacks on inanimate objects along the Pacific coast of North America. In A.P. Klimley & D.G. Ainley (Eds.), *Great white sharks: The biology of* Carcharodon carcharias, pp. 217–221. San Diego: Academic, 518 pp.

Compagno, L.J.V. (1984). FAO Species Catalogue. Vol.4. Sharks of the World. An annotated and illustrated catalogue of sharks species known to date. Parts 1 and 2. *FAO Fisheries Synopsis*, 125: 1–655.

Costantini, M., & Affronte, M. (2003). Neonatal and juvenile sandbar sharks in the northern Adriatic Sea. *Journal of Fish Biology*, 62: 740–743.

Costantini, M., Bernardini, M., Cordone, P., Giulianini, P.G., & Orel, G. (2000). Osservazioni sulla pesca, la biologia riproduttiva ed alimentare di *Mustelus mustelus* (Chondrichtyes, Triakidae) in Alto Adriatico. *Biologia Marina Mediterranea*, 7(1): 427–432.

Cousteau, J.P., & Cousteau, P. (1970). *The shark: Splendid savage of the sea*. Cassell: London, 277pp.

Cugini, G., & De Maddalena, A. (2003). Sharks captured off Pescara (Italy, western Adriatic Sea). *Annales, Series historia naturalis*, 13(2): 201–208.

De La Rosa, F.J.P. (1994). *Tiburones del Mar de Alborán*. Servicio publicaciones Centro de Ediciones de la Diputacion de Malaga (CEDMA).

De La Serna, J. M., Valeiras, J., Ortiz, J. M., & Macias, D. (2002). Large pelagic sharks as by-catch in the Mediterranean swordfish longline fishery: some biological aspects. *Northwest Atlantic Fisheries Organization, Scientific Council Meeting—September 2002*: 1–33.

De Maddalena, A. (1999). *Records of the great white shark in the Mediterranean Sea*. Private publication, Milano, 54 pp.

De Maddalena, A. (2000a). Sui reperti di 28 esemplari di squalo bianco, *Carcharodon carcharias* (Linnaeus, 1758), conservati in musei italiani. *Annali del Museo Civico di Storia Naturale "G. Doria,"* Genova, 93: 565–605.

De Maddalena, A. (2000b). Historical and contemporary presence of the great white shark *Carcharodon carcharias* (Linnaeus, 1758), in the Northern and Central Adriatic Sea. *Annales, Series historia naturalis*, 10(1): 3–18.

De Maddalena, A. (2000c). Il disegno della superficie ventrale delle pinne pettorali dei Selaci come carattere diagnostico per il riconoscimento delle specie. *Annales, Series historia naturalis*, 10(2): 187–198.

De Maddalena, A. (2000d). The Mediterranean Shark Research Group. *Annales, Series historia naturalis*, 10(2): 336–337.

De Maddalena, A. (2001a). *Squali delle acque italiane. Guida sintetica al riconoscimento*. Formello: Ireco, 72 pp.

De Maddalena, A. (2001b). The Mediterranean

Shark Sportfishery Program. *Annales, Series historia naturalis*, 11(2): 315–316.

De Maddalena, A. (2002a). *Lo squalo bianco nei mari d'Italia*. Formello: Ireco, 144 pp.

De Maddalena, A. (2002b). Lo squalo bianco: biologia del predatore e guida al riconoscimento. *Rivista Marittima*, Luglio 2002: 195–205.

De Maddalena, A. (2014). *Biologia dello squalo bianco*. Milano: Magenes Editoriale, 190 pp.

De Maddalena, A., Celona, A., Zuffa, M., & Vanadia, A. (2002). Su alcune catture di notidano cinereo, *Heptranchias perlo* (Bonnaterre, 1788), nelle acque della Sicilia. *Thalassia Salentina*, 26: 39–44.

De Maddalena, A., & Della Rovere, G. (2005). First record of the pigeye shark, *Carcharhinus amboinensis* (Müller & Henle, 1839), in the Mediterranean Sea. *Annales, Series historia naturalis*, 15(2): 209–212.

De Maddalena, A., Glaizot, O., & Oliver, G. (2003). On the great white shark, *Carcharodon carcharias* (Linnaeus, 1758), preserved in the Museum of Zoology in Lausanne. *Marine Life*, 13(1/2): 53–59.

De Maddalena, A., & Heim, W. (2009). *Great White Sharks in United States Museums*. Jefferson, NC: McFarland. 214 pp.

De Maddalena, A., & Heim, W. (2012). *Mediterranean Great White Sharks: A Comprehensive Study Including All Recorded Sightings*. Jefferson, NC: McFarland, 254 pp.

De Maddalena, A., & Piscitelli, L. (2001). Morphometrics of neonate velvet belly, *Etmopterus spinax* (Linnaeus, 1758). *Annales, Series historia naturalis*, 11(1): 17–22.

De Maddalena, A., & Piscitelli, L. (2001). Analisi preliminare dei selaci registrati presso il mercato ittico di Milano (aprile-settembre 2000). *Bollettino del Museo civico di Storia naturale di Venezia*, 52: 129–145.

De Maddalena, A., Piscitelli, L., & Malandra, L. (2001). The largest specimen of smooth-hound, *Mustelus mustelus* (Linnaeus, 1758), recorded from the Mediterranean Sea. *Biljeske–Notes*, 84: 1–7.

De Maddalena, A., Preti, A., & Smith, R. (2005). *Mako sharks*. Malabar: Krieger, 72 pp.

De Maddalena, A., & Reckel, F. (2003). Monstermythos im Mittelmeer. *Unterwasser*, April 2003: 76–81.

De Maddalena, A., & Reckel, F. (2003). Haie im Mittelmeer: Fakten, Forschung, Probleme. *Biologie in unserer Zeit*, 33(4): 257–263.

De Maddalena, A., & Zuffa, M. (2003). A gravid female bramble shark, *Echinorhinus brucus* (Bonnaterre, 1788), caught off Elba Island, Italy, Northern Thyrrenian Sea. *Annales, Series historia naturalis*, 13(2): 193–206.

De Maddalena, A., Zuffa M., Lipej, L., & Celona, A. (2001). An analysis of the photographic evidences of the largest great white sharks, *Carcharodon carcharias* (Linnaeus, 1758), captured in the Mediterranean Sea with considerations about the maximum size of the species. *Annales, Series historia naturalis*, 11(2): 193–206.

Doderlein, P. (1881). *Manuale Ittiologico del Mediterraneo. Parti 1–2*. Palermo.

Dodrill, J.W., & Gilmore, R.G. (1979). First North American continental record of the longfin mako (*Isurus paucus* 1979 Guitart Manday). *Florida Scientist*, 42: 52–58.

Doria, G., & Gestro, R. (1877). Crociera del "Violante" comandato dal capitano armatore Enrico D'Albertis durante l'anno 1876. *Annali del Museo Civico di Storia Naturale "G. Doria,"* Genova, 11: 302–304.

Ebert, D.A. (1994). Diet of the sixgill shark *Hexanchus griseus* off southern Africa. *South African Journal of Marine Sciences*, 14: 213–218.

Ebert, D.A., Compagno, L.J.V., & Cowley, V. (1992). A preliminary investigation of the feeding ecology of squaloid sharks off the west coast of southern Africa. *South African Journal of Marine Sciences*, 12: 601–609.

Ellis, R. (1983). *The book of sharks*. London: Robert Hale, 256 pp.

Ellis, R., & McCosker, J.E. (1991). *Great white shark*. Stanford: Stanford University Press, 270 pp.

Fairfax, D. (1998). *The Basking Shark in Scotland: Natural History, Fishery and Conservation*. East Linton: Tuckwell, 217 pp.

Fergusson, I.K. (1996). Distribution and autecology of the white shark in the Eastern North Atlantic Ocean and the Mediterranean Sea. In A.P. Klimley & D.G. Ainley (Eds.), *Great white sharks: The biology of Carcharodon carcharias*, pp. 321–345. San Diego: Academic, 518 pp.

Fergusson, I.K., & Compagno, L.J.V. (2000). Distributional note on the dusky shark, *Carcharhinus obscurus*, from the Mediterranean Sea, with a first record from the Maltese islands. In B. Sèret & J.-Y. Sire (Eds.), *Proc. 3rd European Elasmobranch Association Meeting, Boulogne-sur-Mer, 1999*, pp. 57–65. Paris: Soc. Fr. Ichthyol. & IRD.

Fourmanoir, P. (1961). Requins de la côte ouest de Madagascar. *Memoires de L'Institut Scientifique de Madagascar*, Ser. F, 4: 1–81.

Francis, M.P. (1996). Observations on a pregnant white shark with a review of reproductive biology. In A.P. Klimley & D.G. Ainley (Eds.), *Great white sharks: The biology of Carcharodon carcharias*, pp. 157–172. San Diego: Academic, 518 pp.

Francis, M.P., & Mulligan, K.P. (1998). Age and growth of New Zealand school shark, *Galeorhinus galeus*. *New Zealand Journal of Marine and Freshwater Research*, 32(3): 427–440.

Francis, M.P., & Stevens, J.D. (2000). Reproduction, embryonic development, and growth of the porbeagle shark, *Lamna nasus*, in the Southwest Pacific Ocean. *Fishery Bulletin*, 98(1): 41–63.

Galaz, T., & De Maddalena, A. (2004). On a great white shark, *Carcharodon carcharias* (Linnaeus,

1758), trapped in a tuna cage off Libya, Mediterranean Sea. *Annales, Series historia naturalis*, 14(2): 159–164.

Garrick, J.A.F (1967). Revision of sharks of genus *Isurus* with description of a new species (Galeoidea, Lamnidae). *Proceedings of the United States National Museum*, 118: 663–690.

Garrick, J.A.F (1982). Sharks of the genus *Carcharhinus*. *NOAA Technical Report NMFS Circular*, 445: 1–194.

George, C.J., Athanassiou, V.A., & Boulos, I. (1964). The fishes of the coastal waters of Lebanon. *Misc. Pap. Nat. Sci. Amer. Univ. Beirut*, 4: 1–27.

Gilat, A., & Gelman, E. (1984). On sharks and fishes observed using underwater photography during a deep-water cruise in the Eastern Mediterranean. *Fisheries Research*, 2: 257–271.

Gilbert, C.R. (1967). A revision of the hammerhead sharks (family Sphyrnidae). *Proceedings of the United States National Museum*, 119(3539): 1–88.

Gilmore, R.G., Dodrill, J.W., & Linley, P.A. (1983). Reproduction and embryonic development of the sand tiger shark, *Odontaspis taurus* (Rafinesque). *Fishery Bulletin*, 81: 201–225.

Girard, M., & Du Buit, M.-H. (1999). Reproductive biology of two deep-water sharks from the British Isles, *Centroscymnus coelolepis* and *Centrophorus squamosus* (Chondrichthyes: Squalidae). *Journal of the Marine Biological Association, UK*, 79: 923–931.

Golani, D. (1986–1987). On deepwater sharks caught off the Mediterranean coast of Israel. *Israel Journal of Zoology*, 34: 23–31.

Golani, D. (1996). The marine ichthyofauna of the Eastern Levant—history, inventory, and characterization. *Israel Journal of Zoology*, 42: 15–55.

Golani, D., & Pisanty, S. (2000). Biological aspects of the gulper shark, *Centrophorus granulosus* (Bloch and Schneider, 1801), from the Mediterranean coast of Israel. *Acta Adriatica*, 41(2): 71–78.

Goldman, K.J., Anderson, S.D., McCosker, J.E., & Klimley, A.P. (1996). Temperature, swimming depth, and movements of a white shark at the South Farallon Islands, California. In A.P. Klimley & D.G. Ainley (Eds.), *Great white sharks: The biology of* Carcharodon carcharias, pp. 111–120. San Diego: Academic, 518 pp.

Goosen, A.J.J., & Smale, M.J. (1997). A preliminary study of age and growth of the smooth-hound shark *Mustelus mustelus* (Triakidae). *South African Journal of Marine Sciences*, 18: 85–91.

Grace, M. (2001). Field guide to requiem sharks (Elasmobranchiomorphi: Carcharhinidae) of the Western North Atlantic. *NOAA Technical Report, NMFS*, 153: 1–32.

Granier, J. (1964). Les euselaciens dans le Golf d'Aigües-Mortes. *Bulletin du Musée Histoire Naturelle Marseille*, 24: 33–43.

Hemida, F., & Capapé, C. (2002). Observations on a female Bramble shark, *Echinorhinus brucus* (Bonnaterre, 1788), caught off the Algerian coast (southern Mediterranean). *Acta Adriatica*, 43(1): 103–108.

Hemida, F., & Labidi, N. (2001). Estimation de la croissance par analyse des fréquences de taille du requin-ha. *Rapport du 36ème Congrès de la CIESM*, Monte-Carlo, 274 pp.

Hemida, F., Seridji, R., Labidi, N., Bensaci, J., & Capapé, C. (2002). Records of *Carcharhinus spp.* (Chondrichthyes: Carcharhinidae) from off the Algerian coast (southern Mediterranean). *Acta Adriatica*, 43(2): 83–92.

Holland, K.N., Wetherbee, B.M., Peterson, J.D., & Lowe, C.G. (1993). Movements and distribution of hammerhead shark pups on their natal grounds. *Copeia*, 1993(2): 495–502.

Houziaux, J.S., & Voss, J. (1997). Première observation filmée des comportements associées à l'accouplement chez la petite roussette, *Scyliorhinus canicula* (Linné, 1758). *Rev. Fr. Aquariol.*, 24(1–2): 15–26.

Jardas, I. (1972). Supplement to the knowledge of ecology of some Adriatic cartilaginous fishes (Chondrichthyes) with special reference to their nutrition. *Acta Adriatica*, 14(7): 1–60.

Jensen, C.F., Natanson, L.J., Pratt, H.L. Jr., Kohler, N.E., & Campana, S.E. (2002). The reproductive biology of the porbeagle shark (*Lamna nasus*) in the western North Atlantic Ocean. *Fishery Bulletin*, 100: 727–738.

Johnson, R.H. (1978). *Sharks of Polynesia*. Papeete: Les Editions du Pacifique, 170 pp.

Jones, T.S., & Ugland, K.I. (2001). Reproduction of female spiny dogfish, *Squalus acanthias*, in the Oslofjord. *Fishery Bulletin*, 99: 685–690.

Joyce, W.N., Campana, S.E., Natanson, L.J., Kohler, N.E., Pratt, H.L. Jr., & Jensen, C.F. (2002). Analysis of stomach contents of the porbeagle shark (*Lamna nasus* Bonnaterre) in the northwest Atlantic. *ICES Journal of Marine Science*, 59: 1263–1269.

Kabasakal, H. (1998). Sharks and rays fisheries in Turkey. *Shark News*, 11: 8.

Kabasakal, H. (2001). Preliminary data on the feeding ecology of some selachians from the north-eastern Aegean Sea. *Acta Adriatica*, 42(2): 15–24.

Kabasakal, H. (2002a). Cephalopods in the stomach contents of four Elasmobranch species from the northern Aegean Sea. *Acta Adriatica*, 43(1): 17–24.

Kabasakal, H. (2002b). Stomach contents of the longnose spurdog, *Squalus blainvillei* (Risso, 1826) from the North-eastern Aegean Sea. *Annales, Series historia naturalis*, 12(2): 161–166.

Kabasakal, H. (2003). Historical records of the great white shark, *Carcharodon carcharias* (Linnaeus, 1758) (Lamniformes: Lamnidae), from the Sea of Marmara. *Annales, Series historia naturalis*, 13(2): 173–180.

Kabasakal, H., & De Maddalena, A. (2011). A huge shortfin mako shark *Isurus oxyrinchus* Rafinesque, 1810 (Chondrichthyes: Lamnidae) from the waters of Marmaris, Turkey. *Annales, Series historia naturalis*, 21(1): 21–24.

Kabasakal, H., & Kabasakal, E. (2002). Morphometrics of young kitefin sharks, *Dalatias licha* (Bonnaterre, 1788), from Northeastern Aegean Sea, with notes on its biology. *Annales, Series historia naturalis*, 12(2): 161–166.

Kabasakal, H., & Kabasakal, E. (2004). Sharks captured by commercial fishing vessles off the Turkish coast of Northern Aegean Sea. *Annales, Series historia naturalis*. In press.

Kabasakal, H., & Ünsal, N. (1999). Observations on *Etmopterus spinax* (Pisces: Squalidae), from the north-eastern Aegean Sea. *Biljeske–Notes*, 81: 1–11.

Kajiura, S.M. (2001). Head morphology and electrosensory pore distribution of carcharhinid and sphyrnid sharks. *Environmental Biology of Fishes*, 61: 125–133.

Kajiura, S.M., & Holland, K.N. (2002). Electroreception in juvenile scalloped hammerhead and sandbar sharks. *The Journal of Experimental Biology*, 205: 3609–3621.

Klimley, A.P., Butler, S.B., Nelson, D.R., & Stull, A.T. (1988). Diel movements of scalloped hammerhead sharks (*Sphyrna lewini* Griffith and Smith) to and from a seamount in the Gulf of California. *Journal of Fish Biology*, 33: 751–761.

Klimley, A.P., Le Boeuf, B.J., Cantara, K.M., Richert, J.E., Davis, S.F., Van Sommeran, S., & Kelly, J.T. (2001). The hunting strategy of white sharks (*Carcharodon carcharias*) near a seal colony. *Marine Biology*, 138: 617–636.

Klimley, A.P., Pyle, P., & Anderson, S.D. (1996). Tail slap and breach: agonistic displays among white sharks? In A.P. Klimley & D.G. Ainley (Eds.), *Great white sharks: The biology of Carcharodon carcharias*, pp. 241–255. San Diego: Academic, 518 pp.

Kohler, N.E., Casey, J.G., & Turner, P.A. (1996). Length-length and length-weight relationships for 13 shark species from the Western North Atlantic. *NOAA Technical Memorandum NMFS-NE-110*: 1–22.

Kolombatović, J. (1894). O navodima vrsti meèi i kraljeznjaka iz Jadranskog mora, *Izvjesæe Vel. Realke*, Split, 58 pp.

Kovacic, M. (1998). Ichthyological collection (Cyclostomata, Selachii, Osteichthyes) of the Natural History Museum Rijeka. In M. Arko-Pijevac, M. Kovacic & D. Crnkovic (Eds.), *Natural History researches of the Rijeka region*, pp. 685–698. Rijeka: Ed. Natural History Library.

La Cascia, P. (1935). Sul *Cetorhinus maximus* Gunn. (*Selache maxima*) nel Mediterraneo. Catture nel mare di Palermo. *Bollettino dell'Istituto di Zoologia dell'Università di Palermo*, 2: 137–176.

Last, P.R., & Stevens, J.D. (1994). *Sharks and rays of Australia*. Australia: CSIRO, 514 pp.

Lawley, R. (1881). *Studi comparativi sui pesci fossili coi viventi dei generi* Carcharodon, Oxyrhina e Galeocerdo. Pisa: Nistri.

Le Boeuf, B. (2004). Hunting and migratory movements of white sharks in the eastern North Pacific. *Mem. Natl. Inst. Polar Res.*, Spec. Issue, 58: 91–102.

Lineaweaver, T.H. III, & Backus, R.H. (1969). *The Natural History of sharks*. Philadelphia: J.B. Lippincott, 256 pp.

Lipej, L., De Maddalena, A., & Soldo, A. (2004). *Sharks of the Adriatic Sea*. Koper: Knjiznica Annales Majora, 254 pp.

Lipej, L., Makovec, T., Orlando, M., & Ziza, V. (2000). Occurrence of the Basking shark, *Cetorhinus maximus* (Günnerus, 1765), in the waters off Piran (Gulf of Trieste, Northern Adriatic). *Annales, Series historia naturalis*, 10(2): 211–216.

Lipej, L., Makovec, T., Soldo, A., & Ziza, V. (2000). Records of the Sandbar shark *Carcharhinus plumbeus* (Nardo, 1827) in the Gulf of Trieste (Northern Adriatic). *Annales, Series historia naturalis*, 10(2): 199–206.

Liu, K. M., Chiang, P.J., & Chen, C.T. (1998). Age and growth estimates of the bigeye thresher shark, *Alopias superciliosus* in the northeastern Taiwan waters. *Fishery Bulletin*, 96: 482–491.

Liu, K. M., & Chen, C.T. (1999). Demographic analysis of the scalloped hammerhead shark, *Sphyrna lewini* in the northwestern Pacific. *Fish. Sci.* 65(2): 218–223.

Lo Bianco, S. (1909). Notizie biologiche riguardanti specialmente il periodo di maturità sessuale degli animali del Golfo di Napoli. *Mittheilungen aus der Zoologischen Station zu Neapel*, 19(4): 513–761.

Lozano Cabo, F. (1945). Nota sobre un caso de bicefalismo en el *Squalus blainvillei*. *Boletín de la Real Sociedad Española de Historia Natural*, 43: 147–148.

Lucifora, L.O., Menni, R.C., & Escalante, A.H. (2003). Reproduction of the shark *Galeorhinus galeus* from Argentina: support for a single Southwestern Atlantic population. *AES Abstracts Manaus, Brazil, June 27–June 30*: 22.

Lucifora, L.O., Menni, R.C., & Escalante, A.H. (2002). Reproductive ecology and abundance of the sand tiger shark, *Carcharias taurus*, from the southwestern Atlantic. *ICES Journal of Marine Science*, 59: 553–561.

Lyle, J.M. (1983). Food and feeding habits of the lesser spotted dogfish, *Scyliorhinus canicula* (L.), in Isle of Man waters. *Journal of Fish Biology*, 23(6): 725–737.

Macpherson, E. (1980). Régime alimentaire de *Galeus melastomus* Rafinesque, 1810 *Etmopterus spinax* (L., 1758) et *Scymnorhinus licha* (Bonnaterre, 1788) en Méditerranée occidentale. *Vie Milieu*, 30(2): 139–148.

Marconi, M., & De Maddalena, A. (2001). On the capture of a young porbeagle, *Lamna nasus* (Bonnaterre, 1788), in the Western Adriatic Sea. *Annales, Series historia naturalis*, 11(2): 179–184.

Martin, R.A. (1995). *Shark smart: The divers' guide*

to understanding shark behaviour. Vancouver: Diving Naturalist, 180 pp.

Martin, R.A. (2003). *Field Guide to the Great White Shark*. ReefQuest Centre for Shark Research, Special Publication No. 1, 192 pp.

Matallanas, J. (1982). Feeding habits of *Scymnorhinus licha* in Catalan waters. *Journal of Fish Biology*, 20: 155–163.

Matthews, L.H. (1962). The shark that hibernates. *New Scientist*, 280: 415–421.

McCosker, J.E. (1987). The white shark, *Carcharodon carcharias*, has a warm stomach. *Copeia*, 1987: 195–197.

McEachran, J.D., & Séret, B. (1987). Allocation of the name *Sphyrna tudes* (Valenciennes, 1822) and status of the nominal species *Sphyrna couardi* Cadenat, 1951 (Chondrichthyes, Sphyrnidae). *Cybium*, 11(1): 39–46.

McFarlane, G.A., & King, J.R. (2003). Migrations patterns of spiny dogfish (*Squalus acanthias*) in the North Pacific Ocean. *Fishery Bulletin*, 101: 358–367.

Megalofonou, P., Damalas, D., & Yannopoulos, C. (2003). Composition and abundance of pelagic shark by-catch in the eastern Mediterranean Sea. *Fisheries Research* (submitted).

Michael, S.W. (1993). *Reef sharks and rays of the world*. Monterey: Sea Challengers, 107 pp.

Mizzan, L. (1994). I Leptocardi, Ciclostomi e Selaci delle collezioni del Museo Civico di Storia Naturale di Venezia–1) Leptocardia, Agnatha, Gnathostomata–Chondrichthyes (esclusi Rajiformes). *Bollettino del Museo Civico di Storia Naturale di Venezia*, 45. 123–137.

Mollet, H.F., & Cailliet, G.M. (1996). Using allometry to predict body mass from linear measurements of the white shark. In A.P. Klimley & D.G. Ainley (Eds.), Great white sharks. The biology of *Carcharodon carcharias*, pp. 81–90. San Diego: Academic, 518 pp.

Mollet, H.F., Cailliet, G.M., Klimley, A.P., Ebert, D.A., Testi, A.D., & Compagno, L.J.V. (1996). A review of length validation methods and protocols to measure large white sharks. In A.P. Klimley & D.G. Ainley (Eds.), *Great white sharks. The biology of* Carcharodon carcharias, pp. 91–108. San Diego: Academic, 518 pp.

Mollet, H.F., Cliff, G., Pratt, H.L. Jr., & Stevens, J.D. (2000). Reproductive biology of the female shortfin mako, *Isurus oxyrinchus* Rafinesque, 1810, with comments on the embryonic development of lamnoids. *Fishery Bulletin*, 98: 299–318.

Monterosso, B. (1931). Notizie e considerazioni su quattro recenti catture di *Selache Maxima* Gunn., nel mare di Catania. *Atti dell'Accademia Gioenia*, Catania, 18(5): 1–29.

Moreno, J.A. (1987). *"JAQUETONES" Tiburones del género Carcharhinus del Atlántico Nororiental y Mediterráneo Occidental*. Ministerio de Agricultura Pesca y Alimentación, 205 pp.

Moreno, J.A. (1989). Biología reproductiva y fenología de *Alopias vulpinus* (Bonnaterre, 1788) en el Atlántico Nororiental y Mediterráneo Occidental. *Scientia Marina*, 1989, 53(1): 37–46.

Moreno, J.A. (1995). *Guía de los tiburones del Atlántico Nororiental y Mediterráneo*. Madrid: Ed. Pirámide, 310 pp.

Moreno, J.A., & Hoyos, A. (1983a). *Carcharhinus acarenatus*, nov sp., noveau requin Carcharhinide de l'Atlantique Nororiental et de la Mediterranée Occidental. *Cybium*, 7(1): 57–64.

Moreno, J.A., & Hoyos, A. (1983b). Premiere capture en eaux espagnoles et de la Mediterranée de *Carcharhinus altimus* (Springer, 1950). *Cybium*, 7(1): 65–70.

Moreno, J.A., & Moron, J. (1992a). Comparative Study of the genus *Isurus* (Rafinesque, 1810) and description of a form ('marrajo criollo') apparently endemic to the Azores. *Australian Journals of Scientific Research*, 43(1): 109–122.

Moreno, J.A., & Moron, J. (1992b). Reproductive biology of the bigeye thresher shark, *Alopias superciliosus* (Lowe 1839). *Australian Journals of Scientific Research*, 43(1): 77–86.

Morey, G., & Massuttí, E. (2004). Record of the copper shark, *Carcharhinus brachyurus*, from the Balearic Islands (Western Mediterranean). *Cybium*, 27(1): 53–56.

Mouneimne, N. (1977). Liste des poissons de la côte du Liban (Méditerranée orientale). *Cybium*, 3e Sér., 1: 37–66.

Muñoz-Chapuli, R. (1984). Ethologie de la reproduction chez qualques requins de l'Atlantique Nord-Est. *Cybium*, 8(3): 1–14.

Myrberg, A. Jr. (1987). Shark behaviour. Pp. 84–92 in: Stevens, J.D. (ed.) *Sharks*. Hong Kong: Intercontinental, 240 pp.

Natanson, L.J., Casey, J.G., & Kohler, N.E. (1995). Age and growth of the dusky shark, *Carcharhinus obscurus*, in the western North Atlantic Ocean. *Fishery Bulletin*, 93: 116–126.

Natanson, L.J., Casey, J.G., Kohler, N.E., & Colket, T. IV (1999). Growth of the tiger shark, *Galeocerdo cuvier*, in the western North Atlantic based on tag returns and length frequencies; and a note on the effects of tagging. *Fishery Bulletin*, 97: 944–953.

Natanson, L.J., Mello, J.J., & Campana, S.E. (2002). Validated age and growth of the porbeagle shark (*Lamna nasus*) in the western North Atlantic Ocean. *Fishery Bulletin*, 100: 266–278.

Ninni, E. (1904). Sulla cattura di un *Echinorhinus spinosus* (Blainv.) (Ronco spinoso) nel mare di Venezia. *Neptunia*, 19(2): 20–21.

Ninni, E. (1912). *Catalogo dei Pesci del Mare Adriatico*. Bertotti, Venezia.

Orsi Relini, L. (1998). *Carcharhinus brachyurus* (Günther, 1870) in the Museum of the Institute of Zoology, University of Genoa. *Boll. Mus. Ist. biol. Univ. Genova*, 62–63: 93–98.

Parker, H.W., & Boeseman, M. (1954). The basking shark, *Cetorhinus maximus*, in winter. *Proceedings of the Zoological Society of London*, 124(1): 185–194.

Pastore, M., & Tortonese, E. (1984). Prima segnalazione in Mediterraneo dello squalo *Rhizoprionodon acutus* (Ruppell). *Thalassia Salentina*, 14: 11–15.

Patokina, F.A., & Litvinov, F.F. (2004). Food composition and distribution of demersal elasmobranches on shelf and upper slope of North-West Africa. *International Council for the Exploration of the Sea, CM 2004/K:19.*

Piscitelli, L., & De Maddalena, A. (2003). Evidence of a predatory attack on a large paromola, *Paromola cuvieri* (Risso, 1816), by a kitefin shark, *Dalatias licha* (Bonnaterre, 1788). *Thalassia Salentina*, 28: 3–8. .

Politi, E. (1997). Analisi dei contenuti gastrici di *Prionace glauca* nell'Alto e Medio Adriatico. *Quaderni della Civica Stazione Idrobiologica di Milano*, 22: 65–78.

Poll, M. (1951). Poissons. 1. Generalités. 2. Sélaciens et Chimères. *Result. Sci. Exped. Oceanogr. Belge*, 4(1): 1–154.

Pomi, C. (1997). Studio morfometrico di *Prionace glauca* (Linnaeus, 1758) nel Medio e Alto Adriatico. *Quaderni della Civica Stazione Idrobiologica di Milano*, 22: 95–105.

Pratt, H.L. Jr. (1996). Reproduction in the male white shark. In A.P. Klimley & D.G. Ainley (Eds.), Great white sharks: The biology of *Carcharodon carcharias*, pp. 131–138. San Diego: Academic, 518 pp.

Preti, A., Smith, S.E., & Ramon, D.A. (2001). Feeding habits of the common thresher shark (*Alopias vulpinus*) sampled from the California-based drift gill net fishery, 1998–99. *California Cooperative Oceanic Fisheries Investigations Reports*, 42: 145–152.

Quignard, J.-P. (1971). Recherches sur la biologie de *Squalus blainvillei* (Risso, 1826). *Travaux du Laboratoire de biologie halieutique, Université Rennes*, 5: 125–141.

Quignard, J.-P., & Capapé, C. (1971). Note preliminaire sur le marquage de Sélaciens des côtes de Tunisie. *Bulletin de l'Institut National Scientifique et Technique d'Océanographie et de Pêche de Salammbô*, 2(2): 143–155.

Quignard, J.-P., & Capapé, C. (1972a). Note sur les espèces méditérraneennes du genre *Mustelus* (Selachii, Galeoidea, Triakidae). *Revue des Travaux de l'Institut des Pêches Maritimes*, 36(1): 15–29.

Quignard, J.-P., & Capapé, C. (1972b). Complement à la liste commentée des Sélaciens de Tunisie. *Bulletin de l'Institut National Scientifique et Technique d'Océanographie et de Pêche de Salammbô*, 2(3): 445–447.

Randall, J.E. (1973). Size of the great white shark (*Carcharodon*). *Science*, 181(4095): 169–170.

Randall, J.E. (1986). *Sharks of Arabia*. London: IMMEL, 148 pp.

Randall, J.E. (1987). Refutation of lenghts of 11.3, 9.0, and 6.4 m attributed to the white shark, *Carcharodon carcharias*. *California Fish and Game*, 73(3): 163–168.

Ranzi, S. (1932–1934). Le basi fisio-morfologiche dello sviluppo embrionale dei Selaci. 1, 2, 3. *Pubbl. Stazione Zoologica di Napoli*, 12–13.

Rey, J., De Sola, L.G., & Massuttí, E. (2004). Distribution and Biology of the Blackmouth Catshark *Galeus melastomus* in the Alboran Sea (Southwestern Mediterranean). *J. Northw. Atl. Fish. Sci.*, Vol. 35: 1–9.

Ribot Carballal, C., Felix Uraga, R., & Galvan Magaña, F. (2003). Age and growth of the shortfin mako, *Isurus oxyrinchus*, from Baja California Sur, Mexico. *AES Abstracts Manaus, Brazil, June 27–June 30*: 6.

Risso, A. (1810). *Ichthyologie de Nice*. Paris: Schoell.

Roedel, P.M., & Ripley, W.E. (1950). California sharks and rays. *Fishery Bulletin*, (75): 1–88.

Roule, L. (1912). Notice sur les Sélaciens conservés dans les collections du Musée Océanographique. *Bulletin de l'Institut Océanographique*, 243: 1–36.

Sacco, U., La Mesa, G., Dalu, & Vacchi, M. (2000). Changes with length of swimming ability in a small benthic elasmobranch (*Galeus melastomus*): a work hypothesis. *Abstract, 4th European Elasmobranch Association Meeting, Livorno, 27–30 September 2000*: 19.

Šanda, R., & De Maddalena, A. (2003). Collection of the sharks of the National Museum in Prague–Part 1. Complete taxiderms and liquid preservations. *Journal of the National Museum, Natural History Series*, 172(1–4): 61–70.

Šanda, R., & De Maddalena, A. (2004). Collection of the sharks of the National Museum in Prague–Part 2. Skeletal preservations. *Journal of the National Museum, Natural History Series*, 173(1–4): 51–58.

Sará, R., & Sará, M. (1990). La collezione ittiologica Doderlein del Museo di Zoologia di Palermo. *Museologia scientifica*, 1989(1990): 1–23.

Sciarrotta, T.C., & Nelson, D.R. (1977). Diel behavior of the blue shark, *Prionace glauca*, near Santa Catalina Island, California. *Fishery Bulletin*, 75(3): 519–528.

Serena, F., Vacchi, M., & Notarbartolo Di Sciara, G. (2000). Geographical distribution and biological information on the basking shark *Cetorhinus maximus* in the Thyrrenian and Ligurian Seas. In B. Sèret & J.-Y. Sire (Eds.), *Proc. 3rd European Elasmobranch Association Meeting, Boulogne-sur-Mer, 1999*, Pp. 47–56. Paris: Soc. Fr. Ichthyol. & IRD.

Seret, B. (1999). *Les requins des côtes françaises*. Rennes: Editions Ouest-France, 32 pp.

Shestopal, I.P., Smirnov, O.V., & Grekov, A.A. (2002).Bottom long-line fishing for deepwater sharks on sea-mounts in the International waters of the North Atlantic. *NAFO SCR Doc. 02/100*, Ser. No. N4721, 5 pp.

Siccardi, E.M. (1971). *Cetorhinus* in el Atlantico sur (Elasmobranchii: Cetorhinidae). *Revista del Museo Argentino de Ciencias Naturales "Bernardino Rivadavia,"* 6(2):61–101.

Sicher, E. (1898). I pesci e la pesca nel compartimento di Catania con due note sui generi *Laemargus* e *Maena*. *Atti Accademia gioenia Scienze Naturali*, 11: 1–71.

Sims, D.W., Southall, E.J., Quayle, V.A., & Fox, A.M. (2000). Annual social behaviour of basking sharks associated with coastal front areas. *Proceedings of the Royal Society of London, B*, 267: 1897–1904.

Sims, D.W., & Quayle, V.A. (1998). Selective foraging behaviour of basking sharks on zooplankton in a small-scale front. *Nature*, 393: 460-464.

Sion, L., D' Onghia, G., & Carlucci, R. (2000). A simple technique for ageing *Etmopterus spinax* (Linnaeus, 1758). *Abstract, 4th European Elasmobranch Association Meeting, Livorno*, 27–30 September 2000: 34.

Skomal, G.B., & Natanson, L.J. (2002). Age and growth of the blue shark, *Prionace glauca*, in the North Atlantic Ocean. *Col. Vol. Sci. Pap. ICCAT*, 54(4): 1212–1230.

Smale, M.J. (1991). Occurrence and feeding of the three shark species, *Carcharhinus brachyurus, C. obscurus* and *Sphyrna zygaena*, on the eastern Cape coast of South Africa. *South African Journal of Marine Sciences*, 11: 31–42.

Smale, M.J., & Compagno, L.J.V. (1997). Life history and diet of two southern African smoothhound sharks, *Mustelus mustelus* (Linnaeus, 1758) and *Mustelus palumbes* Smith, 1957 (Pisces: Triakidae). *South African Journal of Marine Sciences*, 18: 229–248.

Smale, M.J., & Heemstra, P.C. (1997). First record of albinism in the great white shark, *Carcharodon carcharias* (Linnaeus, 1758). *South African Journal of Science*, 93: 243–245.

Sminkey, T.R., & Musick, J.A. (1995). Age and growth of the sandbar shark, *Carcharhinus plumbeus*, before and after population depletion. *Copeia*, 1995: 871–883.

Soldat, V.T. (2002). Spiny dogfish (*Squalus acanthias* L.) of the Northwest Atlantic Ocean (NWA). *Northwest Atlantic Fisheries Organization, Scientific Council Meeting*—September 2002: 1–33.

Soldo, A. (2003). Status of sharks in the Mediterranean. *Annales, Series historia naturalis*, 13(2): 191–200.

Soldo, A., & Jardas, I. (2002a). Large sharks in the Eastern Adriatic. Pp. 141–155 in: *Proc. 4th Elasm. Assoc. Meet., Livorno (Italy) 2000*. ICRAM, ARPAT & SFI.

Soldo, A., & Jardas, I. (2002b). Occurrence of great white shark, *Carcharodon carcharias* (Linnaeus, 1758) and basking shark, *Cetorhinus maximus* (Gunnerus, 1765) in the Eastern Adriatic and their protection. *Periodicum Biologorum*, 104(2): 195–201.

Soldo, A., Peharda, M., Onofri, V., Glavic, N., & Tutman, P. (1999). New record and some morphological data of the basking shark, *Cetorhinus maximus* (Gunnerus, 1765), in the Eastern Adriatic. *Annales, Series historia naturalis*, 9(2): 229–232.

Springer, S. (1948). Oviphagous embryos of the sand shark, *Carcharias taurus*. *Copeia*, 1948(3): 153–157.

Springer, S. (1960). Natural history of the sandbar shark, *Eulamia milberti*. *Fishery Bulletin*, 61: 1–38.

Springer, V.G. (1964). A revision of the Carchahinid shark genera *Scoliodon*, *Loxodon*, and *Rhizoprionodon*. *Proceedings of the United States National Museum*, 115: 559–632.

Stephan, E., Jung, A., & Guerin, S. (2000). Basking shark (*Cetorhinus maximus*) apparent abundance off French coast in 1997 and 1998. In B. Sèret & J.-Y. Sire (Eds.), *Proc. 3rd European Elasmobranch Association Meeting, Boulogne-sur-Mer, 1999*, pp. 84. Paris: Soc. Fr. Ichthyol. & IRD.

Stevens, J.D. (Ed.) (1987). *Sharks*. Hong Kong: Intercontinental, 240 pp.

Stevens, J.D., & Lyle, J. M. (1989). Biology of three hammerhead sharks (*Eusphyra blochii*, *Sphyrna mokarran*, and *S. lewini*), from northern Australia. *Australian Journal of Marine and Freshwater Resources*, 40: 129–146.

Stillwell, C. (1991). The ravenous mako. In S.H. Gruber (Ed.), Discovering sharks, pp. 77–88. *Underwater Naturalist, Bulletin American Littoral Society*, 19(4)-20(1).

Storai, T., Zuffa, M., & Gioia, R. (2001). Evidenze di predazione su odontoceti da parte di *Isurus oxyrinchus* (Rafinesque, 1810) nel Tirreno Meridionale e Mar Ionio (Mediterraneo). *Atti Società toscana Scienze naturali*, Mem., Serie B, 108: 71–75.

Strong, W.R. Jr. (1996). Shape discrimination and visual predatory tactics in white sharks. In A.P. Klimley & D.G. Ainley (Eds.), *Great white sharks. The biology of* Carcharodon carcharias, Pp. 229–240. San Diego: Academic, 518 pp.

Strong, W.R., Snelson, F.F., & Gruber, S.H. (1990). Hammerhead shark predation on stingrays: an observation of prey handling by *Sphyrna mokarran*. *Copeia*, 1990(3): 836–840.

Sund, O. (1943). Et Brugdebarsel. *Naturen*, 67: 285–286.

Torchio, M., & Michelangeli, M. (1971). Prima segnalazione in acque italiane di uno squalide del genere *Centroscymnus*. *Natura*, 62(3): 241–245.

Tortonese, E. (1938). Revisione degli squali del Museo civico di Milano. *Atti della Società Italiana di Scienze Naturali*, 77: 1–36.

Tortonese, E. (1956). *Fauna d'Italia vol.II. Leptocardia, Ciclostomata, Selachii*. Calderini, Bologna, 334 pp.

Tortonese, E. (1985). Gli squali Mediterranei del genere *Hexanchus* (Chondrichthyes). *Atti della Societa Italiana di Scienze Naturali e Museo Civico di Storia Naturale di Milano*, 126 (3–4): 137–140.

Tortonese, E. (1987). *Pesci del Mediterraneo.*

Recenti studi intorno alla sistematica e distribuzione. Il Ventaglio, Roma.

Tricas, T.C., & McCosker, J.E. (1984). Predatory behavior of the white shark (*Carcharodon carcharias*) with notes on its biology. *Proceedings of the California Academy of Sciences*, 43(14): 221–238.

Uchida, S., Toda, M., Teshima, K., & Yano, K. (1996). Pregnant white sharks and full-term embryos from Japan. In A.P. Klimley & D.G. Ainley (Eds.), *Great white sharks: The biology of Carcharodon carcharias*, pp. 139–155. San Diego: Academic, 518 pp.

Ungaro, N., Marano, G., & Marzano, M.C. (2000). On the length-at-maturity of the smallspotted catshark *Scyliorhinus canicula* (L.) in the Southern Adriatic Sea (Mesiterranean Sea). *Abstract, 4th European Elasmobranch Association Meeting, Livorno, 27–30 September 2000*: 46.

Vacchi, M., & Relini Orsi, L. (1979). Aspetti riproduttivi in *Etmopterus spinax* L. (Chondrichthyes, Squalidae). *Quaderni della Civica Stazione Idrobiologica Milano*, 7: 63–74.

Vacchi, M., & Serena, F. (1997). Squali di notevoli dimensioni nel Mediterraneo Centrale. *Quaderni della Civica Stazione Idrobiologica di Milano*, 22: 17–21.

Vacchi, M., & Serena, F. (2000). On a large specimen of bigeye thresher shark, A*lopias superciliosus* (Lowe, 1839) (Chondrichthyes: Alopiidae) stranded in Tavolara Island (Eastern Sardinia, Mediterranean). In B. Sèret & J.-Y. Sire (Eds.), *Proc. 3rd European Elasmobranch Association Meeting, Boulogne-sur-Mer, 1999*, pp. 84. Paris: Soc. Fr. Ichthyol. & IRD.

Vacchi, M., Serena, F., & Biagi, V. (1996). Cattura di *Carcharhinus brachyurus* (Günther, 1870) (Pisces, Selachii, Carcharhinidae), nel Mar Tirreno Settentrionale. *Biologia Marina Mediterranea*, 3(1): 389–390.

Van Deinse, A.B., & Adriani, M.J. (1953). On the absence of gill rakers in specimens of the basking shark, *Cetorhinus maximus* (Gunner). *Zoologische Mededelingen*, 31(27): 307–310.

Vanni, S. (1992). Cataloghi del Museo di Storia Naturale dell'Universita di Firenze, Sezione di Zoologia "La Specola." XI. Chondrichthyes. *Atti della Societa Toscana di Scienze Naturali*, Memorie, Serie B, 99: 85–114.

Vannuccini, S. (1999). Shark utilization, marketing and trade. *FAO Fisheries Technical Paper*, 389: 1–470.

Vinciguerra, D. (1923). Le appendici branchiali nell'*Echinorhinus spinosus* (Gm.) e in altri Elasmobranchi. *Annali del Museo di Storia Naturale di Genova*, 8(3).

Vinciguerra, D. (1923). Nuove catture di *Selache maxima* nel Golfo di Genova. *Annali del Museo di Storia Naturale di Genova*, 1923: 133–144.

Watts, S. (2001). *The end of the line?* San Francisco: WildAid, 62 pp.

White, W.T., & Potter, I.C. (2004). Habitat partitioning among four elasmobranch species in nearshore, shallow waters of a subtropical embayment in Western Australia. *Marine Biology*, 145: 1023–1032.

Whitehead, P.J.P., Bauchot, M.-L., Hureau, J.C., Nielsen, J., & Tortonese, E. (Eds.) (1984). *Fishes of the North-Eastern Atlantic and the Mediterranean. Vol. 1*. Paris: Unesco.

Zogaris, S., & De Maddalena, A. (2014). Sharks, blast fishing and shifting baselines: insights from Hass's 1942 Aegean expedition. *Cahiers de Biologie Marine*, 55: 305–313.

Zuffa, M., Soldo, A., & Storai, T. (2001). Preliminary observations on abnormal abundance of *Cetorhinus maximus* (Gunnerus, 1765) in the Central and Northern Adriatic Sea. *Annales, Series historia naturalis*, 11(2): 185–192.

Index

Numbers in ***bold italics*** indicate pages with illustrations.

aiguillat commun 87
aiguillat coq 89
aiguillat galludo 89
aiguillat nez court 91
alitán 138
Alopias superciliosus see bigeye thresher
Alopias vulpinus see common thresher shark
Alopiidae 68, 72, 116–121
ange de mer commun 110
ange de mer de Bonaparte 108
ange de mer épineux 106
ange de mer ocellé 108
angelote 110
angelote espinoso 106
angular roughshark 28, 40, ***54***, 67, 72, 102–103, ***102***, ***C4***

barbeled houndshark 66
basking shark 5, ***6***, 7, 11, 20, 25, 29, 39, 41, 49, ***55***, 58, 61, 68, 70, 73, 121–123, ***121***, 192, ***C7***
bigeye thresher 5, 20, 68, 72, 116–118, ***117***, 120, ***C6***
bigeyed sixgill shark 15, 40, ***56***, 66, 71, 82–84, ***83***, ***C1***
bignose shark 68, 74, 151–153, ***152***, 171, 173, ***C11***
blackmouth catshark ***6***, ***9***, 41, 68, 73, ***79***, 133–135, ***134***, ***C9***
blackspotted smooth-hound 68, 74, 144, 146, 147–149, ***147***, ***C11***
blacktip reef shark 25, 33, 69, 75, 167–169, ***168***, ***C14***
blacktip shark ***8***, ***26***, 33, 69, 75, 162–164, ***163***, ***C13***
blauhai 176
blue shark ***6***, ***7***, 8, 9, 13, 20, ***21***, 25, 26, 27, 29, 33, ***35***, 36, 37, 40, 41, 42, 44, 69, 76, 176–179, ***177***, ***C15***
bluntnose sixgill shark 5, ***6***, 12, 15, 26, 29, 41, ***52***, ***62***, 66, 71, 80–82, ***81***, 84, ***C1***
boccanera 133

bogenstirn-hammerhai 181
boquidulce 78
bramble shark 40, 66, 71, 85–87, ***85***, ***C2***
bronze whaler *see* copper shark
bull shark 33
bullhead sharks 4

cagnaccio 114
cagnesca 140
cailón 131
cañabota 80
cañabota ojigrande 82
capopiatto 80
Carcharhinidae 42, 68, 74, 149–181
Carcharhiniformes 4, 68, 73, 133–190
Carcharhinus acarenatus see strait shark
Carcharhinus altimus see bignose shark
Carcharhinus amboinensis see pigeye shark
Carcharhinus brachyurus see copper shark
Carcharhinus brevipinna see spinner shark
Carcharhinus falciformis see silky shark
Carcharhinus leucas see bull shark
Carcharhinus limbatus see blacktip shark
Carcharhinus longimanus see oceanic whitetip shark
Carcharhinus melanopterus see blacktip reef shark
Carcharhinus obscurus see dusky shark
Carcharhinus plumbeus see sandbar shark
Carcharias taurus see sandtiger shark
Carcharodon carcharias see great white shark
carpet sharks 4

cazón 140
centrine commune 102
centroforo 93
Centrophoridae 67, 71, 93–95
Centrophorus granulosus see gulper shark
centroscimno 98
Centroscymnus coelolepis see portuguese dogfish
Cetorhinidae 68, 73, 121–123
Cetorhinus maximus see basking shark
cetorino 122
chien espagnol 133
common angelshark ***6***, 40, 67, 72, 107, 109, 110–112, ***111***, ***C5***
common smooth-hound ***6***, ***13***, 29, 40, 41, ***45***, 68, 74, 144–146, ***145***, 148, ***C10***
common thresher shark 5, ***6***, 20, 27, 42, ***46***, 68, 73, 118–121, ***119***, ***C7***
copper shark 33, 69, 75, 151, 155–157, ***156***, ***C12***
cornuda 188
cornuda negra 181
cornuda ojichica 186
cow sharks 3

Dalatias licha see kitefin shark
Dalatiidae 67, 72, 104–106
dogfish sharks 3
dormilón 100
dornhai 87
dusky shark 33, 69, 75, 153, 169–171, ***170***, 173, 174, ***C14***
düsterer hai 169

Echinorhinidae 66, 71, 85–87
Echinorhinus brucus see bramble shark
echinorino 85
emissole lisse 144
emissole pointillée 147
emissole tachetée 142
engelshai 110
Etmopteridae 67, 71, 95–97

205

Index

Etmopterus spinax see velvet belly

fleckhai 133
frilled sharks 3

galeo 140
Galeocerdo cuvieri see tiger shark
Galeorhinus galeus see tope shark
Galeus melastomus see blackmouth catshark
galludo 89
galludo ñato 91
gattopardo 138
gattuccio maggiore 138
gattuccio minore 136
gefleckter glatthai 142
gewöhnlicher fuchshai 118
gewöhnlicher glatthai 144
glatter hammerhai 188
golden hammerhead 69, 76, 183, 185, 186–188, *186*, 190
grand requin blanc 123
grand requin-marteau 183
grande roussette 138
great hammerhead 5, 23, 25, 27, 33, *42*, *47*, 69, 76, 183–185, *186*, 188, 190, *C16*
great white shark 5, *5*, *6*, 7, 11, *11*, 12, 13, 14, 16, 17, *18*, 20, 22, *23*, 24, 25, 26, 27, *27*, 29, 30, 31, 32, 33, *33*, 34, *34*, 36, 37, *40*, *43*, 51, *56*, 57, 58, 59, 60, 61, 68, 73, 123–126, *124*, 128, 131, 133, *147*, *C7*
großaugen-fuchshai 116
großaugen-sechskiemerhai 83
großer hammerhai 183
großgefleckter katzenhai 138
großnasenhai 151
ground sharks 4
gulper shark *10*, 20, 67, 71, 93–95, *94*, *C3*

Heptranchias perlo see sharpnose sevengill shark
heringshai 131
Heterodontiformes 4
Hexanchidae 66, 71, 78–84
Hexanchiformes 3, 66, 71, 78–84
Hexanchus griseus see bluntnose sixgill shark
Hexanchus nakamurai see bigeyed sixgill shark
hundshai 140

Isurus oxyrinchus see shortfin mako
Isurus paucus see longfin mako

jaquetón chato 153
jaquetón cobre 155
jaquetón de ley 164
jaquetón de Milberto 172
jaquetón de puntas negras 167
jaquetón del Estrecho 149
jaquetón lobo 169
jaquetón manchado 162
jaquetón picoto 151
jaquetón picudo 157
jaquetón sedoso 160
Java shark *see* pigeye shark
Javahai 153

kitefin shark 30, 67, 72, 98, 104–106, *104*, *C4*
kleinaugen-hammerhai 186
kleiner schlafhai 100
kleingefleckter katzenhai 136
kupferhai 155
kurzflossenmako 126
kurznasen-dornhai 91

laimargue de la Méditerranée 100
Lamna nasus see porbeagle
Lamnidae 68, 73, 123–133
Lamniformes 4, 67, 72, 112–133
langflossenmako 129
langnasen-dornhai 89
lemargo 100
Leptocharias smithii see barbeled houndshark
little sleeper shark 40, 67, 72, 100–101, *100*, *C4*
longfin mako 5, 9, 68, 73, 126, 128, 129–131, *130*, 133, *C8*
longimano 164
longnose spurdog 66, 71, 89, 89–91, *90*, 93, *C14*

mackerel sharks 4
marrajo 126
marrajo negro 129
meersau 102
mielga 87
milandre 140
milchhai 179
milk shark 69, 76, 179–181, *180*, *C15*
moretto 95
musola 144
musola pimienta 147
musola pinta 142
Mustelus asterias see starry smooth-hound
Mustelus mediterraneus see blackspotted smooth-hound
Mustelus mustelus see common smooth-hound

nagelhai 85
negra 104
negrito 95
notidano cinereo 78
notidano dagli occhi grandi 83
notidano grigio 80

nursehound *6*, 41, 59, 68, 73, 137, 138–140, *139*, *C9*

oceanic whitetip shark 2, 25, 29, *31*, *32*, 33, *35*, 36, *37*, 39, *41*, 69, 75, 164–167, *165*, *C13*
Odontaspididae 67, 72, 112–116
Odontaspis ferox see smalltooth sand tiger
olayo 133
Orectolobiformes 4
Oxynotidae 67, 72, 102–103
Oxynotus centrina see angular roughshark

pailona 98
pailona commun 98
palombo liscio 144
palombo nocciolo 144
palombo punteggiato 147
palombo stellato 142
peau bleue 176
pèlerin 122
peregrino 122
pesce angelo aculeato 106
pesce angelo comune 110
pesce angelo ocellato 108
pesce martello comune 188
pesce martello dorato 186
pesce martello maggiore 183
pesce martello smerlato 181
pesce porco 102
pesce volpe 118
pesce volpe dagli occhi grandi 116
petit taupe 129
petite roussette 136
pez ángel 108
pigeye shark *12*, 40, 41, 69, 74, 153–155, *154*, *C12*
piked dogfish *6*, 9, *16*, 18, 20, 40, 41, 42, 44, 47, 66, 71, 87, 87–89, *88*, 91, 93, *C2*
pintarroja 136
porbeagle *6*, 8, 14, 16, *16*, 20, *28*, 40, 42, 44, *45*, 47, 68, 73, *92*, 126, 128, 131–133, *132*, *C8*
portugiesenhai 98
portuguese dogfish 25, 67, 72, 97–99, *99*, 105, *C3*
Prionace glauca see blue shark
Pristiophoriformes 3

quelvacho 93

renard 118
renard à gros yeux 116
renard de mer 118
requiem sharks 42
requin à museau pointu 179
requin babosse 151
requin balestrine 153
requin bordé 162
requin bouclé 85
requin cuivre 155

requin du Détroit 149
requin féroce 114
requin gris 172
requin griset 80
requin-hâ 140
requin-marteau à petits yeux 186
requin-marteau commun 188
requin-marteau halicorne 181
requin océanique 164
requin perlon 78
requin pointes noires 167
requin sombre 169
requin soyeux 160
requin-taupe commun 131
requin taureau 112
requin tigre 174
requin tisserand 157
requin vache 82
Rhincodon typus see whale shark
Rhizoprionodon acutus see milk shark
riesenhai 122
ronco spinoso 85

sägerückenengelshai 106
sagre commun 95
samtbauchhai 95
sandbankhai 172
sandbar shark 13, 26, 40, 69, 70, 75, 153, 171–174, *172*, *C15*
sandtiger shark 8, 9, 14, 20, 25, 40, 67, 72, 112–114, *113*, 116, *C6*
sandtigerhai 112
saw sharks 3
sawback angelshark 40, 67, 72, 106–108, *107*, 109, 112, *C5*
scalloped hammerhead 25, *36*, 69, 76, 181–183, *182*, 183, 185, 188, 190, *C16*
schildzahnhai 114
schlinghai 93
schokoladenhai 104
schwarzpunkt-glatthai 147
schwarzspitzen-riffhai 167
schwarzspitzenhai 162
scimnorino 104
Scyliorhinidae 68, 73, 133–140
Scyliorhinus canicula see small-spotted catshark
Scyliorhinus stellaris see nursehound
sechskiemerhai 80
seestraßenhai 149
seidenhai 160
sharpnose sevengill shark 15, 66, 71, 78–80, *79*, *C1*
shortfin mako 5, *6*, 9, *12*, *13*, *14*, *15*, 16, 20, 26, 30, 33, 36, 37, 40, 42, 47, 68, 73, 126–129, *127*, 131, 133, 180, *C8*

shortnose spurdog 66, 71, 89, 91–93, *92*, *C2*
silky shark 36, 69, 75, 159, 160–162, *160*, *C13*
small-spotted catshark *6*, 8, *19*, 28, 29, 41, 59, *62*, 68, 73, *81*, *102*, 103, 135–138, *137*, 140, *C9*
smalleye hammerhead *see* golden hammerhead
smalltooth sand tiger 5, *6*, 40, 67, 72, 114–116, *115*, *C6*
smeriglio 131
smooth hammerhead *6*, 35, 40, 42, 44, 69, 76, 183, 185, 188–190, *189*, *C16*
smoothback angelshark 40, 67, 72, 107, 108–110, *109*, 112, *C5*
solrayo 114
Somniosidae 67, 72, 97–101
Somniosus rostratus see little sleeper shark
Sphyrna lewini see scalloped hammerhead
Sphyrna mokarran see great hammerhead
Sphyrna tudes see golden hammerhead
Sphyrna zygaena see smooth hammerhead
Sphyrnidae 69, 76, 181–190
spinarolo 87
spinarolo bruno 89
spinarolo dalla testa grande 91
spinner shark *28*, 69, 75, 157–159, *158*, 162, 164, *C12*
spinnerhai 157
spiny dogfish *see* piked dogfish
spitzkopf-siebenkiemerhai 78
squadro aculeato 106
squadro comune 110
squadro ocellato 108
squale-chagrin commun 93
squale licha 104
Squalidae 44, 66, 71, 87–93
Squaliformes 3, 66, 71, 85–106
squalo azzurro 176
squalo bianco 123
squalo bronzeo 155
squalo bruno 169
squalo dal muso lungo 151
squalo dall'occhio di porco 153
squalo dalle pinne corte 157
squalo dalle pinne nere di scogliera 167
squalo dalle pinne orlate di nero 162
squalo di Giava 153
squalo di Gibilterra 149
squalo elefante 122
squalo gigante 122
squalo grigio 172
squalo latteo 179

squalo mako dalle pinne corte 126
squalo mako dalle pinne lunghe 129
squalo ramato 155
squalo sericeo 160
squalo tigre 174
squalo toro 112
Squalus acanthias see piked dogfish
Squalus blainvillei see longnose spurdog
Squalus megalops see shortnose spurdog
Squatina aculeata see sawback angelshark
Squatina oculata see smoothback angelshark
Squatina squatina see common angelshark
Squatinidae 44, 67, 72, 106–112
Squatiniformes 3, 67, 72, 106–112
starry smooth-hound 25, 40, 41, *45*, 59, 68, 74, 142–144, *143*, 146, 148, *C10*
strait shark 68, 74, 149–151, *150*, 157, *C11*

taupe bleu 126
tiburón blanco 123
tiburón cerdo 102
tiburón de clavos 85
tiburón lechoso 179
tiburón martillo 183
tiburón tigre 174
tiburón toro 112
tiger shark 5, 11, 14, *24*, 29, 33, 39, 41, 69, 75, 174–176, *175*, *C15*
tigerhai 174
tintorera 176
tope shark *6*, 25, 40, 68, 74, 140–142, *141*, *C10*
Triakidae 68, 73, 140–149

velvet belly 5, *6*, 9, 26, 41, 67, 71, 95–97, *96*, *104*, *C3*
verdesca 176

weichrückiger engelshai 108
weißer hai 123
weißspitzen-hochseehai 164
whale shark 5, 40, 66
whaler sharks 12, 15, *22*, *24*, 33, 34, 70

zorro 118
zorro negro 116